——ARRL's——
Small Antennas
for Small Spaces

Projects and Advice for Limited-Space Stations

2nd Edition

Steve Ford, WB8IMY

Production Staff:

Michelle Bloom, WB1ENT, Production Supervisor, Layout

Jodi Morin, KA1JPA, Assistant Production Supervisor, Layout

David Pingree, N1NAS, Senior Technical Illustrator

Sue Fagan, KB1OKW, Graphic Design Supervisor, Cover Design

Table of Contents

Foreword

As much as amateurs admire the tall towers and large antenna arrays they see in *QST* magazine and elsewhere, the reality for most of them is altogether different. An increasingly large portion of the Amateur Radio population finds itself running out of room – literally – to erect effective antennas. Hams find themselves living in environments that severely curtail their activities, either because of homeowner association restrictions, landlord rules or simply lack of space.

Small Antennas for Small Spaces was written with these amateurs in mind. Author Steve Ford, WB8IMY, has been licensed for several decades, yet has spent much of that time operating from apartments, condominiums or small houses. Despite this handicap, he has made thousands of contacts and earned a number of operating awards.

Steve brings his experience, along with the experiences of other amateurs, to create a book of ideas and options for the space-restricted ham. Regardless of your living situation, or whether your interest is HF or VHF, *Small Antennas for Small Spaces* has advice and projects that you can put to use right away!

David Sumner, K1ZZ
ARRL Chief Executive Officer
November 2015

Acknowledgements

This book is the sum of its parts and those "parts" came from many sources, not just my own knowledge and experience. *QST* Technical Editor Joel Hallas, W1ZR, provided a much-needed sanity check for all my ramblings. In addition to providing corrections and inspiration, Joel also created an HF antenna project specifically for this book. Thanks, Joel!

I'm grateful to Jeff Blaine, AC0C and Les Rayburn, N1LF, for their contributions to Chapter 2. Both are masters of indoor antennas – Jeff on HF and Les on VHF+.

Finally, a number of individuals and manufacturers contributed photography that you'll see throughout this book: Doc Searle; MFJ Enterprises; S9 Antennas; Zero Five Antennas; DX Engineering; Bilal Company; Bob Locher, W9KNI; Super Antennas; John Reisenauer, KL7JR; NCG Company and Quicksilver Radio.

ARRL Member Services

 **Get Involved**
www.arrl.org/get-involved

 **Join or Renew**
www.arrl.org/join

 **Donate**
www.arrl.org/donate

 **Shop**
www.arrl.org/shop

Membership Benefits

Your ARRL membership includes *QST* magazine, plus dozens of other services and resources to help you **Get Started**, **Get Involved**, and **Get On the Air**. ARRL members enjoy Amateur Radio to the fullest!

Members-Only Web Services

Create an online ARRL Member Profile, and get access to ARRL members-only web services. Visit **www.arrl.org/myARRL** to register.

- **QST Digital Edition – www.arrl.org/qst**
  All members can access the enhanced digital edition of *QST* from a web browser. Apps are available for *iOS* and *Android* devices.

- **QST Archive and Periodicals Search – www.arrl.org/qst**
  Browse ARRL's extensive online *QST* archive. A searchable index for *QEX* and *NCJ* is also available.

- **Free E-Newsletters**
  Subscribe to a variety of ARRL e-newsletters and e-mail announcements: ham radio news, radio clubs, public service, contesting, and more!

- **Product Review Archive – www.arrl.org/qst**
  Download and view *QST* Product Reviews.

- **E-Mail Forwarding Service**
  E-mail sent to your **arrl.net** address will be forwarded to any e-mail account you specify.

ARRL Technical Information Service — www.arrl.org/tis

Call or e-mail our expert ARRL Technical Information Service specialists for answers to all your technical and operating questions. This service is FREE to ARRL members.

ARRL as an Advocate — www.arrl.org/regulatory-advocacy

ARRL supports legislation and regulatory measures that preserve and protect meaningful access to the radio spectrum. Our **ARRL Regulatory Information Branch** answers member questions concerning FCC rules and operating practices. ARRL's **Volunteer Counsel** and **Volunteer Consulting Engineer** programs open the door to assistance with antenna regulation and zoning issues.

ARRL Group Benefit Programs* — www.arrl.org/benefits

- **ARRL Ham Radio Equipment Insurance Plan**
  Insurance is available to protect you from loss or damage to your station, antennas, and mobile equipment by lightning, theft, accident, fire, flood, tornado, and other natural disasters.

- **The ARRL Visa Signature® Card**
  Every purchase supports ARRL programs and services.

- **Liberty Mutual Auto and Home Insurance**
  ARRL members may qualify for special group discounts on home and auto insurance. Get a free quote.

  * ARRL Group Benefit Programs are offered by third parties through contractual arrangements with ARRL. The programs and coverage are available in the US only. Other restrictions may apply.

Programs

Public Service — www.arrl.org/public-service
Amateur Radio Emergency Service® – **www.arrl.org/ares**
Emergency Communications Training – **www.arrl.org/emcomm-training**

Radiosport
Awards – **www.arrl.org/awards**
Contests – **www.arrl.org/contests**
QSL Service – **www.arrl.org/qsl**
Logbook of The World – **www.arrl.org/lotw**

Community
Radio Clubs (ARRL-affiliated clubs) – **www.arrl.org/clubs**
Hamfests and Conventions – **www.arrl.org/hamfests**
ARRL Field Organization – **www.arrl.org/field-organization**

Licensing, Education, and Training
Find a License Exam Session – **www.arrl.org/exam**
Find a Licensing Class – **www.arrl.org/class**
ARRL Continuing Education Program – **www.arrl.org/courses-training**
Books, Software, and Operating Resources – **www.arrl.org/shop**

Quick Links and Resources
QST – ARRL members' journal – **www.arrl.org/qst**
QEX – *A Forum for Communications Experimenters* – **www.arrl.org/qex**
NCJ – *National Contest Journal* – **www.arrl.org/ncj**
The ARRL Library – **www.arrl.org/library**
Support for Instructors – **www.arrl.org/instructors**
Support for Teachers – **www.arrl.org/teachers**
ARRL Volunteer Examiner Coordinator (ARRL VEC) – **www.arrl.org/vec**
Public and Media Relations – **www.arrl.org/media**
Forms and Media Warehouse – **www.arrl.org/forms**
FCC License Renewal – **www.arrl.org/fcc**
Foundation, Grants, and Scholarships – **www.arrl.org/arrl-foundation**
Advertising – **www.arrl.org/ads**

Interested in Becoming a New Ham?

www.arrl.org/newham · newham@arrl.org · 1-800-326-3942 (US)

Contact Us

ARRL, the national association for Amateur Radio®
225 Main Street, Newington, CT 06111-1494 USA
Tel 1-860-594-0200, Mon-Fri 8 AM to 5 PM ET (except holidays)
FAX 1-860-594-0259, e-mail **hqinfo@arrl.org**
Website – **www.arrl.org/contact-arrl**

 Facebook
www.facebook.com/ARRL.org

 Follow us on Twitter
twitter.com/arrl · **twitter.com/w1aw** · **twitter.com/arrl_pr**
twitter.com/arrl_youth · **twitter.com/arrl_ares**
twitter.com/arrl_dxcc

YouTube
www.youtube.com/ARRLHQ

The American Radio Relay League, Inc.

The American Radio Relay League, Inc. is a noncommercial association of radio amateurs, organized for the promotion of interest in Amateur Radio communication and experimentation, for the establishment of networks to provide communication in the event of disasters or other emergencies, for the advancement of the radio art and of the public welfare, for the representation of the radio amateur in legislative matters, and for the maintenance of fraternalism and a high standard of conduct.

ARRL is an incorporated association without capital stock chartered under the laws of the State of Connecticut, and is an exempt organization under Section 501(c)(3) of the Internal Revenue Code of 1986. Its affairs are governed by a Board of Directors, whose voting members are elected every three years by the general membership. The officers are elected or appointed by the directors. The League is noncommercial, and no one

with a pervasive and continuing conflict of interest is eligible for membership on its Board.

"Of, by, and for the radio amateur," the ARRL numbers within its ranks the vast majority of active amateurs in the nation and has a proud history of achievement as the standard-bearer in amateur affairs.

A *bona fide* interest in Amateur Radio is the only essential qualification of membership; an Amateur Radio license is not a prerequisite, although full voting membership is granted only to licensed amateurs in the US.

Membership inquiries and general correspondence should be addressed to the administrative headquarters: ARRL, 225 Main Street, Newington, Connecticut 06111-1494.

About the ARRL

The seed for Amateur Radio was planted in the 1890s, when Guglielmo Marconi began his experiments in wireless telegraphy. Soon he was joined by dozens, then hundreds, of others who were enthusiastic about sending and receiving messages through the air—some with a commercial interest, but others solely out of a love for this new communications medium. The United States government began licensing Amateur Radio operators in 1912.

By 1914, there were thousands of Amateur Radio operators—hams—in the United States. Hiram Percy Maxim, a leading Hartford, Connecticut inventor and industrialist, saw the need for an organization to band together this fledgling group of radio experimenters. In May 1914 he founded the American Radio Relay League (ARRL) to meet that need.

Today ARRL, with approximately 165,000 members, is the largest organization of radio amateurs in the United States. The ARRL is a not-for-profit organization that:
• promotes interest in Amateur Radio communications and experimentation
• represents US radio amateurs in legislative matters, and
• maintains fraternalism and a high standard of conduct among Amateur Radio operators.

At ARRL headquarters in the Hartford suburb of Newington, the staff helps serve the needs of members. ARRL is also International Secretariat for the International Amateur Radio Union, which is made up of similar societies in 150 countries around the world.

ARRL publishes the monthly journal *QST*, as well as newsletters and many publications covering all aspects of Amateur Radio. Its headquarters station, W1AW, transmits bulletins of interest to radio amateurs and Morse code practice sessions. The ARRL also coordinates an extensive field organization, which includes volunteers who provide technical information and other support services for radio amateurs as well as communications for public-service activities. In addition, ARRL represents US amateurs with the Federal Communications Commission and other government agencies in the US and abroad.

Membership in ARRL means much more than receiving *QST* each month. In addition to the services already described, ARRL offers membership services on a personal level, such as the Technical Information Service—where members can get answers by phone, email or the ARRL website, to all their technical and operating questions.

Full ARRL membership (available only to licensed radio amateurs) gives you a voice in how the affairs of the organization are governed. ARRL policy is set by a Board of Directors (one from each of 15 Divisions). Each year, one-third of the ARRL Board of Directors stands for election by the full members they represent. The day-to-day operation of ARRL HQ is managed by an Executive Vice President and his staff.

No matter what aspect of Amateur Radio attracts you, ARRL membership is relevant and important. There would be no Amateur Radio as we know it today were it not for the ARRL. We would be happy to welcome you as a member! (An Amateur Radio license is not required for Associate Membership.) For more information about ARRL and answers to any questions you may have about Amateur Radio, write or call:

ARRL—The national association for Amateur Radio
225 Main Street
Newington CT 06111-1494
Voice: 860-594-0200
   Fax: 860-594-0259
   E-mail: **hq@arrl.org**
   Internet: **www.arrl.org/**

Prospective new amateurs call (toll-free):
800-32-NEW HAM (800-326-3942)
You can also contact us via e-mail at **newham@arrl.org**
or check out *ARRLWeb* at **www.arrl.org/**

Getting Started

1

Amateur Radio operators dearly love antennas. To us, antennas are more than mere functional devices for radiating signals; they are beautiful works of engineering art. A gorgeous antenna system will stop us cold in our tracks, utterly transfixed by the wonder of its design.

Hams are the people who nearly cause traffic accidents because they are gaping at awesome antennas when they should be paying attention to their driving. A few years ago I alarmed my family by abruptly swerving off Interstate 78 in eastern Pennsylvania, grabbing my camera and leaping from the car. The object of my insane desire was the spidery curtain antenna of shortwave broadcaster WMLK (see the accompanying photo).

As the Editor of *QST* magazine, I know how much hams enjoy seeing photographs of antennas. Nothing lights up a page like a forest of sky high aluminum silhouetted against a setting sun. The higher and more impressive the towers and the antennas they support, the longer we gaze in admiration, tinged with a bit of envy.

But even the most delightful dreams end with the chime of the alarm clock. Against our will we're forced to sit upright, yawn and face reality. For many, reality means

The impressive antenna of shortwave broadcaster WMLK beside Interstate 78 in eastern Pennsylvania.

Who doesn't love the beauty of an antenna at sunset?

chapter may be rightly called the most critical part of this book.

IT ALL COMES DOWN TO CHOICES

There is a lot of pleasure to be had while operating in a limited-space environment, be it on a small piece of property or even indoors. No, you won't have the muscle of the big boys with acres of land and towers reaching for the heavens, *but you can put a signal on the airwaves regardless of your circumstances.* The key is to make choices that will improve your odds of success. To squeeze the full measure of fun from your station there are several factors you'll need to consider:

■ Antenna design — which is what most of this book is about.

■ Feed lines — getting the signals to and from your antenna with the least amount of loss.

■ Power — how much is enough; how much is too much?

■ Modes — which operating mode will give you the best bang for the buck?

We'll spend subsequent chapters talking about antennas, so let's jump the queue and go after the second topic bullet from the top: Feed lines.

YOUR FEED LINE: THE CRITICAL LINK

Feed lines are the unsung heroes of antenna systems. Unlike antennas, they aren't physically attractive. You don't usually see hams gazing in rapturous awe at feed lines. To most of us, feed lines are simply the wires that transport our signals. We may not give them much consideration, but that would be a grave mistake.

Coaxial Cable

At the most basic level, coaxial cable, or simply "coax" for short, consists of one conductor — the *center conductor* — surrounded by another — the *shield* — and separated by some sort of insulating material. In the types of coax hams most often encounter, the insulating material is either solid or foam plastic of one type or another, or it may be an open space, filled with ordinary air.

The type of insulating material used, the composition of the shield (solid metal or

that their antennas are far removed from the stunning images they glimpse in magazines. These amateurs don't live on endless tracts of land ideal for "antenna farms." In fact, quite a few of them don't enjoy the luxury of private land at all. Their homes are apartments or condominiums.

Believe me, I feel your pain. For the last 20 years I've lived in a house that sits on a patch of soil measuring 90 feet in length by 70 feet in width. We're talking something on the order of ⅕ of an acre. My tiny house is approximately 50 feet long and 25 feet wide. Do the math and you can see that there is little property remaining for grand antenna projects.

Prior to purchasing this home, I spent my entire life in apartments of one type or another. I've dwelled in everything from cramped "studio" apartments to two-bedroom condos.

And yet …

I've been active in Amateur Radio for almost 40 years. I have earned a DX Century Club award with various endorsements, a VHF/UHF Century Club award for 6 meters and satellites, and bagged my Worked All States and Worked All Continents certificates. A 100-foot tower and a stack of

gleaming Yagi antennas certainly would have made these achievements easier, but the fact remains that I earned these awards, and made many friends along the way, with antennas that squeezed into whatever spaces I had available at the time.

The secret of my success, if you can call it that, is using the best antenna possible for a given circumstance. For two years that meant a wire dangling from the rafters of a claustrophobic condo attic. Modest as it was, I used that antenna system to get on the air and make contacts — quite a few contacts.

There is no one-size-fits all solution when it comes to antennas. Of course, if you are like me, you know that part of the enjoyment of Amateur Radio is trying one antenna design after another. We're all in search of the *One True Antenna* that will perform spectacularly on every band of interest. (Hint: It doesn't exist, but chasing the mirage is a lot of fun anyway!)

Before we begin exploring various products and projects, there are several important topics we need to cover. They are so important, in fact, that this

RG-8 coaxial cable with the insulating outer jacket stripped away to reveal the shield braid and center conductor.

TABLE 1-1

Nominal Characteristics of Commonly Used Transmission Lines

RG or Type	Part Number	Nom. Z_0 Ω	VF %	Cap. pF/ft	Cent. Cond. AWG	Diel. Type	Shield Type	Jacket Matl	OD inches	Max V (RMS)	Matched Loss (dB/100')			
											1 MHz	10	100	1000
RG-6	Belden 1694A	75	82	16.2	#18 Solid BC	FPE	FC	P1	0.275	600	0.2	.7	1.8	5.9
RG-6	Belden 8215	75	66	20.5	#21 Solid CCS	PE	D	PE	0.332	2700	0.4	0.8	2.7	9.8
RG-8	Belden 7810A	50	86	23.0	#10 Solid BC	FPE	FC	PE	0.405	600	0.1	0.4	1.2	4.0
RG-8	TMS LMR400	50	85	23.9	#10 Solid CCA	FPE	FC	PE	0.405	600	0.1	0.4	1.3	4.1
RG-8	Belden 9913	50	84	24.6	#10 Solid BC	ASPE	FC	P1	0.405	600	0.1	0.4	1.3	4.5
RG-8	CXP1318FX	50	84	24.0	#10 Flex BC	FPE	FC	P2N	0.405	600	0.1	0.4	1.3	4.5
RG-8	Belden 9913F7	50	83	24.6	#11 Flex BC	FPE	FC	P1	0.405	600	0.2	0.6	1.5	4.8
RG-8	Belden 9914	50	82	24.8	#10 Solid BC	FPE	FC	P1	0.405	600	0.2	0.5	1.5	4.8
RG-8	TMS LMR400UF	50	85	23.9	#10 Flex BC	FPE	FC	PE	0.405	600	0.1	0.4	1.4	4.9
RG-8	DRF-BF	50	84	24.5	#9.5 Flex BC	FPE	FC	PE	0.405	600	0.1	0.5	1.6	5.2
RG-8	WM CQ106	50	84	24.5	#9.5 Flex BC	FPE	FC	P2N	0.405	600	0.2	0.6	1.8	5.3
RG-8	CXP008	50	78	26.0	#13 Flex BC	FPE	S	P1	0.405	600	0.1	0.5	1.8	7.1
RG-8	Belden 8237	52	66	29.5	#13 Flex BC	PE	S	P1	0.405	3700	0.2	0.6	1.9	7.4
RG-8X	Belden 7808A	50	86	23.5	#15 Solid BC	FPE	FC	PE	0.240	600	0.2	0.7	2.3	7.4
RG-8X	TMS LMR240	50	84	24.2	#15 Solid BC	FPE	FC	PE	0.242	300	0.2	0.8	2.5	8.0
RG-8X	WM CQ118	50	82	25.0	#16 Flex BC	FPE	FC	P2N	0.242	300	0.3	0.9	2.8	8.4
RG-8X	TMS LMR240UF	50	84	24.2	#15 Flex BC	FPE	FC	PE	0.242	300	0.2	0.8	2.8	9.6
RG-8X	Belden 9258	50	82	24.8	#16 Flex BC	FPE	S	P1	0.242	600	0.3	0.9	3.1	11.2
RG-8X	CXP08XB	50	80	25.3	#16 Flex BC	FPE	S	P1	0.242	300	0.3	0.9	3.1	14.0
RG-9	Belden 8242	51	66	30.0	#13 Flex SPC	PE	SCBC	P2N	0.420	5000	0.2	0.6	2.1	8.2
RG-11	Belden 8213	75	84	16.1	#14 Solid BC	FPE	S	PE	0.405	600	0.2	0.4	1.3	5.2
RG-11	Belden 8238	75	66	20.5	#18 Flex TC	PE	S	P1	0.405	600	0.2	0.7	2.0	7.1
RG-58	Belden 7807A	50	85	23.7	#18 Solid BC	FPE	FC	PE	0.195	300	0.3	1.0	3.0	9.7
RG-58	TMS LMR200	50	83	24.5	#17 Solid BC	FPE	FC	PE	0.195	300	0.3	1.0	3.2	10.5
RG-58	WM CQ124	52	66	28.5	#20 Solid BC	PE	S	PE	0.195	1400	0.4	1.3	4.3	14.3
RG-58	Belden 8240	52	66	28.5	#20 Solid BC	PE	S	P1	0.193	1900	0.3	1.1	3.8	14.5
RG-58A	Belden 8219	53	73	26.5	#20 Flex TC	FPE	S	P1	0.195	300	0.4	1.3	4.5	18.1
RG-58C	Belden 8262	50	66	30.8	#20 Flex TC	PE	S	P2N	0.195	1400	0.4	1.4	4.9	21.5
RG-58A	Belden 8259	50	66	30.8	#20 Flex TC	PE	S	P1	0.192	1900	0.4	1.5	5.4	22.8
RG-59	Belden 1426A	75	83	16.3	#20 Solid BC	FPE	S	P1	0.242	300	0.3	0.9	2.6	8.5
RG-59	CXP 0815	75	82	16.2	#20 Solid BC	FPE	S	P1	0.232	300	0.5	0.9	2.2	9.1
RG-59	Belden 8212	75	78	17.3	#20 Solid CCS	FPE	S	P1	0.242	300	0.6	1.0	3.0	10.9
RG-59	Belden 8241	75	66	20.4	#23 Solid CCS	PE	S	P1	0.242	1700	0.6	1.1	3.4	12.0
RG-62A	Belden 9269	93	84	13.5	#22 Solid CCS	ASPE	S	P1	0.240	750	0.3	0.9	2.7	8.7
RG-62B	Belden 8255	93	84	13.5	#24 Flex CCS	ASPE	S	P2N	0.242	750	0.3	0.9	2.9	11.0
RG-63B	Belden 9857	125	84	9.7	#22 Solid CCS	ASPE	S	P2N	0.405	750	0.2	0.5	1.5	5.8
RG-142	CXP 183242	50	69.5	29.4	#19 Solid SCCS	TFE	D	FEP	0.195	1900	0.3	1.1	3.8	12.8
RG-142B	Belden 83242	50	69.5	29.0	#19 Solid SCCS	TFE	D	TFE	0.195	1400	0.3	1.1	3.9	13.5
RG-174	Belden 7805R	50	73.5	26.2	#25 Solid BC	FPE	FC	P1	0.110	300	0.6	2.0	6.5	21.3
RG-174	Belden 8216	50	66	30.8	#26 Flex CCS	PE	S	P1	0.110	1100	1.9	3.3	8.4	34.0
RG-213	Belden 8267	50	66	30.8	#13 Flex BC	PE	S	P2N	0.405	3700	0.2	0.6	1.9	8.0
RG-213	CXP213	50	66	30.8	#13 Flex BC	PE	S	P2N	0.405	600	0.2	0.6	2.0	8.2
RG-214	Belden 8268	50	66	30.8	#13 Flex SPC	PE	D	P2N	0.425	3700	0.2	0.6	1.9	8.0
RG-216	Belden 9850	75	66	20.5	#18 Flex TC	PE	D	P2N	0.425	3700	0.2	0.7	2.0	7.1
RG-217	WM CQ217F	50	66	30.8	#10 Flex BC	PE	D	PE	0.545	7000	0.1	0.4	1.4	5.2
RG-217	M17/78-RG217	50	66	30.8	#10 Solid BC	PE	D	P2N	0.545	7000	0.1	0.4	1.4	5.2
RG-218	M17/79-RG218	50	66	29.5	#4.5 Solid BC	PE	S	P2N	0.870	11000	0.1	0.2	0.8	3.4
RG-223	Belden 9273	50	66	30.8	#19 Solid SPC	PE	D	P2N	0.212	1400	0.4	1.2	4.1	14.5
RG-303	Belden 84303	50	69.5	29.0	#18 Solid SCCS	TFE	S	TFE	0.170	1400	0.3	1.1	3.9	13.5
RG-316	CXP TJ1316	50	69.5	29.4	#26 Flex BC	TFE	S	FEP	0.098	1200	1.2	2.7	8.0	26.1
RG-316	Belden 84316	50	69.5	29.0	#26 Flex SCCS	TFE	S	FEP	0.096	900	1.2	2.7	8.3	29.0
RG-393	M17/127-RG393	50	69.5	29.4	#12 Flex SPC	TFE	D	FEP	0.390	5000	0.2	0.5	1.7	6.1
RG-400	M17/128-RG400	50	69.5	29.4	#20 Flex SPC	TFE	D	FEP	0.195	1400	0.4	1.1	3.9	13.2
LMR500	TMS LMR500UF	50	85	23.9	#7 Flex BC	FPE	FC	PE	0.500	2500	0.1	0.4	1.2	4.0
LMR500	TMS LMR500	50	85	23.9	#7 Solid CCA	FPE	FC	PE	0.500	2500	0.1	0.3	0.9	3.3
LMR600	TMS LMR600	50	86	23.4	#5.5 Solid CCA	FPE	FC	PE	0.590	4000	0.1	0.2	0.8	2.7
LMR600	TMS LMR600UF	50	86	23.4	#5.5 Flex BC	FPE	FC	PE	0.590	4000	0.1	0.2	0.8	2.7
LMR1200	TMS LMR1200	50	88	23.1	#0 Copper Tube	FPE	FC	PE	1.200	4500	0.04	0.1	0.4	1.3
Hardline														
1/2"	CATV Hardline	50	81	25.0	#5.5 BC	FPE	SM	none	0.500	2500	0.05	0.2	0.8	3.2
1/2"	CATV Hardline	75	81	16.7	#11.5 BC	FPE	SM	none	0.500	2500	0.1	0.2	0.8	3.2
7/8"	CATV Hardline	50	81	25.0	#1 BC	FPE	SM	none	0.875	4000	0.03	0.1	0.6	2.9
7/8"	CATV Hardline	75	81	16.7	#5.5 BC	FPE	SM	none	0.875	4000	0.03	0.1	0.6	2.9
LDF4-50A	Heliax –1/2"	50	88	25.9	#5 Solid BC	FPE	CC	PE	0.630	1400	0.05	0.2	0.6	2.4
LDF5-50A	Heliax –7/8"	50	88	25.9	0.355" BC	FPE	CC	PE	1.090	2100	0.03	0.10	0.4	1.3
LDF6-50A	Heliax – 1¼"	50	88	25.9	0.516" BC	FPE	CC	PE	1.550	3200	0.02	0.08	0.3	1.1

wire mesh or both) and the distance separating the center conductor from the shield are major factors in determining the overall *characteristics* of a given type of coax. We use the word "characteristics" to mean all the various factors that determine how coaxial cable behaves when RF energy is applied to

it. There are a number of different characteristics, but the most important ones for our discussion are the characteristic impedance of the cable in ohms (Ω) and the degree of loss you can expect over a certain length.

If you look at **Table 1.1** you'll see a list of many types of coaxial cable along with their

primary characteristics. Pay special attention to the right hand columns that list "Matched Loss" in "dB per 100 feet." This is a measure of how much RF — both transmitted *and received* — you will lose in 100 feet of cable. The individual columns are labeled according to the frequency in question: 1, 10, 100 and

1000 MHz. The loss specification assumes that the impedance of the cable — usually 50 Ω — is perfectly matched to a 50 Ω load (the antenna). If it isn't, all bets are off, but we'll address that situation in a moment. For now, assume that the cable is connected to an ideal 50 Ω load.

As you examine the table carefully, you'll notice some interesting things:

▌ **Loss varies quite a bit depending on the type of cable you are using.** RG174, for example, is a thin variety of coax that's great for short connections inside pieces of equipment, but it absorbs RF energy like a sponge when the length goes beyond several feet, depending on the frequency (see below). At the opposite extreme you have *Hardline*, the lowest loss coaxial feed line available. See **Figure 1.1**. Hardline is great stuff, but it is expensive and difficult to work with. The only time you usually find hams using Hardline is when they need to feed antennas that are considerable distances from their transceivers.

▌ **Loss increases with frequency.** This is an inviolate rule of feed lines. The higher the frequency, the greater the loss. A few comparisons will demonstrate this fact.

Let's say you are feeding a 50 Ω antenna with 100 feet of RG-58 coax and transmitting at 14 MHz. That calculates to a loss of 1.33 dB. So, if you have 100 W at your transceiver, you'll end up with about 74 W at the antenna.

Now let's ramp up the frequency to 144 MHz and leave everything else the same. The loss skyrockets to 4.6 dB. Of the 100 W at the transmitter, only 35 W is arriving at the antenna! All the rest is being dissipated as heat along the length of the cable.

As you can see, when choosing coax one must choose wisely. If your antenna is less than 100 feet from your station and you're operating at HF frequencies, you can get away with something inexpensive such as RG-58. There will always be a certain amount of loss, but it will be so small as to be unimportant in the greater scheme of things. Remember, however, that loss increases with frequency. The loss in 100 feet of RG-58 when operating at 3.5 MHz may be negligible, but jump to the 10 meter band and it becomes significant.

Needless to say, if you are considering VHF over the same distance, you'll need to step up to something like LMR-400 or 9913 to keep your loss to a minimum.

Veteran hams will say that you should always use the lowest loss coax you can afford. This is generally true ... to a point. Low-loss coax often comes with a "high loss" price tag and there is most definitely a point of diminishing returns.

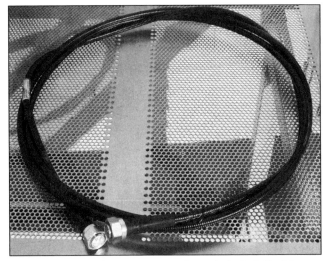

Figure 1.1 — Hardline — an expensive, relatively inflexible cable with very low RF loss.

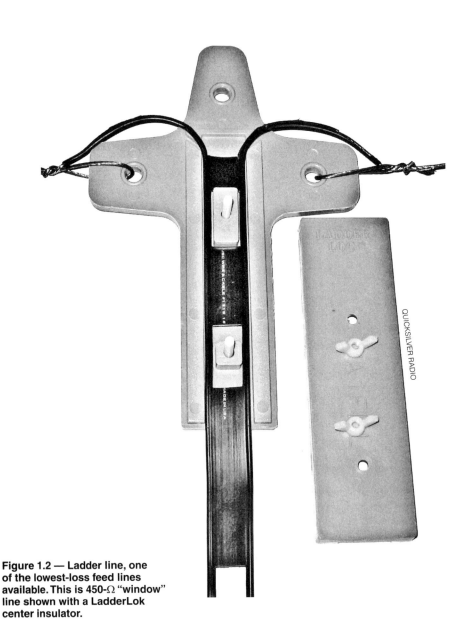

Figure 1.2 — Ladder line, one of the lowest-loss feed lines available. This is 450-Ω "window" line shown with a LadderLok center insulator.

QUICKSILVER RADIO

Let's say you have a 10 meter antenna that you are feeding with 100 feet of coaxial cable. Here is the cost breakdown vs the expected loss (in dB), assuming a matched load. The costs were current when this book was written in late 2010.

- RG58   Cost = $24   Loss = 2.0 dB
- RG8X   Cost = $29   Loss = 1.6 dB
- RG213   Cost = $89   Lost = 1.0 dB
- LMR400 Cost = $119   Loss = 0.7 dB

One hundred feet of LMR400 will cost you $119 and the loss is 0.7 dB compared to a loss of 2 dB with RG58. This may look good at first glance, but a 1.3 dB difference is not worth paying nearly five times as much. The ham at the other end of your signal path wouldn't notice the change on his S meter!

Ladder Line

A feed line doesn't need to consist of one conductor within another. That's how coaxial cable is designed because it makes the feed line easy to work with. Since the shield entirely surrounds the center conductor, interactions with the outside environment are minimized. As a result, you can bend coax (within reason), run it across a sheet metal roof and commit other abuses without substantially changing its impedance. That's what makes coax so popular.

But there is another type of feed line that has its roots in the early days of Amateur Radio. Back then hams often fed their antennas by simply running two wires in parallel, using insulators to keep the wires separated by a specific distance to maintain the impedance. The result was a feed line that resembled a rope ladder hanging from the antenna — *ladder line*.

We use the term "ladder line" today to mean any type of feed line comprised of two parallel wires. Traditional "true" ladder line is still available from a few vendors, but you rarely see it in use. Instead, the most popular variety is "windowed line" (see **Figure 1.2**). In windowed line the parallel conductors are separated by a plastic insulating material that features open sections every inch or so.

The advantage of ladder line over coax is its relative lack of loss. Ladder line has extraordinarily low RF loss, even at VHF frequencies, over astonishing lengths. Considering this fact, you're probably wondering why ladder line isn't used everywhere. It seems like the ideal feed line, doesn't it?

Not so fast. There are a couple of issues with ladder line that greatly diminish its utility.

- **Impedance.** Ladder line impedance is typically in the neighborhood of several hundred ohms. For instance, windowed line is often 450 Ω and true ladder line is about 600 Ω. This is a serious problem when your transceiver is designed to expect a 50 Ω coaxial feed line.
- **Ease of use.** Unlike coax, ladder line must be kept reasonably straight and well away from metal or lossy objects such as the ground. The parallel conductors generate fields that effectively balance each other (which is why it is referred to as a "balanced line"). A sizeable hunk of metal within a few inches is sufficient to disrupt the fields, changing the characteristics of the feed line at that point. A ladder line encased in ice or snow will also change its characteristics for the same reason.

These shortcomings notwithstanding, ladder line remains attractive for amateur use, so long as you can work within the restrictions. As you'll see elsewhere in this book, one of the most efficient multiband HF antennas you can build is fed with ladder line.

SWR — The Joker in the Deck

No discussion of feed lines is complete without introducing the concept of *Standing Wave Ratio*, or SWR. Entire books have been devoted to the subject of SWR and feed lines, so I won't go into great detail here. Instead, try this bit of visualization.

Imagine a small pond with a vibrating motor in the center, just at the surface of the water (**Figure 1.3**). There is nothing special about the motor; all it does is vibrate. When you start the motor, its vibrations cause ripples to radiate outward in all directions. The ripples strike the soil along the edge of the pond and bounce backward in the general direction of the motor. These reflected ripples collide with the "new" ripples being generated by the motor. As they collide they add or subtract from one another. The motor keeps vibrating and these wave interactions continue.

As we stand on the shore and observe, we see the first ripples striking the pond edge and returning, but within seconds it is apparent that we can no longer see moving ripples at all. Instead, we see what appears to be a fixed, non-moving pattern of waves on the surface of the pond. All the traveling waves have collided and merged into a series of *standing waves*. These standing waves will remain in place so long as nothing changes, including the vibrating frequency of the motor.

Now substitute RF waves in a feed line for water, a transceiver for the motor and an antenna for the edge of the pond. The energy your transceiver sends into the feed line, the *forward power*, travels to the antenna. Some of the energy is radiated, but a portion is reflected. This *reflected power* goes racing back down the feed line toward the transceiver where it will ultimately bounce back to the antenna. Along the way it encounters forward power from the transceiver. Just like our pond analogy, the waves of energy interact, adding and subtracting. The result is standing waves on the feed line.

Some amateurs believe that SWR is a simple ratio of forward to reflected power. Not quite. SWR is an expression of the complex interaction (amplitude and phase) between waves of RF energy in a feed line. We measure SWR with SWR meters, typically installed at the transceiver (many transceivers have SWR metering built in).

The reason SWR is important is because it can play an enormous role in determining how much RF energy is lost in a feed line.

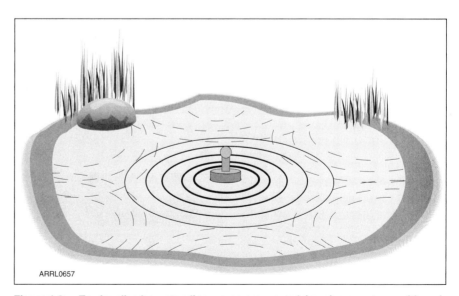

ARRL0657

Figure 1.3 — To visualize how standing waves are created, imagine a motor positioned in the center of a pond. As it vibrates, the waves radiate outward, reflect off the edges and bounce back. On the way back, they combine with other waves and the result is a pattern on the water that appears to be frozen in place. These are *standing waves*.

The loss figures you see in Table 1.1 all assume that the SWR is 1:1. In other words, the feed line impedance is the same as the transceiver and antenna impedances and the RF energy flows from the transceiver to the antenna with little, if any, reflection. That's an ideal situation, the *matched* condition, and it is one you'll rarely enjoy!

In real-world antenna systems, things are usually not perfect. As impedances in an antenna system become mismatched, SWR begins to rise. As the SWR increases, more RF energy is "tied up," so to speak, in the standing waves along the feed line. This wouldn't be a problem if you were using an exotic superconducting feed line with zero RF loss. All the RF would be radiated by the antenna eventually regardless of the SWR. (If you find a zero-loss feed line, there may be a Nobel Prize waiting for you.) But in our real-world feed line that RF energy will lost as heat.

Assume 100 feet of RG58 coax with 100 W at 14 MHz applied by the transceiver (**Figure 1.4**). The characteristic impedance of the coax is 50 Ω and the antenna has been designed and adjusted to present a 50 Ω load. Congratulations, you have a matched condition and you can expect a total feed line loss of 1.33 dB, or 27 W. Your SWR meter at the transceiver dutifully reports an SWR of about 1.2:1. You are smiling.

But now assume that a mischievous crow has landed on the antenna and tampered with the construction. As he flies away laughing, you notice that the SWR at your radio has suddenly jumped to 6:1. The impedance of the antenna at the feed point has strayed some distance from 50 Ω and now you have considerable amounts of 14 MHz RF energy in the form of standing waves between your radio and the antenna. That RG58 coax is dissipating your precious energy, resulting in a staggering loss of almost 10 dB. The 100 W produced by your radio has been reduced to a mere 10 W at your antenna. You are no longer smiling and your friends on the air are wondering what happened to your formerly strong signal.

Like all RF losses, the loss caused by SWR increases with frequency, the type of feed line and the length of the feed line. Also, a high SWR condition can cause high voltage to exist at certain points, including at the output of your transceiver. This can easily damage modern solid-state radios. To protect your investment, many manufacturers have added so-called "SWR fold back" circuitry. When the SWR at the radio rises above about 1.5:1, the radio automatically begins to reduce (fold back) its output power.

You can negate the impact of SWR by adjusting the impedance at the antenna so

The MFJ-929 antenna tuner.

that it more closely matches the feed line impedance. Many of the antennas and antenna designs in this book use this approach. Another technique is to disregard the mismatch at the antenna and instead transform the impedance mismatch to 50 Ω. This is when the *antenna tuner* comes into play.

An antenna tuner is really little more than a variable impedance transformer. It takes whatever impedance it finds on the feed line and matches it to 50 Ω for your transceiver.

There are manual tuners that you adjust yourself, or automatic tuners that determine the correct settings at the press of a button, or at the moment you transmit. Combining an antenna tuner with low loss feed line seems like a sure cure for high SWR, but that isn't necessarily true.

Study **Figure 1.5**. The problem with an antenna tuner is that it only creates a 50 Ω impedance and a 1:1 SWR between its input and your transceiver. The SWR between

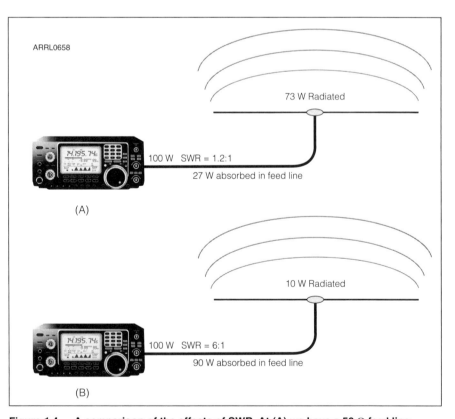

Figure 1.4 — A comparison of the effects of SWR. At (A) we have a 50 Ω feed line attached to the feed point of a dipole antenna, which is also approximately 50 Ω. The resulting SWR measured at the radio is about 1.2:1 and approximately 27 W is lost in the feed line. At (B) the SWR at the radio has jumped to 6:1 and now only 10 W is being radiated by the antenna. Of course, in the real world, the fold back circuit in the transceiver would never have permitted the radio to supply 100 W into a 6:1 SWR!

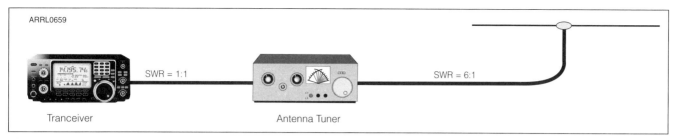

Figure 1.5 — Although an antenna tuner can provide a 50 Ω impedance and a 1:1 SWR to your transceiver, it does nothing whatsoever about the conditions that exist between the antenna tuner and the antenna. The SWR in that part of the antenna system remains unchanged.

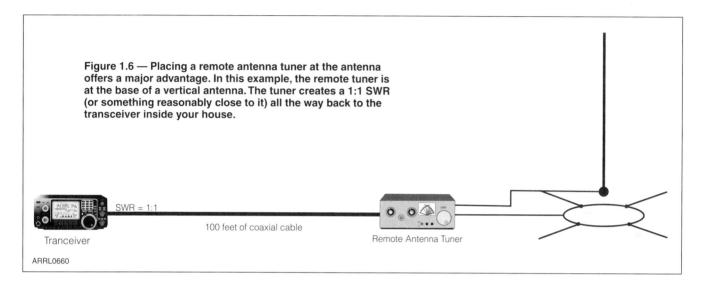

Figure 1.6 — Placing a remote antenna tuner at the antenna offers a major advantage. In this example, the remote tuner is at the base of a vertical antenna. The tuner creates a 1:1 SWR (or something reasonably close to it) all the way back to the transceiver inside your house.

the tuner output and the antenna *remains unchanged.* If you had a 6:1 SWR before you bought the antenna tuner, you'll have a 6:1 SWR after. The loss in the feed line is the same as it always was. The only difference is that now the transceiver fold back circuit will not reduce its output. Instead, it will deliver its full measure of power to the feed line. More power is indeed reaching the antenna, but an awful lot is also still being wasted, especially if the feed line is lossy.

This is not to say that antenna tuners are worthless. As I just mentioned, they make it possible to deliver more power to the feed line. And if you are using an extremely low-loss feed line such as ladder line, you can use an antenna tuner to match the ladder line impedance to your transceiver and take advantage of the fact that so little RF is lost even under extremely high SWR conditions. There are many hams who use ladder line and antenna tuners in exactly this fashion with excellent results. Sure, the SWR is high, but with the low loss of ladder line, it really doesn't matter.

There are also antenna tuners that are designed to be placed at or near the antenna itself. These remote antenna tuners adjust themselves automatically when they sense transmitted RF on the feed line, or when they

receive a command from the transceiver. The great advantage of a remote tuner is that it creates a match between the feed point of the antenna (or at a point very close to it) and the feed line. This means that the resulting low SWR exists on the feed line all the way back to your transceiver, keeping loss to a bare minimum so that you can get away with using a feed line that is inexpensive and easy to install, such as coaxial cable. (See **Figure 1.6**.) We'll include remote antenna tuners with some of the antenna system designs in this book.

So let's condense our discussion of feed lines to four pertinent bullet points:
- The higher the frequency of the RF applied to a feed line, the greater the loss.
- The greater the length of a feed line, the greater the loss.
- The higher the SWR, the greater the loss.
- An antenna tuner does nothing to reduce feed line loss between the tuner and the antenna.

Keep these points in mind when choosing a feed line for your antenna. If you're thinking of setting up a VHF/UHF antenna, always chose a low-loss cable such as 9913 or LMR-400 unless the antenna is within 15 or 20 feet of your operating position. For HF you can get away with RG-58 or an RG-8 va-

riety, again depending on the overall length — and assuming a low SWR on the feed line.

Ladder line is terrific for HF use if you can manage to get it back to your station without bending it at sharp angles or allowing it to come too close to lossy or metallic objects. Keep in mind, however, that you will *most definitely* need an antenna tuner at your radio to bridge the impedance gap between the ladder line and the 50-Ω output of your transceiver. This can't be a tuner designed for coax; it must have a *balanced* input.

But what about transceivers with built-in antenna tuners? Many of these tuners are designed to handle limited impedance mismatches, like those typically resulting in a maximum SWR of 3:1. They are also designed for use with coaxial cable. These tuners were intended to "touch up" minor mismatches, such as when you choose to operate on a frequency that is a bit outside the SWR bandwidth of your antenna (for instance, when jumping from CW on 3.560 MHz where an antenna SWR might be 1.3:1 to SSB on 3.910 MHz where the SWR may rise to nearly 3:1).

On the other hand, it is possible to add a 4:1 balun (see **Figure 1.7**) to make the transition between the balanced ladder line and the unbalanced coaxial output. However, it is

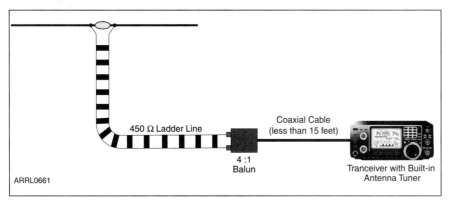

Figure 1.7 — If you can't bring ladder line all the way back to your radio, here is an alternative. Use a 4:1 external balun to make the transition between the ladder line and a *short* (less than 15 foot) length of low loss coaxial cable. With luck, the antenna tuner at your station will be able to find an acceptable match on several bands this way. The reason for keeping the coax very short is because the SWR may be quite high at times. High SWR isn't a problem for ladder line, but it is for coax and the resulting loss may be substantial.

quite likely that the resulting impedance will still be outside the range of the transceiver tuner on some frequencies.

TO AMPLIFY OR NOT TO AMPLIFY

A compromise antenna will always offer a compromised radiation pattern — either it will not focus your RF energy in a specific direction, or it may do so in an environment filled with obstacles that absorb and scatter the energy. This isn't a huge problem *per se*; you'll still make plenty of contacts. But when the going gets tough — poor propagation, heavy interference, or both — your only remaining option may be to increase your output power.

The seductive lure of this line of thinking is the fact that there is a large grain of truth in it. If you can't improve your antenna, you can indeed compensate by generating more RF. The laws of physics support this notion wholeheartedly. For example, assume that you've purchased an amplifier to boost the 100 W at your transceiver to 600 W. That represents a gain factor of six, translating to about 7.8 dB. The result is a gain of about 1.3 S units at the other guy's receiver, which can make a real difference, about the same as going from a dipole to a good 3-element Yagi. That's significant, especially if conditions are marginal.

The problem with doing this is that you also greatly increase the RF in your local environment. The typical result is interference to the electronics in your home and in the homes of your neighbors. It also raises RF Safety issues, which we'll discuss shortly.

Then there is the economics of adding power. I don't just mean the cost of the amplifier itself. If you're looking at a VHF/

UHF amplifier, you may need to purchase a high-current power supply to run it. HF amplifiers usually include their own power supplies, but many of these supplies require 240 V ac, so include the cost of an electrician to run a 240 V line to your station. If your antenna system relies on an antenna tuner, the tuner will need to be capable of handling high power, as will the feed line. So, you may well be required to make more purchases beyond the amplifier itself.

Finally, and importantly, always keep in mind that while adding an amplifier will improve your transmitted signal, it will do *absolutely nothing* to improve your ability to receive. In the worst case scenario, you could become what in Amateur Radio lore is known as an "alligator" — all mouth and no ears.

I don't mean to shoot holes in your dreams of RF conquest. If you have the financial wherewithal to install an amplifier, and if you are willing to tackle the interference and

safety issues, an amplifier is a worthy investment and it *will* make a positive difference. Just choose carefully and make sure you examine your options thoroughly.

RF SAFETY

This book is all about enjoying Amateur Radio with antennas that you can squeeze into small spaces. So, by default, we're talking about antennas that will be pretty close to you and your fellow humans. Every time you transmit, you'll be bathing the entire area, and everyone within it, in RF energy.

In years gone by, no one worried about RF Safety beyond the admonition not to grab an antenna when someone was transmitting. I once met an elderly amateur who was on the air in the ancient days of spark-gap transmitters. He identified himself as R. F. Burns, and then added with a smile, "And it does, too!"

I doubt that Mr Burns concerned himself with thoughts of how RF energy might be affecting his body at the molecular level. Today, however, all that has changed. Within the last couple of decades scientific studies have pointed to a *possible* association between RF exposure and some forms of cancer. Association is not the same as causation, though. To date, no studies have conclusively demonstrated that RF energy causes malignancies. In fact, a number of studies have shown no link whatsoever.

But the controversy lingers, stoked by the mainstream media and the Internet. In 1996 the Federal Communication Commission issued a requirement that all amateurs conduct RF Safety evaluations.

The evaluation process isn't as serious as it sounds. You don't need test equipment and you don't have to submit paperwork to the FCC (although you are required to log your evaluation results and keep them at your station). An RF Safety evaluation amounts to plugging some numbers into an online

The Alpha 9500 RF power amplifier can generate up to 1500 W.

Amateur Radio RF Safety Calculator

Calculation Results

Average Power at the Antenna	100 watts
Antenna Gain in dBi	0 dBi
Distance to the Area of Interest	10 feet 3.048 metres
Frequency of Operation	28 MHz
Are Ground Reflections Calculated?	Yes
Estimated RF Power Density	0.2193 mW/cm²

	Controlled Environment	Uncontrolled Environment
Maximum Permissible Exposure (MPE)	1.153 mW/cm²	0.2346 mW/cm²
Distance to Compliance From Centre of Antenna	4.4206 feet 1.3474 metres	9.8229 feet 2.994 metres
Does the Area of Interest Appear to be in Compliance?	yes	yes

Interpretation of Results

1. The power value entered into these calculations should be the average power seen at the antenna and not Peak Envelope Power (PEP). You should also consider feedline loss in calculating your average power at the antenna.

2. If you wish to estimate the power density at a point below the main lobe of a directional antenna, and if the antenna's vertical pattern is known, recalculate using the antenna's gain in the relevant direction.

3. Please also consult FCC OET Bulletin 65 Supplement B, the Amateur Radio supplement to FCC OET Bulletin 65. It contains a thorough discussion of the RF Safety regulations as they apply to amateur stations and contains numerous charts, tables, worksheets and other data to help determine station compliance.

Perform another computation

Figure 1.8 — The RF Power Density calculator created by Paul Evans, VP9KF, at http://hintlink.com/power_density.htm.

calculator to determine whether your station is in compliance. Yes, it is really that simple.

See **Figure 1.8**. This is the RF Power Density calculator created by Paul Evans, VP9KF, at **http://hintlink.com/power_density.htm**. Give this calculator a try, plugging in various values. For many of the antennas described in this book, you can assume the gain is 0 dB. The exception is a directional antenna where the gain may be substantially higher in the direction where it is pointing.

You'll notice that VP9KF's calculator mentions *controlled* and *uncontrolled* environments. In a controlled RF environment people know that RF is present and can take steps to control their exposure. These are primarily occupational environments, but the FCC includes amateurs and their immediate households (families). This applies to areas where you control access. The limits for controlled environments are evaluated differently (less stringently) than those for uncontrolled environments.

Uncontrolled RF environments are those open to the general public, where persons would normally be unaware of exposure to RF energy. This applies to all property near your station where you don't control public access: sidewalks, roads, neighboring homes and properties that might have some degree of public access.

Try the calculator with 100 W at 28 MHz to a 0 dBi antenna with the "distance to the area of interest" set to 10 feet. This might be an indoor antenna. Run the calculator and you'll see that such an installation would be in compliance in both environments. Print the screen to paper and you've just performed

an RF Safety evaluation for this particular installation.

If you try the calculator with different frequencies, power levels and distances, it quickly becomes obvious that you have to be running substantial power at VHF frequencies or higher, and be fairly close to the antenna, to be out of compliance. Even so, it pays to perform and log the evaluation anyway — not just because it is the law, but also to have on hand in case someone becomes concerned about your station and its effects on their health. Being able to show that you're in compliance with the FCC goes a long way.

FINDING A LOCATION FOR YOUR ANTENNA

Even though you probably haven't yet browsed the other chapters where we discuss specific commercial and homebrew antennas, it helps to take a moment and consider your installation options.

If you live in an apartment or condominium, do you have an attic space overhead? If so, find the access door. It is often hidden away in a closet or utility room. With a ladder or stepstool, grab a flashlight, open the hatch and take a look around. If you can easily (and safely) climb into the attic, go ahead and take some measurements. How much height is available? How much horizontal length? What does the insulation look like? Is it just blown-in fiberglass or other material, or do you see sections of insulation with reflective metallic backing? (The metallic backing is bad news for antennas, so much so that it pretty much rules out the attic as an antenna farm.)

If you don't have an attic, scope out the inside of your apartment. Are there any rooms that might accommodate an antenna secured to the ceiling? If so, how much space is available? If you are considering VHF/UHF antennas, don't neglect the windows, especially if you live in a second story apartment, or a two-story townhouse. In which directions do the windows face? Do they have metal screens? If so, can the screens be removed? I know amateurs who have enjoyed great success pointing directional VHF/UHF antennas out of windows. One gentleman has almost clinched his VUCC award on 2 meters in this fashion. During one band opening, he used his "window Yagi"

Investigating a condominium attic as a possible "antenna farm" — with a little help from my cat.

to work a station 1500 miles away!

Finally, apartment and condo dwellers should examine the property for nearby trees. Depending on how restrictive the landlord or condo association might be, trees provide excellent opportunities for discreet long-wire antennas. I once lived in an apartment with a gorgeous towering pine tree about 60 feet from my bedroom window. One night I took an innocent stroll to visit the tree. While there, I quickly tossed a weight attached to a thin wire high into the branches. I snaked the wire back to my apartment window and used it as a classic long-wire antenna on every band from 40 through 10 meters. If the maintenance crew ever noticed my wire, they didn't say anything.

If you're lucky enough to live in a house, your antenna location options expand considerably. Take a walk around the yard and make some measurements. Look for convenient supports such as trees and note their distances from each other and your house. It is helpful to carry along a clipboard or pad of paper and draw a crude map as you survey your property.

Don't neglect the roof of your home. A chimney can support small VHF antennas, although I recommend against using chimneys to support larger antennas. Big antennas put a lot of mechanical stress on chimneys, stress they were never designed to handle. The results can be catastrophic. If your roof is available (not restricted by association rules, local ordinances or angry spouses), consider a roof tripod instead. These metal tripods are inexpensive and commonly available. Just be sure to secure it properly with sufficient sealant around the leg bolts to prevent water from entering your attic and add lumber in the attic between the rafters to brace the roof. When in doubt, call an expert for this job. Besides, working on rooftops can be hazardous. It's often best if you direct the activity from the ground and let a bonded expert handle the antenna installation.

INTERFERENCE TO AND FROM

When picking out the location for your limited-space antenna, keep in mind that it will likely be within easy striking distance of today's plethora of consumer electronics.

I could spend the rest of this book talking about radio frequency interference (RFI) issues. It is an extremely common problem among hams who operate with antennas installed in proximity to homes or apartments. Depending on how much power you intend to generate, chances are excellent that you will cause interference. Chances are also excellent that you will be on the receiving

Trees make excellent antenna supports. If you're careful, you can blend in a wire antenna so that hardly anyone will notice. Can you see the wire in the upper right corner?

end of interference from your own devices or your neighbor's.

If you're lucky, received interference will be minimal. Perhaps it will occur on frequencies that you can avoid without hampering your on-air enjoyment. If received interference becomes too much to bear, I strongly recommend picking up a copy of the *ARRL RFI Book*. It is your best guide as you take on the role of detective and try to track down the offending signals.

Curing interference that *you* generate is a more serious matter. When your transmissions ruin television viewing or disrupt Internet connections, your family and neighbors will be extremely unhappy, to say the least. In this situation, the *RFI Book* can again come to the rescue. In a real life example that occurred while writing this book, I discovered that the 20-meter transmissions from my backyard vertical antenna were playing havoc with my newly installed AT&T U-Verse TV, telephone and Internet service. Every time I transmitted, the U-Verse decoders at two bedroom televisions would instantly shut down. Consulting the *RFI Book*, I applied ferrite cores to the cables at each decoder. That cured the problem.

As you choose the location for your antenna, one rule of thumb is to keep it as far as possible from your residence or your neighbor's. Even moving the antenna location 10 or 20 feet can make a great deal of difference. Of course, if your antenna is indoors, your options are much more limited. If that is the case, consider reducing your power output. As you'll see in a moment, some modes of communication work wonders even at relatively low output power.

THE MODE IS THE MESSAGE

You should spend some time considering which modes of communication you intend to use. This decision can have a strong bearing on the amount of interference you may cause to others and the effectiveness of your limited-space antenna system.

Most hams want to talk. They want to grab their microphones and chat with the world, or at least with others in their vicinities. This is a fine thing, but effective, reliable voice communication with a compromise antenna requires substantial power. On SSB we're talking at least 100 W. On FM you can use less, especially if you can access a repeater to relay your signal. But if you want to enjoy reliable direct (*simplex*) FM voice communication, 50 to 100 W is probably necessary.

The reason has to do with the relative bandwidth of your transmitted signal. An SSB signal typically spreads its power over about 2.5 kHz of spectrum; amateur FM is about 10 kHz. When you use a wide-bandwidth mode, your RF energy is effectively "diluted," in a manner of speaking. Think of it in the same way that the light from a distant planet is diluted or dispersed as it travels through space. To your unaided eyes, Saturn appears as nothing more than a bright dot in the sky. You need a telescope to concentrate the light and reveal the majesty of its rings. The same is true for radio. That's why many hams rely on directional antennas (analogous to telescopes) to concentrate the dispersed RF energy and render an intelligible signal. These same antennas concentrate transmitted energy as well.

If you can't erect a directional antenna — most limited-space antennas are nondirectional or *omnidirectional* — your ability to communicate by voice will be somewhat limited. That's not to say that you won't work plenty of DX, but you won't do it as consistently or as easily as the guys with directional antennas.

The alternative is to try other communication modes that use your signal energy more efficiently. I'm talking about digital modes such as PSK31, or Morse code CW. Both of these modes confine your RF energy to bandwidths of less than 50 Hz. The difference at the receiving end can be spectacular. It is common to experience conditions in which a CW or digital signal can be copied easily while an SSB signal is unusable.

Hams who specialize in low power (QRP) operating rely on CW or digital modes for precisely this reason. QRP operators are able to communicate successfully with 5 W of output power or less, and with compromise antennas, when SSB would be impossible. Better yet, low output power also means that you'll greatly reduce interference to nearby electronic devices.

As I discussed earlier in this chapter, using low power with a compromise antenna will significantly reduce your chances of being able to communicate whenever you desire, but it certainly beats the alternative, which is no communication at all. If you can run 100 W or more on SSB without tearing up all the consumer electronic devices in the vicinity, by all means do so. On the other hand, if interference becomes a problem, consider CW or digital. CW has a bit of a learning curve and operating digital requires a computer and software, but the long-run payoff is considerable.

Indoor Antennas

Outdoor antennas are almost always superior to indoor designs because they are usually larger and blessed with not having to push and pull signals through various types of building materials. Outdoor antennas are also further away from sources of interference (read: computers and other consumer electronics) and less likely to cause interference to those devices.

But sometimes outdoor antennas are simply impossible. You may have a landlord or home/condo association blocking your every move. Or you may not have enough open property to erect an antenna of any kind. Either way, your only remaining option is to head indoors.

HF ON THE INSIDE

Let's start with wire. The nice thing about wire is that you can bend and shape it to fit your requirements. Even the smallest indoor rooms can accommodate an HF wire antenna if you are willing to be creative.

The easiest indoor wire antenna is the dipole — a center insulator (where the feed line attaches) and two wires of equal length. If you only care about operating on one band, you can try a single-band half wavelength

design. The classic formula to determine its length is:

468 / Frequency (MHz)

However, this formula was created with outdoor antennas in mind. It doesn't take nearby wood, drywall, electrical wiring or heating ducts into account. You can use the formula to get into the ballpark, but count on having to lengthen or shorten the wires considerably as you tweak the antenna for the lowest SWR.

Unless you live in a mansion with enormous rooms, some folding of the dipole will be necessary. The final shape of the antenna will depend on the dimensions and configuration of the room. Remember that the center of the dipole carries the most current and therefore does most of the radiating. This part should be as high and unfolded as possible. Because the ends of the dipole radiate less energy than the center, their orientation is not as important. They do carry the maximum voltage, however, so care should be taken to position the ends far enough from other conductors to avoid arcing, or contact with people or animals.

The dipole may end up being L-shaped, Z-shaped, U-shaped or some indescribable

corkscrew shape, depending on what space is available. As an example, consider the 20-meter dipole shown in **Figure 2.1**. Using the formula, we find that each leg is about 16 feet in length, yet it can squeeze into a small 10 × 10 foot bedroom with some creative folding.

I used an antenna like this to work many stations from a second story apartment while running about 25 W output (mostly CW at the time). To keep my wife happy, I made the dipole out of ordinary two-conductor speaker wire that I painted white to match the walls and ceiling. White thumbtacks held the wires along the corners where the walls met the ceiling. I even painted the coaxial feed line white to help camouflage it against the drywall. An alternative to consider, if you are running low power, is flat wire adhesive tape. It comes in large rolls and is easy to stick to a wall.

The most difficult aspect of setting up a single-band resonant dipole is trimming it for lowest SWR. You have to add or subtract wire in equal lengths from each leg of the antenna while taking SWR measurements to observe the results. On the other hand, one of the great things about indoor wire antennas is that they are easy to adjust — no need to climb ladders or brave inclement weather.

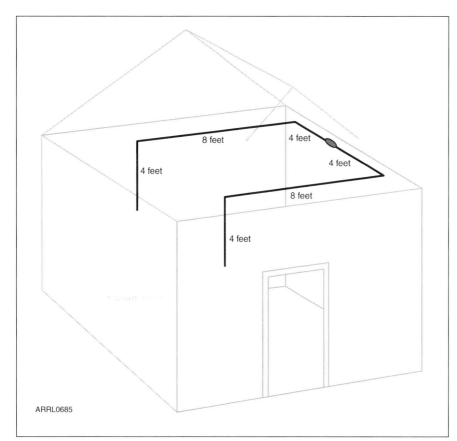

Figure 2.1 — Even a dipole antenna for the 20 meter band can fit into a small room with a bit of folding.

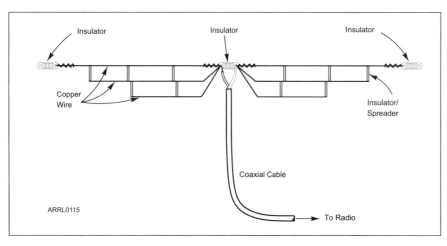

Figure 2.2 — The classic fan dipole brings several dipoles together at a single feed point.

Flat conductors with adhesive backing can be used to create low-power antennas in any room.

So what if you want to operate on more than one band with your wire antenna? One approach is a variation on the venerable fan dipole that essentially amounts to two or more dipoles attached to the same feed point (see **Figure 2.2**). When used outdoors, a fan dipole can present a challenge because the individual wire dipoles tend to interact, making adjustment an exercise in frustration. One way to reduce interaction is to have the dipoles arranged at right angles to each other.

Indoors, separating the dipoles can be a difficult proposition, but not impossible. **Figure 2.3** illustrates a design that makes the best use of two rooms. In this example, the 20 meter dipole is installed and folded into one room. The 15 meter dipole attaches to the same feed point, but extends into adjacent living room (more small wires and white paint).

The easiest way to get multiband perfor-

mance from a wire dipole antenna is to use an antenna tuner. See **Figure 2.4**. Here we have a 20-meter dipole along the ceiling, but notice that it is being fed with 450 Ω windowed ladder line rather than coaxial cable. Instead of the feed line snaking all the way back to the transceiver, it connects to the antenna tuner instead (a tuner with a balanced output port). The tuner, in turn, connects to the transceiver. As we discussed in Chapter 1, you can use a setup like this to operate on any frequency at which the antenna tuner can provide a sufficiently low SWR for your radio. Since you are using a short length of ladder line, the losses between the tuner and the antenna caused by high SWR are almost irrelevant.

If you want to have your radio in a separate room, but don't want to run bulky, highly visible ladder line through your home, look at the alternative in **Figure 2.5**. The antenna tuner can reside in a discrete location near the antenna, but thin coax such as RG-58 can make the rest of the journey back to the transceiver.

The configuration in Figure 2.5 is not ideal. Every time you change frequency at the transceiver, you'll probably have to go into the other room and adjust the antenna tuner. You can mark the positions of the tuner knobs to make this somewhat easier, but it is still an annoyance. The solution is to use a remote automatic antenna tuner (**Figure 2.6**). Depending on the type of automatic tuner you purchase, all you have to do is send a switching command from your radio or simply begin transmitting. The tuner will automatically seek the best SWR and you won't have to move a muscle. Remote automatic tuners are also an excellent device for attic antennas, as you'll see later. Like the antenna analyzers, automatic tuners are not cheap. They typically cost $200 to $400. Even so, the sheer

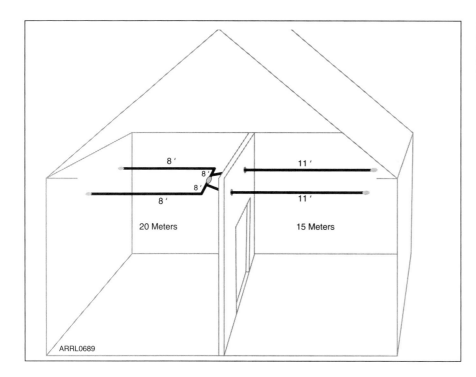

Figure 2.3 — In this example we have a 20 meter dipole in one room and a 15 meter dipole in an adjoining room — both connected at the same feed point.

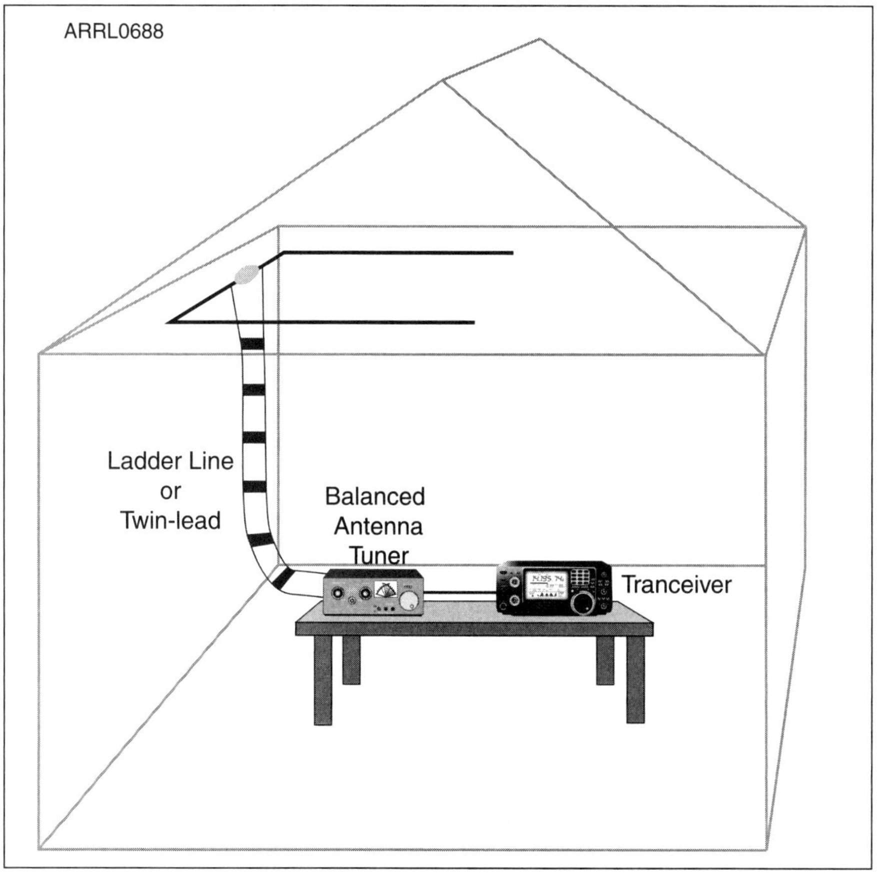

convenience is well worth the price.

So far we've been talking about dipoles, but that isn't the only option for wire antennas inside your home. Another option to consider is the loop antenna.

A loop antenna is exactly as it appears to be. It is a loop of wire connected to the feed line, which must seem pretty strange at first glance. Looking at a loop antenna, it appears to be a dead short, electrically speaking. But on the contrary, when RF is applied to a loop of wire, it sees that wire not as a dead short, but as a load with a specific impedance. When you consider an ordinary room, you can see that there are many opportunities for loop antennas. Take a look at **Figure 2.7** for just one example. In this example, the loop wire travels along the edge of the entire ceiling, connecting to a short length of 450 Ω windowed line that attaches to an antenna tuner. This is the same type of balanced antenna tuner we discussed before. Despite the relatively small diameter of this loop, an antenna tuner with a wide tuning range should be able to find a match on several different bands. This same loop antenna could just as easily be installed vertically on the wall; it all depends on the layout of your house or apartment. As with all antennas, higher is always better. If you live in a structure with aluminum siding, attaching the loop antenna to the ceiling rather than the wall is the best choice.

Figure 2.4 — A multiband ceiling dipole fed with 450-Ω ladder line. Unlike a tuned dipole, the length isn't critical. As a rule of thumb, make each leg of the dipole as long as the space allows and make sure both legs are of equal lengths.

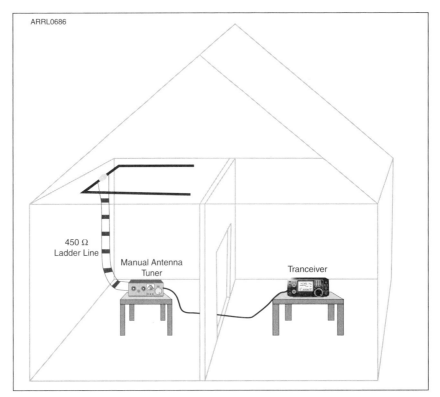

Figure 2.5 — If your station and your multiband antenna are in separate rooms, consider placing the manual antenna tuner close to the antenna, feeding the antenna with 450-Ω ladder line and then using thin RG-58 coaxial cable between the tuner and the radio.

Figure 2.6 — An automatic antenna tuner will seek the best match automatically whenever you transmit. This type of tuner is extremely convenient when your antenna is located in a separate area, such as an attic. This particular model is the MFJ-927.

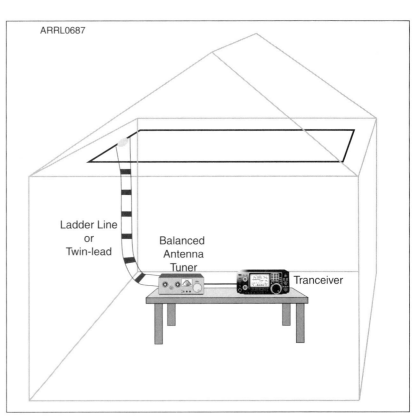

Figure 2.7 — A loop antenna is a continuous circle of wire that attaches at either side of an insulator at the feed point. In this example we have a loop installed within a room, typically on the ceiling. The loop should be as large as the room can accommodate. In this example, we're feeding the loop with 450-Ω ladder line and an antenna tuner for multiband operation.

If you like to play with different antenna designs, I'd strongly recommend investing in an antenna analyzer. These are wonderful devices for antenna experimenters. An antenna analyzer is essentially a low power transmitter coupled to a circuit that analyzes the reflected power (among other things) and displays the SWR. With a twist of a knob or the push of a button, you can sweep through a wide frequency range and determine the point where the SWR is lowest.

Let's use a folded 20 meter wire dipole as an example. You've connected your trusty antenna analyzer and set it for 14.050 MHz — the frequency you want as the "center frequency" of your antenna. You press the button to measure the SWR and…*uh-oh!*…your analyzer is displaying a 12:1 SWR. It is time to conduct a sweep and determine what is really going on.

Some analyzers sweep through a range of frequencies automatically and display a handy SWR plot on an LCD screen; others require you to sweep manually. Let's say you try a manual sweep, slowly adjusting the frequency

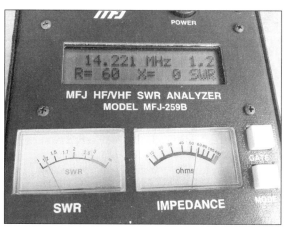

A close-up look at an MFJ antenna analyzer in action.

upward. Pretty soon you are beyond 16 MHz and the SWR just keeps climbing. This is a clear indicator that you need to reverse direction. As you sweep back down to 14.050 MHz and continue lower, you suddenly notice that the SWR is starting to fall. Keep going. Pretty soon the SWR is dropping below 3:1 and finally seems to bottom out at 1.5:1 at 13 MHz.

The analyzer is showing you that your dipole is actually resonant at 13 MHz, not 14.050 MHz. Since lower frequencies translate to longer antenna elements, your dipole is obviously too long. Trim a few inches from each of the ends and sweep again. Soon you will see the low SWR point "moving" upward. Keep sweeping and trimming until you finally see a 1.5:1 SWR reasonably close to 14.050 MHz.

A good antenna analyzer will cost you around $200 or more, but if you think you'll be doing interesting things with antennas now and in the future, an antenna analyzer is well worth the investment. What you'll spend for the instrument will save you time and frustration.

COMMERCIAL ANTENNAS INDOORS

Our discussion has centered on antennas that you have to build yourself, but you can just as easily use commercial antennas indoors as well. In fact, as long as the antenna is small enough to fit inside the room of your choice, any antenna can be used.

One idea to consider is a mobile antenna. Even though these antennas are designed for use on cars, they can function just as well without being attached to a vehicle. The difference is that instead of a car body acting as a ground plane, you must use radial wires or perhaps a single wire known as a counterpoise attached to the ground point of the antenna. Some mobile antenna manufacturers have anticipated that their products would be used this way and they've provided supports such as tripods to make this possible. The Sidekick by High Sierra is a typical example of a mobile antenna that can be attached to a tripod and used indoors in a room with sufficiently high ceilings (9 to 10 feet).

Depending on the mobile antenna design, you may need to adjust a tap or coil whenever you wish to change bands. However, other mobile antennas use motorized mechani-

cal adjustments that can even be performed remotely using a small control box that you would keep by your radio.

It is interesting to note that you can also take two single-band mobile antennas and use them together as a dipole antenna. Manufacturers such as MFJ and High Sierra sell special mounting brackets that allow you to connect two mobile antennas together in this fashion. The mobile antennas screw into the bracket and then you simply attach a coaxial feed line. As handy as this arrange-

John Reisenauer, KL7JR, took two Citizens Band mobile antennas, trimmed them slightly, and then mounted both in a bracket to create a 10-meter dipole for apartment hamming.

ment might be, two mobile antennas back to back can still make for a rather long dipole antenna. For example, two Hamstick-style mobile antennas together for the 20-meter band are approximately 14 feet in length. In addition, these antennas tend to be inefficient, lossy radiators. The 2:1 SWR bandwidth is on the order of about 150 kilohertz at best. Even so, they offer an alternative approach for indoor operating, especially if you have sizable attic space available.

There are other small antenna designs that do not require radials or any other type of ground system. One well known example is the Bilal Isotron antenna. The Isotron has been around for many years. Without oversimplifying, the Isotron is an extremely compact design comprised of a loading coil and metal plates (depending on the model). The Isotron can be placed on a short mast and set up just about anywhere in a room. Depending on how much power you're running, it is best to keep the Isotron well away from nearby objects and people. High voltages can develop and they could be hazardous, not to mention the RF exposure concerns we discussed in Chapter 1.

Yet another antenna to consider for use indoors is a so-called magnetic loop. The antenna itself is not magnetic in any way. When used as a receiving antenna, however, it's said that the antenna primarily responds to the magnetic component of the received signal. Magnetic loop antennas have been around for decades and are popular mainly because they are highly portable. During

WWII and even throughout the Vietnam War era the military used magnetic loop antennas for this very reason. Compared to a dipole antenna, a magnetic loop antenna is not a very efficient radiator, but it can be effective when tuned properly. Perhaps the most popular commercially available loop is the MFJ-1788 Super Hi-Q loop. This magnetic loop is only about 4 feet in diameter yet it can operate on every band from 30 through 10 meters. The antenna has a built-in tuning mechanism consisting of a large variable capacitor attached to an electric motor. By operating the motor by remote control you can adjust the antenna for the lowest SWR. Like the Isotron, the MFJ loop does not require a ground system or radial wires. It does pose the same voltage and RF exposure concerns.

Speaking of tuning, it is important to note that small antennas tend to have very narrow 2:1 SWR bandwidths. Magnetic loop antennas in particular can have extremely narrow bandwidths on the order of just a few kHz. You may find that you must frequently retune whenever you change frequency.

The type of indoor antenna you choose, of course, depends on your circumstances and the size of your wallet. Wire antennas are obviously the least expensive, but for easy multiband operation you may have to also invest in an antenna tuner. Yes, some transceivers have built-in tuners, but most of these do not have the impedance range necessary for the task.

And wire antennas don't lend themselves

to being easily put up or taken down at a moment's notice. When you install a wire antenna in a room, you do it with the expectation that it is going to be there for a long time, hence the need to camouflage it — unless you have a very understanding spouse. Smaller freestanding antennas such as mobile antennas, the Bilal Isotron or the MFJ loop are much easier to set up or put away as required, but they may be more expensive than a simple do-it-yourself antenna.

As you are examining your indoor antenna options, don't forget your windows. Depending how strict your landlord or homeowner association may be, it is certainly possible to mount a mobile antenna on a windowsill with the radiating portion outside the window and the radials or counterpoise wire inside the room. See **Figure 2.8**. You will also find a number of HF portable antennas designed for low power outdoor operating that can also serve indoors or as window antennas. These antennas may be too tall to fit inside the average room, but they can certainly be mounted on a windowsill. Take a look at **Figure 2.9**. This is the model MP-1 portable HF antenna manufactured by Super Antennas. The MP-1 comes with a mounting bracket and clamp that are ideal for use in a window mounting situation. To change bands you simply move the metal sleeve up and down the loading coil. The MP-1 can also be removed quickly if necessary.

MFJ Enterprises offers an antenna known as the MFJ-1622 that is specifically de-

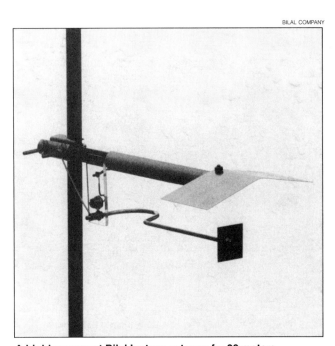

A highly compact Bilal Isotron antenna for 20 meters.

BILAL COMPANY

MFJ

The MFJ-1786 is a small loop antenna with a remotely tuned capacitor to resonate it on 30 through 10 meters.

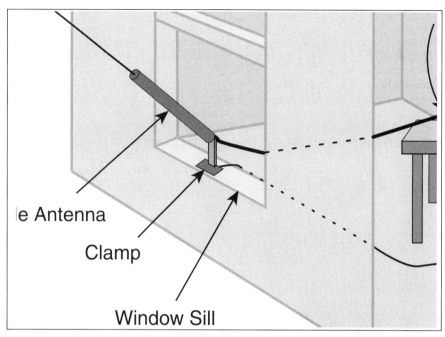

e Antenna

Clamp

Window Sill

Figure 2.8 — A mobile antenna can clamp to a windowsill and extend outdoors. To provide an RF current "return," a counterpoise wire attaches to the antenna ground point (where it would normally attach to a car body). This wire should be at least ¼ wavelength at the desired frequency if the mobile antenna is a single-band design. If it is a multiband tunable antenna, it will work best with a ¼ wave counterpoise for each band you intend to use.

Figure 2.9 — The Super Antennas MP-1 is a multiband HF antenna intended for portable operating. However, it can also be used indoors.

signed for apartment window installations. The mount attaches to the window and the antenna is adjusted for the lowest SWR by selecting coil taps. See **Figure 2.10**.

Once again, none of these very small HF antennas are particularly efficient. But as we discussed in chapter one, when used with a narrow bandwidth mode such as CW or PSK 31, they will provide hours of enjoyment.

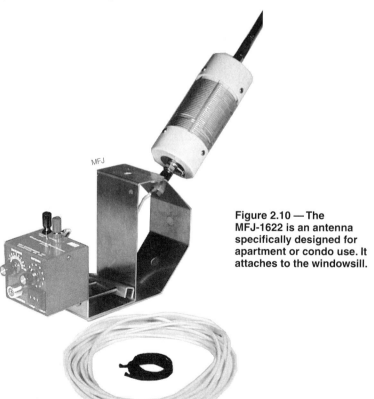

Figure 2.10 — The MFJ-1622 is an antenna specifically designed for apartment or condo use. It attaches to the windowsill.

INTO THE ATTIC

If you're fortunate enough to live in a home, apartment, or condominium that has an attic space, you may find that you have an excellent location for an antenna farm right over your head!

Attics in modern homes tend to be rather small. Count yourself lucky if you have an attic that will allow you to stand upright; most modern attics offer, at most, 4 or 5 feet of headroom between the attic floor and the peak of the roof. Attics in newer homes also tend to be unfinished. This means that instead of a floor you will find only lumber joists packed with insulation.

The truly lucky hams are the ones who live in older homes with large finished attics. Some of these old attics are rooms unto themselves with high ceilings, finished floors and plenty of horizontal space. Hams with attics like these have room not only for wire antennas, but also even for small directional arrays.

If you live in an apartment or condominium and you're on the top floor, it's time to do some detective work. Access to the

Even a partially finished attic is ideal for an antenna farm. Notice the TV antenna (or at least half of one) pointing out the window.

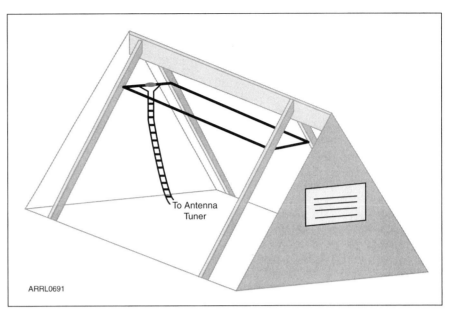

ARRL0691

Figure 2.11 — An HF loop antenna can be easily installed within an attic by stringing the wire along the rafters. You can feed it with 450-Ω ladder line and use an antenna tuner for multiband operation.

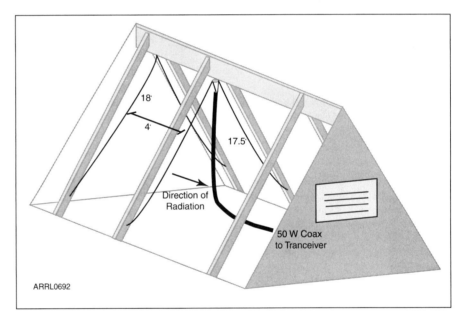

ARRL0692

Figure 2.12 — If you have a sufficiently large attic, you can even construct a wire Yagi antenna by using rafters as supports. This example is a 10-meter version. Dimensions shown are approximate.

attic is typically provided by a small door, a hatchway really, that you'll find tucked away in a closet or utility room. In many instances, however, these attics are shared, which means that you don't have the attic all to yourself. Approach this type of attic with special care. If you're considering the idea of stringing a wire antenna along the length of the attic, keep in mind that you'll be walking right over your neighbor's rooms as you are putting it up. They aren't likely to appreciate this and there is always the danger that your foot may slip off a joist, smash through the drywall and appear in their home as an uninvited guest. It is one thing to slip and punch a hole through your own ceiling; some handiwork with a drywall patch will set it right. Your neighbor won't be nearly as understanding!

But having said all that, a shared attic is still an excellent place for an antenna. At the very least you could install a commercial antenna such as a Bilal Isotron, a remotely adjustable mobile antenna (in a horizontal orientation, perhaps) or even a magnetic loop antenna (assuming you can get it through the hatch and into the attic). Of course, a long wire antenna is still possible in a shared attic if you are careful and considerate.

Before you start planting antennas in your attic, take a look around. Check the underside of the roof in particular. Is the underside packed with insulation? If the answer is "yes," gently pull down a small corner of the insulating material and see what is on the other side. Some types of insulation have a metal backing and, for obvious reasons, this is not a good situation for antennas. You may decide to remove such insulation, but it may have a strong negative impact on your utility

bills. And if you're a renter, your landlord may be displeased if he or she finds out.

It pays to take a glance at your roof from the outside as well. You don't have to scale a ladder, but take a good look from ground level and see if you can determine whether the roof is overlaid with asphalt shingles or something similar. If your attic space is under a metal roof, that's bad news since it renders your attic unusable as an antenna farm.

Assuming that you can use your attic, what's the best antenna to put up there? The answer is easy: the largest antenna that will

fit the space. Even if you have a relatively small attic chances are good that you can install the same wire dipole or loop that you would use indoors. For example, I have used remote automatic antenna tuners in attics with good success. In one townhouse attic I installed a small wire loop antenna in the 20 foot by 20 foot attic, stringing the wires along the rafters and holding them in place with nylon string (**Figure 2.11**). At the feed point I ran a 6 foot length of ladder line to a remote automatic antenna tuner. From the antenna tuner I snaked 30 feet of RG-58

Jeff Blaine, AC0C, has one of the most elaborate HF attic antenna installations known. With it he has worked a ton of DX and has been a competitive presence in a number of contests — all with a ham station that is utterly invisible to his neighbors.

My #1 advice to guys working on attic antennas is to view the project as an iterative experiment. You won't know exactly what will work best until you try to build the first antenna. And that experience will lead you to take new paths; consider new ideas. I'm on the 4th generation of antennas now at my current home and each generation is higher in performance and capability than the one before it.

There is an upside for an interior antenna that is pretty significant: If you love to fiddle with antennas, the attic provides a great environment because you don't need to be worried about the weather, and you can work on your antennas when your friends are "grounded" due to weather! You'll really appreciate that fact when wind or ice storms strike.

Questions and Answers

Isn't the performance of an HF attic antenna always inferior to that of an outdoor antenna?

Not necessarily. I've seen HF dipoles in attics *outperform* outdoor dipoles because the attic antennas had a height advantage. If the concern is attenuation caused by wood roofs and asphalt or slate shingles, you should know that at HF frequencies the impact is insignificant.

On the other hand, if the attic antenna is a compromise, compact design, it will almost always underperform a full-sized outdoor antenna (unless your attic is atop a 20-story building!).

Aren't the interference problems caused by attic antennas insurmountable?

Not at all. There are a few problem areas for the HF attic antenna farmer and RFI in the house is indeed one. Fortunately, these issues are not as serious as they may seem, especially with so much modern consumer technology shifting to VHF and microwave spectrum for communication (the typical consumer Wi-Fi computer network operates at 2.4 GHz).

That said, interference can become an issue if you insist on using higher power levels (50 W and up). The good news is that most problems can be easily remedied with the application of ferrite chokes on the afflicted devices (usually telephones or televisions). Pick up a copy of *The ARRL RFI Book* and keep it on hand as your reference for diagnosis and treatment.

Won't the RF energy radiated by an attic antenna be dangerous to the people in the house?

As discussed in Chapter 1 of this book, the FCC requires amateurs to perform an assessment of RF levels called Maxi-mum Permissible Exposure (MPE). If you read Chapter 1, you also learned that at HF frequencies — even with substantial RF power output — the exposure level for the inhabitants of your home will likely be well below the permitted threshold.

Are attic antennas fire hazards?

In most instances, no.

For the most common type of HF antenna, the dipole, the high voltage points are at the ends of the antenna. The conductivity of open air is roughly 0.3 to 0.8 $\times$ 10^{-14} Siemens per Meter. That is a very poor degree of conductivity, so it requires a large amount of electrical energy to create a spark across a one-inch gap.

But a spark to *where*? Critics fail to consider that electricity can only flow when it has a path to ground. The end of an antenna may be at a high voltage potential, but to where is that spark going to jump? Dry wood has an extremely high resistance value, so even with a bare wire connected directly to wood, the resistance in the return path to ground is essentially infinite. Current won't flow and the wood won't heat to the point of combustion.

Now this is not a free pass to ignore good engineering and safety practices. And to the extent local regulations or perhaps insurance company considerations exist, you may be required to expand your precautions.

When building attic antennas we often want to keep the wires away from the wood structure, especially at the ends, because of the capacitive detuning effects. This is good antenna building logic and it gives you some additional peace of mind should you ever attempt to run high power levels with your attic installation. Also keep your antenna wires away from any metal pipes, duct work or electrical wiring that may be in your attic.

Aren't attics awfully hot environments in which to work on antennas?

Well, yes, they can be. If you need to be told "Don't climb your outside tower in an ice storm," you should also appreciate the advice "Don't build attic antennas in the heat of the summer." Common sense applies here. If you must work in your attic during the summer, do it in the early morning or at night.

By working in my attic don't I run the risk of falling?

Yes, that can happen. In most cases, the injuries will be more to your dignity and bank account. Attic antenna farming requires the ability to negotiate rafters and keep your feet on the floor joists. If you slip and fall, your foot will easily go through the sheetrock ceiling. If you aren't sufficiently nimble, find someone else to do it.

What if my house has a metal roof and is covered with wire-impregnated stucco on the sides?

Okay. I give up on that one!

coaxial cable all the way back to my radio. With this arrangement I was able to operate on 30 through 10 meters.

Depending on the size and the design of your attic you can do some amazingly creative things. For instance, let's say that you have a sizable attic in a house with wood or vinyl siding. It is possible to use such an attic to install a wire Yagi antenna for 20 meters or the higher bands by draping wires for the antenna element along the rafters. See **Figure 2.12**. To be sure, this would be a challenging antenna design. You would have to do quite a bit of trimming and repositioning of wires to finally achieve the best result. And it goes without saying that this antenna would have a fixed pattern since you wouldn't be able to rotate it. Even so, a large directional antenna can be built within an attic and it will work quite well. I once installed an antenna like this for the 10 meter band while I was living in a condominium with a relatively small attic. It took me all day, even with an antenna analyzer, to finally get all the wires in the right places and the antenna adjusted for the lowest SWR, but DX stations within the pattern of my antenna reported that I often had a booming signal while running just 100 W.

INDOOR ANTENNAS ABOVE 50 MHZ

So far we've concentrated on HF antennas for indoor applications, but that's not to say that you can't enjoy VHF operating as well. VHF antennas are certainly smaller and easier to install indoors, but signal attenuation caused by the materials in the surrounding walls is a serious problem at VHF and above. Also, antenna height plays a much more critical role at VHF. There are exceptions to the rule, as we'll see shortly, but generally speaking the higher the antenna at VHF, the better the performance.

If you live on the top floor of an apartment building and you have access to the attic, you may be in luck. The same holds true if you live in a house with an attic, particularly if the house is at a high elevation. Either situation lets you take advantage of the available height, allowing you to work some serious VHF and UHF DX. Les Rayburn, N1LF, lives in a home that is only about 400 feet above sea level, but he has turned his attic into a highly effective VHF/UHF antenna farm. See the sidebar, "Les Rayburn, N1LF, on Attic Antennas Above 50 MHz."

Antennas for FM and Digital

For most FM and digital applications (such as the Automatic Packet Reporting System, better known as APRS), a sturdy antenna that radiates in all directions is good enough for the job. I'll assume that there is a repeater or packet digipeater reasonably close by to pick up and relay your signals. If that's the case, antenna height is usually not critical.

One of the most common omnidirectional antenna designs for VHF and UHF is the *ground plane*. This antenna is easy to build and can be installed almost anywhere. A ground plane antenna for 2 meters is only about 19 inches tall (a quarter wavelength for this band) and sports four sloping radials. See the diagram for a ground plane in **Figure 2.13**. You can even make a ground plane antenna out of an SO-239 coaxial connector and some stiff wire, or you can buy one from your local Amateur Radio dealer. As you might imagine, these simple antennas are not expensive.

Like all antennas designed for FM use, the ground plane is vertically polarized. There is nothing magical about vertically polarized radio waves, but if the polarization of your antenna doesn't match the polarization of the antenna at the other end of the path, the result is a large loss of signal strength, possibly on the order of 20 dB. Vertical polarization was chosen for FM work because most operation is conducted from automobiles and their antennas are vertical.

Another popular vertically polarized design is the J-Pole. This is an end-fed omnidirectional dipole matched to the feed line

Les Rayburn, N1LF, on Attic Antennas Above 50 MHz

My VHF/UHF antenna farm is in the attic space above an unused bedroom at the rear of my house. The antennas are about 25 feet above ground; the house itself is at 425 feet above sea level.

I had the luxury of building our new home "around" my indoor antenna requirements. This allowed me to specify the type of roof shingles that would cause the least amount of signal attenuation. I chose my shingles by doing a "poor man's" RF test. I took samples of all the shingles the builder recommended and placed them, one at a time, into glasses of water inside my microwave oven. I heated them for 60 seconds and then measured their surface temperatures. I selected the shingle that had the lowest temperature because, according to my theory, it had absorbed the lowest level of microwave energy. I have no scientific proof that the test was accurate, but I notice no significant degradation in antenna performance unless the roof is wet.

Whenever we have rainfall, all bands above 222 MHz are lost causes. I live in the South and rarely experience ice or snow, but under these conditions I'm sure the attenuation would be much worse. Fortunately, most enhanced VHF propagation goes hand-in-hand with the dog days of summer, and we don't get a lot of rain here during the warmer months.

RF exposure was a top concern as I planned the installation. Fortunately, I found that beyond a normally empty guest bedroom I would be well within FCC guidelines as long as power was kept below 200 W. As it turns out, I run 160 W on 2 meters and 100 W on 6 meters. I keep my output at 125 W on 222 MHz and cap it at just 30 W on 902 and 1296 MHz. Of course, I avoid operating whenever we have guests occupying the bedroom!

My attic antenna system consists of a 3-element 6-meter Yagi, a 6-element 2-meter Yagi, an 8-element 222 MHz Yagi, an 11-element 432-MHz Yagi and an 18-element loop Yagi

for 1296 MHz. I have also installed preamplifiers at several of these antennas.

How well does it work? Remarkably well! When this book went to press, I had worked stations in 98 grid squares on 2 meters and more than 270 grid squares on 6 meters. My grid square totals on 432 and 1296 are equally impressive, especially when you consider the fact that all these contacts were made with attic Yagi antennas.

N1LF

N1LF has stuffed his attic full of VHF, UHF and microwave beam antennas like the ones shown here.

This attic would be a ham's nightmare. The proliferation of foil-backed insulation makes it useless as a location for antennas.

ing, my experience has shown that you are better off using directional antennas for indoor VHF work. At 6 meters a directional antenna such as a Yagi can be quite large and only suitable for the biggest attics. Antennas for 2 meters and up, however, become much smaller and more manageable indoors.

As N1LF mentions in his sidebar, the higher you go in frequency, the more attenuation you'll suffer from the building materials that surround you. In addition, moisture can compound the problem. A wet or snow-covered roof will effectively shut down attic antennas at UHF and above. I used to enjoy amateur satellite operation with a small 435 MHz Yagi antenna in my attic, but whenever it rained or snowed, I was off the air!

In an attic installation, you may have the luxury of being able to rotate your directional antennas with an electric antenna rotator. Check the turning radius of your largest an-

by a quarter wavelength "stub." That's what gives the antenna its name since it looks like the letter **J**. (See **Figure 2.14**.) The J-Pole is a half-wavelength antenna and provides some gain compared to the quarter wavelength ground plane. A J-Pole tends to be sensitive to surrounding metal objects, so beware of this fact as you choose a location.

Edison Fong, WB6IQN, designed a dual-band (2 meter and 70-cm) J-pole made from 300 Ω twinlead, the kind of feed line ordinarily used with TV antennas. You'll find his article titled "The DBJ-2 A Portable VHF-UHF Roll-up J-pole Antenna for Public Service" in the Appendix of this book.

"Weak Signal" Antennas

As the term suggests, weak signal operating on VHF and above takes place using SSB, CW or digital modes without the assistance of repeaters or digipeaters. This means that antenna performance becomes particularly critical. Since weak-signal operators use horizontal polarization, it also means that your antennas have to be polarized accordingly.

It is possible to use horizontally polarized omnidirectional antennas for weak signal work. On 6 meters in particular, an omnidirectional antenna such as a loop or even a dipole will provide many contacts. When Sporadic E propagation is in play on 6 meters, any antenna — indoors or out — will do. While writing this book I happened to work a Canadian station during a 6-meter Sporadic E opening. He was 800 miles away and using just a wire dipole antenna in his attic, yet his signal was pinning the S meter on my transceiver at 20 dB over S9.

But the magic of 6 meters notwithstand-

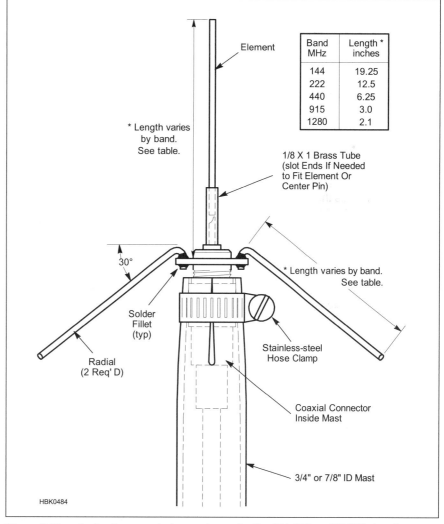

Band MHz	Length * inches
144	19.25
222	12.5
440	6.25
915	3.0
1280	2.1

Element

* Length varies by band. See table.

1/8 X 1 Brass Tube (slot Ends If Needed to Fit Element Or Center Pin)

* Length varies by band. See table.

30°

Solder Fillet (typ)

Stainless-steel Hose Clamp

Radial (2 Req' D)

Coaxial Connector Inside Mast

3/4" or 7/8" ID Mast

HBK0484

Figure 2.13 — A simple ground-plane antenna for the 144, 222 or 440-MHz bands. The feed line and connector are inside the PVC mast, and a hose clamp squeezes the slotted mast end to tightly grip the plug body. Vertical element and radial dimensions given in the drawing are good for the entire band.

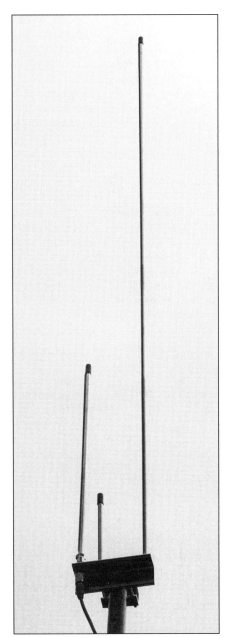

Figure 2.14 — The J-Pole is a popular omnidirectional antenna design that can be used indoors or out. This model is made by Arrow Antennas (www. arrowantennas.com).

A typical 6-meter horizontal full wave loop antenna. An antenna like this can be used indoors as well.

The 2-meter PortaQuad by National RF isn't intended for permanent outdoor use, but it would be a fine directional antenna inside a room (by a window), or within an attic.

tenna and see if it can rotate without slamming into the rafters. If its rotational path is clear, you're good to go. You'll have to string the rotator cable along with the coaxial feed line, but since you're already punching one hole into your drywall, another hole won't make much difference!

If you can't rotate your directional antenna, don't despair. Mount it permanently, pointing in the best direction possible depending on where you believe most of your contacts will take place. Another possibility

is to buy or build several antennas and switch between them using a remote antenna switch that is rated for VHF or UHF applications

For all your indoor VHF antennas, rotating or fixed, I strongly recommend the use of receive preamplifiers. These will give your received signals a much needed boost. Install these preamps directly at the antennas. You may need to string a separate dc power cable to the preamp, but there are

also models that will allow you to apply power through the coaxial cable itself. You'll also need some means to remove the preamplifier from the circuit each time you transmit. Preamps from manufacturers such as Downeast Microwave, SSB Electronic and Advanced Receiver Research often include the ability to sense the presence of transmitted RF and switch out of line automatically.

Outdoor Antennas for the HF Bands

If you're like me, you may be living on a piece of land that barely accommodates the house that sits on it. Or you may be living in an apartment or condominium with little or no land to speak of; perhaps just a balcony, a deck or a window facing an open yard with a few trees. Assuming that you aren't hampered by local ordinances, landlord rules or homeowner association restrictions, you can almost always put up an outdoor antenna *somewhere*. All you have to do is find the right antenna design to fit the available space!

THE CLASSIC MULTIBAND DIPOLE

When it comes to HF antennas, I tend to prefer multiband designs. After all, if you have little room for antennas to begin with, it makes sense to erect one antenna that covers as many frequencies as possible.

One of the simplest, most effective antennas in this category is a multiband random-length dipole fed with an open-wire feed line. This design has been around for close to 100 years and it remains a favorite today. See **Figure 3.1**.

You'll notice that Figure 3.1 doesn't specify a length for this antenna. Here is the

Figure 3.1 — The classic multiband dipole antenna. Simply make it as long as space allows and feed it with 450 Ω ladder line. With a good antenna tuner you'll be able to operate on several HF bands.

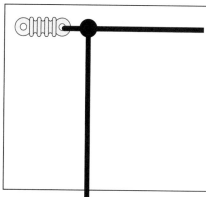

Figure 3.2 — Ladder line dipoles don't have to be installed in straight lines. You can droop the ends, for example.

formula to calculate it (written with tongue firmly planted in cheek):

Antenna Length = W × R / FT

W = The amount of wire you have available
R = The amount of room available
FT = Family Tolerance factor

In other words, you want as much wire as

possible, as high as possible. This antenna is not particularly "stealthy"; it is easy to see with its dangling feed line. So, the Family (or Spouse, or Neighbor) Tolerance factor may play a key role.

All kidding aside, my rule of thumb for the length of this antenna is to make it at least ½ wavelength for the lowest frequency band

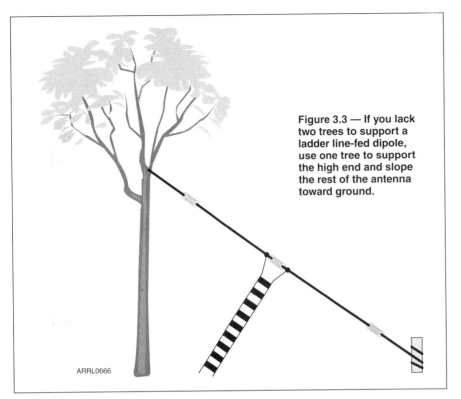

Figure 3.3 — If you lack two trees to support a ladder line-fed dipole, use one tree to support the high end and slope the rest of the antenna toward ground.

ARRL0666

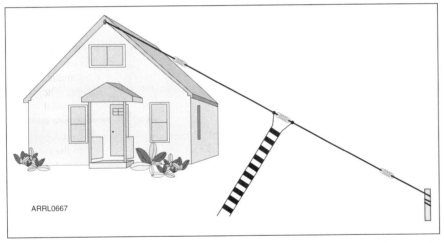

ARRL0667

Figure 3.4 — If you don't have trees at all, you can use your house to support one end of a sloping ladder-line fed dipole.

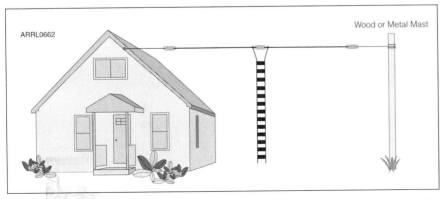

ARRL0662

Wood or Metal Mast

Figure 3.5 — Sometimes sloping an antenna to ground isn't a good solution, especially if you have a lot of human traffic in your yard. An alternative is to use a wood, metal or fiberglass mast to support one end and your house to support the other.

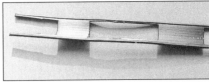

A section of 450 Ω "windowed" ladder line.

I intend to use. For 40 meters that would be 66 feet; for 20 meters, it would be 33 feet. As mentioned in Chapter 2, the half wavelength formula is:

Length = 468 / Frequency (MHz)

If you have two trees in your yard, they will make good supports for the classic multiband dipole. See the sidebar, "Trees as Antenna Supports." If you want to use this design at a low frequency such as 3.5 MHz, but you don't have 134 feet of open space between trees, don't worry. This antenna does *not* have to be deployed in a straight, horizontal line. Take a look at **Figure 3.2**. You can bend the wires in various directions to squeeze the antenna into the available space.

If you have only one tree, put it to good use. Get one end of the antenna as high as possible and slope the rest down to the ground (**Figure 3.3**). Or use the Inverted V approach by hauling the feed point of the antenna as high as possible and sloping both legs of the dipole to the ground.

No trees at all? No problem. Use your house to support one end and slope downward (**Figure 3.4**). Or plant a wood or metal mast in your yard (if the family will tolerate it) and use it to support one end of the dipole with the other end attached to your house (**Figure 3.5**). Just roam your property and open your mind to the possibilities that present themselves.

But what about that feed line?

The open-wire feed line is the "secret" of the success of this antenna. If you read Chapter 1, you know that balanced feed lines exhibit astonishingly low RF loss in the presence of high SWR. That characteristic is at the heart of this antenna's multiband performance.

Most hams feed this dipole with a type of balanced line known as 450 Ω *windowed ladder line*. It is a thin, flat line with open slots in the plastic insulation spaced every inch or so, hence the "window" reference. This feed line is commonly available from Amateur Radio dealers. You'll find it for sale at hamfest fleamarkets as well. With the "station end" of the feed line connected to a wide impedance range antenna tuner (one with a balanced input), you can find a 50 Ω impedance match for your transceiver on many bands.

Note that some antenna tuners, especially those that are internal to radios, are only rated

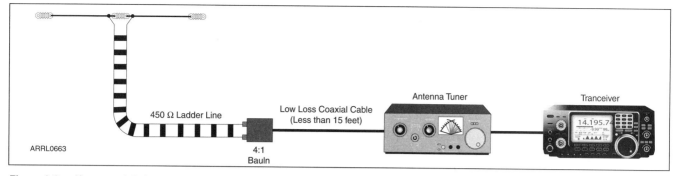

Figure 3.6 — If you can't bring 450 Ω ladder line all the way to your antenna tuner, try using a 4:1 balun, perhaps installed outside in a weatherproof enclosure. From the balun to the antenna tuner, you can use 50 Ω coaxial cable. Be sure to keep the coaxial cable short — preferably no more than 15 feet.

to match a 3:1 SWR. These are not suitable for this application.

Yes, the SWR on the feed line between the tuner and the antenna will be very high at times, but resulting RF loss in the ladder line is usually inconsequential. You wouldn't be able to say that about ordinary coaxial cable!

With the proper antenna tuner (automatic or manual) at your radio, you'll be able to easily hop from band to band. Let's say you installed a 34 foot dipole and fed it with ladder line. With luck your tuner should be able

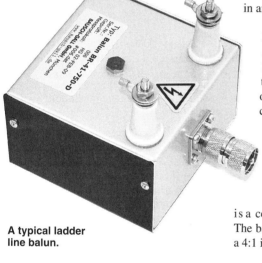

A typical ladder line balun.

to find an acceptable match (SWR less than 2:1) on 20 through 10 meters. Of course, depending on the variables inherent in your particular antenna installation, you may not be able to achieve a match on every band. Even so, it is a good bet that you will be able to operate on several bands — all through a single antenna system.

As we discussed in Chapter 1, getting ladder line into a home and to your station can be a challenge. You must keep ladder line several inches from metal objects such as aluminum siding, electrical wiring, etc. Nearby metal upsets the balance of the RF fields that surround the feed line, resulting in an impedance mismatch.

If you don't want to bring the ladder line all the way to the radio, there are alternatives. One is shown in **Figure 3.6**. In this example we're bringing the ladder line to a 4:1 *balun* installed outside the house in a weatherproof enclosure. From the balun there is a short (10 foot) run of coaxial cable to the antenna tuner. The balun acts as a transformer to make the transition from the balanced ladder line to the unbalanced coaxial cable. That's why it is called a balun; "balun" is a contraction of "balanced-unbalanced." The balun in this example is also providing a 4:1 impedance transformation.

The problem with this approach is two-fold: (1) High SWR will exist on the length of coaxial cable and the resulting loss could be substantial. That's why it must be kept as short as possible. My rule of thumb is to use low loss coax such as Belden 9913 and not exceed 15 feet. (2) The 4:1 impedance transformation may result, on some frequencies, in an impedance your antenna tuner can't accommodate. You could try other balun ratios such as 1:1 or even 9:1, but baluns come at a price and the cost of your experiments could begin to add up.

Another alternative appears in **Figure 3.7**. Instead of having the antenna tuner at the radio, and bringing the ladder line all the way to the station, put a remote automatic antenna tuner outside near the antenna. The ladder line would connect to the tuner and the tuner would find the low SWR match at that point. From the tuner ordinary coaxial cable would make the rest of the journey to the radio.

We discussed a similar setup for indoor antennas in Chapter 2 and the same issues apply here. That is, remote autotuners can be expensive, typically ranging from $170 to $500. Depending on the design and power rating, you may need to run separate wiring to provide dc power and/or control signals. The lower priced tuners are only rated at about 100 W, so you wouldn't be able to use an RF power amplifier.

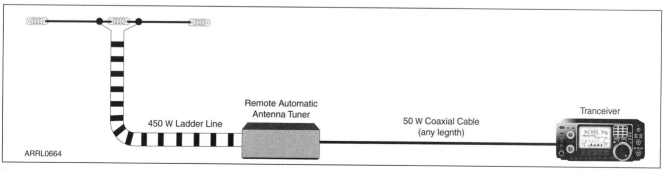

Figure 3.7 — Another approach to using an antenna tuner with a ladder line-fed dipole is to purchase a remote automatic antenna tuner and place it outside near the antenna. Connect the ladder line to the tuner and then use 50 Ω coaxial cable to the radio.

An MFJ remote automatic antenna tuner installed outdoors in a weatherproof container along with a small 4:1 balun.

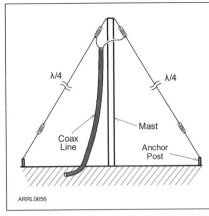

Figure 3.9 — A single-band Inverted-V antenna. Keeping the ends about 8 feet above ground will help reduce ground losses.

COAX-FED INVERTED V AND SLOPING DIPOLES

If multiband operation isn't your top priority, there is no need to feed a dipole with open-wire line, or even use an antenna tuner. You could simply install a standard "flat top" dipole between two supports and feed it at the center with the 50-Ω coaxial cable of your choice (**Figure 3.8**). When erected in horizontal fashion at a sufficient height, this antenna should provide a decent impedance match on one band (or in the case of a 40-meter dipole, two bands since it is often resonant on 15 meters as well, especially if you trim it at the low end of 40). You will probably have to lengthen or trim both ends of the antenna to achieve the lowest SWR; the 468/F formula will only get you within "spitting distance."

But this book is about antennas for small spaces and unless you have enough room to accommodate a horizontal dipole you'll need to consider alternatives. High on the list of single-band designs are the Inverted V and sloping dipoles.

An Inverted-V dipole (**Figure 3.9**) is supported at the center with a single support, such as a tree or mast. Not only are you spared from having to find two supports with the proper separation, the fact that the legs of the Inverted-V dipole slope downward makes it easier to fit this antenna into a small lot.

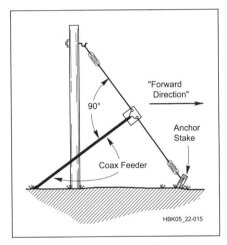

Figure 3.10 — If you have only one support, consider the sloping single-band dipole. Note the direction of radiation.

The inverted-V's radiation pattern and feed point impedance depend on the *apex angle* between the legs. As the apex angle decreases, so does feed point impedance, and the radiation pattern becomes less directive. At apex angles below 90°, the antenna efficiency begins to decrease substantially.

The proximity of ground to the antenna ends will lower the resonant frequency of the antenna so that a dipole cut to the standard formula may have to be shortened in the inverted-V configuration. Losses in the ground also increase when the antenna ends are close to the ground. Keeping the ends eight feet or higher above ground reduces ground loss and also prevents humans and animals from coming in contact with the antenna.

Keeping in mind that antenna current produces the radiated signal, and current is maximum at the dipole center, you'll get the best performance by installing the center of

Figure 3.8 — The standard coaxial fed "resonant" dipole antenna. This antenna needs to be ½ wavelength for the band of your choice. It can be fed directly with 50 Ω coaxial cable without an antenna tuner.

the antenna as high as you can get it. In Figure 3.9 the Inverted V is shown being supported by a pole, but it can also be supported by a tree, or even by your house. Just avoid getting the antenna too close to metal objects.

We've already addressed the sloping dipole in our discussion of open-wire fed dipoles, but this type of antenna can be created in a single-band version and fed with coaxial cable. What is interesting about the sloping dipole is that it can be used to skew your radiation pattern in a particular direction. See **Figure 3.10**. With a non-conducting support and poor ground, signals off the back are weaker than those off the front.

A conductive support such as an aluminum sided house or a metal mast acts as a parasitic element. (So does the coax shield, unless it is routed at 90° from the antenna.) The parasitic effects vary with ground quality and support height. With such variables, performance is very difficult to predict. Losses increase as the antenna ends approach the support or the ground, so the same cautions about the height of the antenna ends applies as for the Inverted-V antenna. To prevent feed line radiation, route the coax away from the feed point at 90° from the antenna as far as possible.

THE HALF-WAVE VERTICAL DIPOLE

Who said that a dipole had to be horizontal or sloping? Couldn't a dipole be vertical instead?

You bet it can!

If you have a tall tree in your yard, and if you can a get rope over one of the high branches, nothing would stop you from installing a dipole antenna in a vertical orientation (**Figure 3.11**). Height is the issue, however. To put up a vertical dipole for 40 meters, you'd better have a strong branch that is at least 74 feet high so that there is enough vertical space for the dipole, leaving an 8-foot gap between the end and the ground. Also, you need to bring the 50-Ω coaxial feed line away from the antenna horizontally for a substantial distance.

MULTIBAND COAXIAL-FED DIPOLES

For the moment let's assume that you have some horizontal space at your disposal between two supports — two trees, a single tree and a house, a tree and a mast, or whatever. Depending on how much space is available, it is possible to install a multiband dipole antenna and feed it with a single coaxial cable. It all depends on how you wish to approach the problem.

Parallel Dipoles

We briefly discussed the parallel or *fan* dipole design in Chapter 2. See **Figure 3.12**. This is certainly an odd looking antenna, but there is a method to its madness.

Consider the center-fed dipole. It has a low feed point impedance (something close to 50 Ω) near the fundamental frequency and its and its odd harmonics. That's why a 40-meter (7 MHz) dipole can also be used at 15 meters (21 MHz). The 15 meter frequency is an odd (third) harmonic of the 7 MHz frequency. High impedances exist at other frequencies. This impedance arrangement lets us construct simple multiband systems that automatically select the appropriate antenna.

Think about a 50-Ω resistor connected in parallel with a 5-kΩ resistor. A generator connected across the two resistors will see 49.5 Ω, and 99% of the current will flow through the 50-Ω resistor (**Figure 3.13**). When resonant and non-resonant antennas

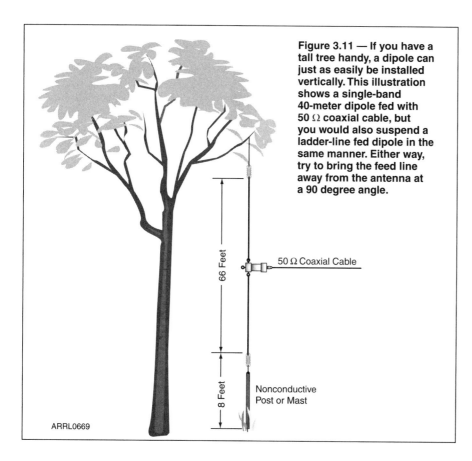

Figure 3.11 — If you have a tall tree handy, a dipole can just as easily be installed vertically. This illustration shows a single-band 40-meter dipole fed with 50 Ω coaxial cable, but you would also suspend a ladder-line fed dipole in the same manner. Either way, try to bring the feed line away from the antenna at a 90 degree angle.

66 Feet

50 Ω Coaxial Cable

8 Feet

Nonconductive Post or Mast

ARRL0669

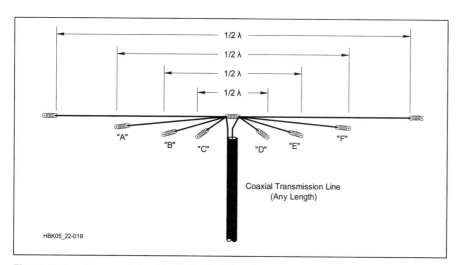

1/2 λ
1/2 λ
1/2 λ
1/2 λ

"A" "B" "C" "D" "E" "F"

Coaxial Transmission Line (Any Length)

HBK05_22-019

Figure 3.12 — The parallel or "fan" dipole. When it works correctly, the dipole that is resonant at the operating frequency presents the lowest impedance to the RF current. Each dipole — A through F — is cut for resonance on separate bands.

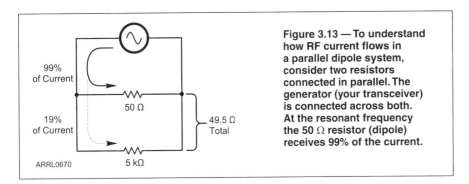

Figure 3.13 — To understand how RF current flows in a parallel dipole system, consider two resistors connected in parallel. The generator (your transceiver) is connected across both. At the resonant frequency the 50 Ω resistor (dipole) receives 99% of the current.

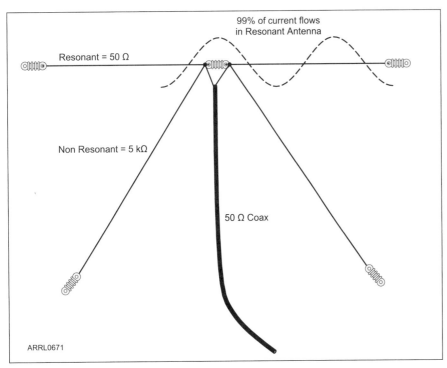

Figure 3.14 — A group of parallel dipoles behaves just like the parallel resistors in Figure 3.13. The resonant 50 Ω dipole receives most of the current.

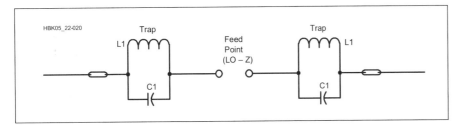

Figure 3.15 — A two-band trap antenna. A trap consists of inductance and capacitance in parallel with a resonant frequency on the higher of the two bands of operation. The high impedance of the trap at its resonant frequency effectively disconnects the wire beyond the trap.

length of the shorter dipoles lengthens a few percent. The shorter antennas don't affect longer ones much, so trim the individual dipoles for resonance *in order from longest to shortest*. The antenna analyzer described in Chapter 2 comes in *really* handy here — so much so that I personally wouldn't attempt to build a parallel dipole antenna without one.

Mutual inductance also reduces the bandwidth of shorter dipoles, so you may need an antenna tuner at the station to achieve an acceptable SWR across all bands covered. These effects can be reduced by spreading the ends of the dipoles apart. Note that perpendicular antennas have no coupling.

Also, the power-distribution mechanism requires that only one of the parallel dipoles is near resonance on any amateur band. Separate dipoles for 80 and 30 meters should not be connected in parallel because the higher band is near an odd harmonic of the lower band ($80/3 \approx 30$) and center-fed dipoles have low impedance near odd harmonics. (The 40 and 15 meter bands have a similar relationship.) This means that you either have to accept the performance of the low-band antenna operating on a harmonic or erect a separate antenna for those odd-harmonic bands. For example, four parallel-connected dipoles cut for 80, 40, 20 and 10 meters (fed by a single antenna tuner unit and coaxial cable) work reasonably on all HF bands from 80 through 10 meters.

Trap Dipoles

Trap dipoles (also called "trapped dipoles") provide multiband operation from a coax-fed single-wire dipole. **Figure 3.15** shows a two-band trap antenna. A trap consists of inductance and capacitance in parallel with a resonant frequency on the higher of the two bands of operation. The high impedance of the trap at its resonant frequency effectively disconnects the wire beyond the trap, not unlike a mechanical switch. So, on the higher of the two bands of operation at which traps are resonant, only the portion of the antenna between the traps is active.

Above resonance, the trap presents a capacitive reactance. Below resonance, the trap is inductive. On the lower of the two bands of operation, then, the inductive reactance of the trap acts as a loading coil to create a shortened or loaded dipole with the wire beyond the trap.

In the **Appendix** of this book you'll find a project article by Al Buxton, W8NX, which shows you how to build a 6-band trap dipole from scratch. This can be rather tricky, especially when it comes to building the traps themselves. For instance, you may need to check trap resonance before installation by using a grid-dip meter or an antenna analyzer.

are connected in parallel, the same result occurs: The non-resonant antenna has a high impedance, so little current flows in it and it has little effect on the total feed point impedance. As a result, we can connect several dipoles together at the feed point, and power naturally flows to the resonant antenna (**Figure 3.14**). Pretty nifty, isn't it?

There is no such thing as a free lunch, though. Wires in proximity to each other tend to couple due to mutual inductance. In parallel dipoles, this means that the resonant

For this reason many amateurs choose to buy pre-made traps or entirely pre-built trap dipole systems.

A trap dipole is a reasonable solution when you want to operate on several bands with a single antenna in less horizontal space than you'd normally need. On the other hand, the 2:1 SWR bandwidth on each band tends to be somewhat narrow and changing the frequency coverage within each band can be difficult. Also, if visibility is a concern, be forewarned that trap dipoles are very easy to see compared to a single, trapless wire suspended in the air.

OCF — Off Center Fed Dipole

Earlier I stated that the impedance at the center of a dipole antenna was somewhere in the neighborhood of 50 Ω. When attached to a 50 Ω coaxial cable the resulting SWR tends to be low (below 2:1), the transceiver loads its full output into the antenna system and all is right with the world.

But there is no law that dictates that you must feed a dipole at its center. If you feed the dipole at a different point, you will encounter a different impedance, but it is still possible to match that impedance to a 50 Ω coaxial line.

In **Figure 3.16** you'll see an Off Center Fed dipole design in which the feed line connects to the antenna ⅓ of its length from one end. This antenna can be used on its fundamental and *even* harmonics. For this antenna, the impedance at 3.5, 7 and 14 MHz is on the order of 150 to 200 Ω. A 4:1 balun at the feed point should offer a reasonably good match to 50- or 75-Ω coax. Some commercially made OCF dipoles use 6:1 baluns. At the 6th harmonic, 21 MHz, the antenna is three wavelengths long and fed at a voltage loop (maximum), instead of a current loop. The feed-point impedance at this frequency is high, a few thousand ohms, so the antenna is unusable on that band.

Because the OCF dipole is not fed at the center of the radiator, the RF impedance paths of the two wires at the feed point are unequal. If the antenna is fed directly with coax, voltages of equal magnitude (but opposite polarity) are applied to the wires at the feed point. Because of unequal impedances, the resulting antenna currents flowing in the two wires will not be equal. The bottom line is that current will likely flow on the outside shield of the coaxial cable, which is not good.

How much current flows on the coax shield depends on the impedance of the RF current path down the outside of the feed line. At any rate, to prevent this from happening, you need to use a *current* or *choke* balun at the feed point, *not* a so-called *voltage* balun. Current/choke baluns are available from a number of amateur dealers. Some

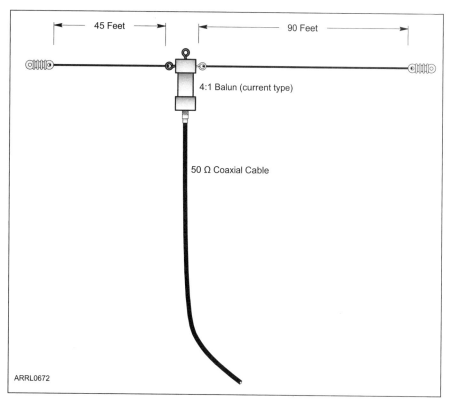

Figure 3.16 — In this example, we have an 80-meter Off Center Fed dipole with the feed point at ⅓ wavelength from the end.

OCF dipole designs place the current choke part way down the coax to take advantage of the coax current as an additional "antenna".

So what is the advantage of an OCF dipole in a limited-space situation? It is primarily the ability to enjoy multiband operation with a single antenna without a highly visible feed line dangling from its center. With the OCF you can place the feed point at a more convenient location in terms of hiding it from view and routing the feed line into the house.

The Legend of the G5RV

If you haven't heard of the G5RV dipole, you will. It has achieved legendary status in the amateur community with some hams ascribing almost magical properties to its design.

In truth, the virtue of the G5RV is that it is a multiband antenna that does not require a lot of space It is simple to construct and is low in cost. The antenna was designed in England by the late Louis Varney, G5RV. See **Figure 3.17**. It can be used from 3.5 through 30 MHz. Although some amateurs claim that the antenna can be fed directly with 50-Ω coax and operated on several amateur bands with a low SWR, Varney himself recommended the use of an antenna tuner on bands other than 14 MHz. In practice, you'll find that the SWR will exceed 2:1 on most

bands, so you will definitely need an antenna tuner at the radio. If your transceiver has a built-in antenna tuner, that may be sufficient.

As you'll see in Figure 3.17, the antenna is fed with a specific length of 450-Ω ladder line that connects to a 1:1 *current* or *choke* balun. From there it is standard 50-Ω coaxial cable all the way back to the station. It is a good idea to use low-loss (9913 or LMR 400) coax for this portion of the feed line

The portion of the G5RV antenna shown as horizontal in Figure 3.17 may also be installed in an Inverted-V arrangement. Or instead, up to ⅙ of the total length of the antenna at each end may be dropped vertically, semivertically, or bent at a convenient angle to the main axis of the antenna, to cut down on the requirements for real estate.

The W1ZR Folded Skeleton Sleeve 40 and 20 Meter Dipole

QST Technical Editor Joel Hallas, W1ZR, devised an interesting approach to a dual-band dipole antenna that's easy to build, can be fed with coaxial cable and doesn't require an antenna tuner. The result is an antenna that is somewhat different from ordinary dipoles in two regards:

1. It uses the parasitic *skeleton sleeve* coupling to a single higher frequency element to

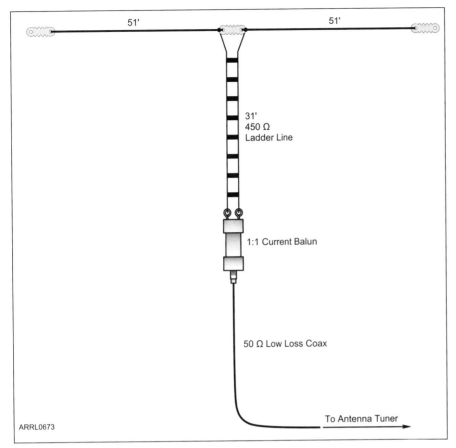

51'   51'

31'
450 Ω
Ladder Line

1:1 Current Balun

50 Ω Low Loss Coax

To Antenna Tuner

ARRL0673

Figure 3.17 — The legendary G5RV dipole antenna.

JOEL HALLAS, W1ZR

The W1ZR skeleton sleeve dipole.

provide the second band — rather than the more common parallel connection.

2. The ends of the lower frequency dipole are bent back to almost reach the higher frequency one. This results in an antenna about 10 feet shorter than the usual 40 meter dipole.

The first change avoids the narrow bandwidth usually encountered in closely spaced parallel wired dipoles. The close spacing allows the whole antenna to be constructed from a single piece of 450 Ω window line. In the interests of structural integrity, while the 40 meter section is enter fed, the parallel 20 meter dipole has a solid connection at the center.

This antenna provides gain and directivity comparable to a full size dipole on both 40 and 20 meters. At its design height of 30 feet, the SWR across both bands is 2:1 or less to 50 Ω coax. There is a small variation in resonance predicted at heights from 20 through 50 feet, however, at the end of 100 feet of RG-8X coax it is still within a 2:1 SWR across both bands. So, with this antenna you get two popular HF bands in a relatively short horizontal space — all without having to use an antenna tuner.

You can easily build this antenna from materials you may have at hand. You'll find complete details in the **Appendix** of this book.

BUILDING WIRE DIPOLES

When building any kind of wire dipole antenna one of the top considerations is the wire itself. Choosing the right type of wire for the project at hand is the key to a successful antenna — the kind that works well and stays up through a winter ice storm or a gusty spring wind storm.

When deciding what gauge of wire to use the answer depends on strength, ease of handling, cost, availability and visibility. Generally, antennas that are expected to support their own weight, plus the weight of the feed line should be made from #12 AWG wire. Horizontal dipoles fall into this category. Antennas supported in the center, such as Inverted-V dipoles may be made from lighter material, such as #14 AWG wire — the minimum size called for in the National Electrical Code.

The type of wire to be used is the next important decision. One of the strongest wires suitable for antenna service is copper-clad steel, also known as *Copperweld*. The copper coating is necessary for RF service because steel is a relatively poor conductor. Practically all of the RF current is confined to the copper coating because of the skin effect.

Copper-clad steel is outstanding for permanent installations, but it can be difficult to work with because of the stiffness of the steel core. Stranded wire made of copper-clad steel wire is also available and is more flexible and easier to work with. Solid-copper wire, either hard-drawn or soft-drawn, is another popular material. Easier to handle than copper-clad steel, solid copper is available in a wide range of sizes. It is usually more expensive, however, because it is all copper. Soft-drawn tends to stretch under tension, so you may find that your dipole seems to become longer over time!

Enamel-coated *magnet-wire* is a suitable choice for experimental antennas because it is easy to manage, and the coating protects the wire from the weather. Although it stretches under tension, the wire may be pre-stretched before final installation and adjustment. A local electric motor rebuilder might be a good source for magnet wire.

Hook-up wire, speaker wire or even ac lamp cord are suitable for temporary antennas. Frankly, almost any copper wire may be used, as long as it is strong enough for the demands of the installation.

Aluminum wire can be used for antennas, but is not as strong as copper or steel for the same diameter and soldering it to feed lines requires special techniques.

Galvanized and steel wire, such as that used for electric fences, is inexpensive, but it is a much poorer conductor at RF than copper and should be avoided.

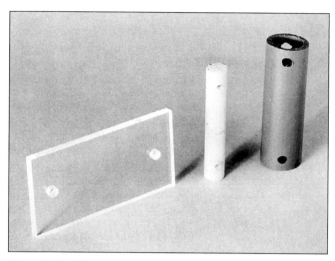
Figure 3.18 — You can make antenna insulators from just about any nonconductive materials.

Kinking, which severely weakens wire, is a potential problem when handling any solid conductor. When uncoiling solid wire of any type — copper, steel, or aluminum — take care to unroll the wire or untangle it without pulling on a kink to straighten it. A kink is actually a very sharp twist in the wire and the wire will break at such a twist when flexed, such as from vibration in the wind.

Solid wire also tends to fail at connection or attachment points at which part of the wire is rigidly clamped. The repeated flexing from wind and other vibrations eventually causes metal fatigue and the wire breaks. Stranded wire is preferred for antennas that will be subjected to a lot of vibration and flexing. If stranded wire is not suitable, use a heavier gauge of solid wire to compensate.

Insulated vs Bare Wire

Losses are the same (in the HF region at least) whether the antenna wire is insulated or bare. If insulated wire is used, a 3 to 5% shortening from the length calculated for a bare wire is required to obtain resonance at the desired frequency. This is caused by the increased distributed capacitance resulting from the dielectric constant of the plastic insulating material. The actual length for resonance must be determined experimentally by pruning and measuring because the dielectric constant of the insulating material varies from wire to wire. Wires that might come into contact with humans or animals should definitely be insulated to reduce the chance of shock or burns.

Insulators

Wire antennas must be insulated at the ends. Commercially available insulators are made from ceramic, glass or plastic. Insulators are available from many Amateur Radio dealers. RadioShack and local hardware stores are other possible sources. I prefer glass or ceramic insulators in situations where I will be soldering wires near the insulators; plastic has a tendency to become soft and melt in the presence of a torch or heavy duty soldering iron.

Of course, you can also make your own insulators from a variety of material including (but not limited to) acrylic sheet or rod, PVC tubing, wood, fiberglass rod or even stiff plastic from a discarded container. **Figure 3.18** shows some homemade insulators. Ceramic or glass insulators will usually outlast the wire, so they are highly recommended for a safe, reliable, permanent installation. Other materials may tear under stress or break down in the presence of sunlight. Many types of plastic do not weather well. If your antenna ends are supported with synthetic rope, separate insulators are not needed — just count on the rope as insulation, but be sure the rope is protected from the wire wearing through it.

Most wire antennas require an insulator at the feed point. Although there are many ways to connect the feed line, there are a few things to keep in mind. If you feed your antenna with coaxial cable, you have two choices. You can install an SO-239 connector on the center insulator and use a PL-259 on the end of your coax, or you can separate the center conductor from the braid and connect the feed line directly to the antenna wire.

Although it costs less to connect directly, the use of connectors offers several advantages. Coaxial cable braid acts as a wick to soak up water. If you do not adequately seal the antenna end of the feed line, water will find its way into the braid. Water in the feed line will lead to contamination, rendering the coax useless. It is not uncommon for water to drip from the end of the coax inside the shack after a year or so of service if the antenna connection is not properly waterproofed. Use of a PL-259/SO-239 combination (or other connector of your choice) makes the task of waterproofing connections much easier.

Another advantage to using the PL-259/SO-239 combination is that feed line replacement is much easier, should that become necessary.

Whether you use coaxial cable, ladder line, or twin lead to feed your antenna, an often overlooked consideration is the mechanical strength of the connection. Wire antennas and feed lines tend to move a lot in the breeze, and unless the feed line is attached securely, the connection will weaken with time. The resulting failure can range from a frustrating intermittent electrical connection to a complete separation of feed line and antenna. **Figure 3.19** illustrates several different ways of attaching the feed line to the antenna. You'll also find a project by the late Richard Peacock, W2GFF, in the **Appendix** titled "An Improved Center Insulator for Wire Antennas Fed with Window Line" that shows you how to build a high-strength center insulator.

Putting It All Together

As you begin assembling your antenna, here are some bits of advice gleaned from 40 years of occasionally painful experience.

First and perhaps foremost, don't cut the antenna exactly to the length determined by the formula. Remember that the result of the formula is just an approximation. So, cut the wires 2 to 3% longer than the calculated length. Measure the total constructed length, with insulators attached, and write this down. (The constructed length is measured between the ends of the loops at each end of the wire.) Next, raise the dipole to the working height and find the frequency at which minimum SWR occurs. Multiply the frequency of the SWR minimum by the antenna length and divide the result by the desired frequency. The result is the finished length; trim both ends equally to reach that length and, with luck, you're done.

In determining how well your antenna will work over the long term, how well you put the pieces together is second only to the ultimate strength of the materials used. Even the smallest details, such as how you connect the wire to the insulators, contribute significantly to antenna longevity. By using plenty of wire at the insulator and wrapping it tightly, you will decrease the possibility of

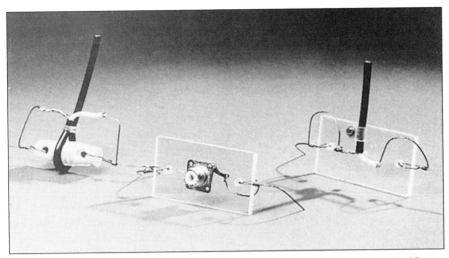

Figure 3.19 — Here are some clever designs for dipole center insulators intended for use with coaxial cable.

the wire pulling loose in the wind. There is no need to solder the wire once it is wrapped. There is no electrical connection here, only mechanical. The high heat needed for soldering can anneal the wire, significantly weakening it at the solder point.

Similarly, the feed line connection at the center insulator should be made to the antenna wires after they have been secured to the insulator. This way, you will be assured of a good electrical connection between the antenna and feed line without compromising the mechanical strength.

Do a good job of soldering the antenna and feed line connections. Use a heavy iron or a torch, and be sure to clean the materials thoroughly before starting the job. If possible, solder the connections at a workbench,

Trees as Antenna Supports

From the beginning of Amateur Radio, trees have been used widely for supporting wire antennas. Trees cost nothing to use, and often provide a means of supporting a wire antenna at considerable height. As antenna supports, trees are unstable in the presence of wind, except in the case of very large trees used to support antennas well down from the top branches. As a result, tree-supported antennas must be constructed much more sturdily than is necessary with stable supports. Even with rugged construction, it is unlikely that an antenna suspended from a tree, or between trees, will stand up indefinitely. Occasional repair or replacement usually must be expected.

At bare minimum, you can simply run the support rope over the highest branch and then bring it down to eye level, securing it to the tree trunk with an eyelet screw and carabineer.

A more elegant method is to use a pulley system. There are two general methods of securing a pulley to a tree. If the tree can be climbed safely to the desired level, a pulley can be attached to the trunk of the tree. To clear the branches of the tree, the antenna end of the halyard can be tied temporarily to the tree at the pulley level. Then the remainder of the halyard is coiled up, and the coil thrown out horizontally from this level, in the direction in which the antenna runs. It may help to have the antenna end of the halyard weighted.

After attaching the antenna to the halyard, the other end is untied from the tree, passed through the pulley, and brought to ground along the tree trunk in as straight a line as possible. The halyard need only be long enough to reach the ground after the antenna has been hauled up. (Additional rope can be tied to the halyard when it becomes necessary to lower the antenna.)

The other method consists of passing a line over the tree from ground level, and using this line to haul a pulley up into the tree and hold it there. Several ingenious methods have been used to accomplish this. The simplest method employs a weighted pilot line, such as fishing line or mason's chalk line.

By grasping the line about two feet from the weight, the weight is swung back and forth, pendulum style, and then heaved with an underhand motion in the direction of the treetop. Several trials may be necessary to determine the optimum size of the weight for the line selected, the distance between the weight and the hand before throwing, and the point in the arc of the swing where the line released. The weight, however, must be sufficiently large to carry the pilot line back to ground after passing over the tree. Flipping the end of the line up and down so as to put a traveling wave on the line often helps to induce the weight to drop down if the weight is marginal. The higher the tree, the lighter the weight and the pilot line must be. A glove should be worn on the throwing hand, because a

A carabiner and an eyelet screwed into a tree truck can make a good anchor for an antenna rope.

where the best possible joints can be made. Poorly soldered connections will become headaches as the wire oxidizes and the electrical integrity degrades with time. Besides degrading your antenna performance, poorly made joints can even be a cause of TVI because of rectification. Spray the connections with a UV-resistant acrylic coating for waterproofing.

If the supports for the antenna move in the wind, such as trees do, leave enough slack in the antenna that it is not pulled overly tight in normal winds. Other options are to use pulleys and counterweights to allow the antenna supports to flex without pulling on the antenna. If made from the right materials and installed in the clear, the dipole should give years of maintenance-free service. As you build your antenna, keep in mind that if you get it right the first time, you won't have to do it again for a long time!

COMMERCIAL DIPOLES

Some hams look down their noses at folks who buy their dipole antennas off the shelves rather than building them with their bare hands. I disagree. Although building your own dipole saves money and is an educational process by itself, many of us simply don't have the free time to buy materials and assemble dipoles. When I was a child I was told that as an adult I would have extraordinary amounts of leisure time at my disposal. Those visions of the future were a little cloudy to say the least. They didn't anticipate, for example, an economy where some people were required to hold down two jobs just to get by!

Glance through the advertising pages of *QST* magazine and you find many dealers and manufacturers that sell dipole antennas. The designs range from simple single-band antennas fed with coaxial cable to multiband parallel dipoles. One interesting variation is provided by NCG Company — the Comet H-422 rotatable dipole (**Figure 3.20**). This is essentially a trap dipole for 40, 20, 15 and 10 meters built with aluminum tubing. It is 33 feet long horizontally, but you can raise the dipole legs to form a V, allowing the antenna to fit into a much smaller space.

Since the H-422 is supported at the center rather than at the ends like a traditional wire dipole, you can easily rotate the antenna manually or by using an electrical rotator. Dipoles have radiation patterns with gain

line running swiftly through the bare hand can cause a severe burn.

If there is a clear line of sight between ground and a particularly desirable crotch in the tree, it may eventually be possible to hit the crotch after a sufficient number of tries. Otherwise, it is best to try to heave the pilot line completely over the tree, as close to the centerline of the tree as possible. If it is necessary to retrieve the line and start over again, the line should be drawn back very slowly or better yet, with the weight removed; otherwise the swinging weight may wrap the line around a small limb, making retrieval impossible.

Stretching the line out straight on the ground before throwing may help to keep the line from snarling, but it places extra drag on the line, and the line may snag on obstructions overhanging the line when it is thrown. Another method is to make a stationary reel by driving eight nails, arranged in a circle, through a 1-inch board. After winding the line around the circle formed by the nails, the line should reel off readily when the weighted end of the line is thrown. The board should be tilted at approximately right angles to the path of the throw.

Other devices that have been used successfully to pass a pilot line over a tree are a bow and arrow with heavy thread tied to the arrow, and a short casting rod and spinning reel used by fishermen. The Wrist Rocket slingshot made from surgical rubber tubing and a metal frame has proved highly effective as an antenna-launching device.

Still another method that has been used where sufficient space is available is flying a kite or a large weather balloon to sufficient altitude, walking around the tree until the kite string lines up with the center of the tree, and paying out string until the kite falls to the earth. This method can be used to pass a line over a patch of woods between two higher supports, which may be impossible using any other method. The pilot line can be used to pull successively heavier lines over the tree until one of adequate size to take the strain of the antenna has been reached. This line is then used to haul a pulley up into the tree after the antenna halyard has been threaded through the pulley. The line that holds the pulley must be capable of withstanding considerable chafing where it passes through the crotch, and at points where lower branches may rub against the standing part. For this reason, it may be advisable to use galvanized sash cord or stranded guy wire for raising the pulley.

Larger lines or cables require special attention when they must be spliced to smaller lines. A splice that minimizes the chances of coming undone when coaxed through the tree crotch must be used. If, however, the line has been passed over (or close to) the center line of the tree, it will usually break through the lighter crotches and come to rest in a stronger one lower in the tree.

Needless to say, any of the suggested methods should be used with due respect to persons or property in the immediate vicinity. A child's sponge-rubber ball (baseball size) makes a safe weight for heaving a heavy thread line or fishing line. If the antenna wire snags in the lower branches of the tree when the wire is pulled up, or if other trees interfere with raising the antenna, a weighted line thrown over the antenna and slid to the appropriate point is often helpful in pulling the antenna wire to one side to clear the interference as the antenna is being raised.

Wind Compensation

The movement of an antenna suspended between supports that are not stable in the wind can be reduced by the use of heavy springs, such as screen-door springs under tension, or by a counterweight at the end of one halyard. The weight, which may be made up of junkyard metal, window sash weights, or a galvanized pail filled with sand or stone, should be adjusted experimentally for best results under existing conditions.

Figure 3.20 — The Comet H-422 rotatable dipole shown in its V configuration.

lobes broadside to their lengths and nulls at the ends. So, rotating the H-422 allows you to position the antenna for the greatest gain in the direction you wish (or to null interference coming from other directions). At the time of this writing, the H-422 sold for $360. You'll find more information online at **www. cometantenna.com**.

THE MULTIBAND INVERTED L ANTENNA

Hams enjoy describing antenna designs according to how they resemble letters of the English alphabet. The Inverted L antenna looks like … well … an upside down capital L. Part of the antenna is vertical while the rest is horizontal.

Inverted L antennas aren't normally considered to be limited space designs. In fact, they are commonly used for 80 and 160 meter operating where the horizontal portion of the antenna can exceed 100 feet in length. The reason for its popularity for low-band operating has to do with its relatively small size (compared to a 160 meter dipole at 260 feet!) and the fact that its radiation pattern combines vertically and horizontally polarized fields, giving the antenna a bit of an edge under dicey propagation conditions.

A few years ago, *QST* Technical Editor Joel Hallas, W1ZR, and I were discussing antenna options for my tiny swatch of property. Noting that I had two trees available, Joel suggested a short Inverted L with a remote automatic antenna tuner at the base (**Figure 3.21**).

The result was an antenna with a 20-foot vertical section and an 80 foot horizontal portion that stretched over the top of the house to a pine tree on the corner of the

lot. An MFJ-927 remote automatic antenna tuner was housed in a plastic weatherproof box at the base of the vertical section. The vertical wire attached to the tuner's "long wire" connection. I laid 20 radial wires on the ground, each about 30 feet in length, and attached them to the ground side of the tuner.

My Inverted L was more than a ½ wave-

length on 40 meters, but shorter than ½ wavelength on 80 meters. Perhaps that was the "magic" length for my installation, one that provided an impedance on every band that was well within the range of the MFJ tuner. Regardless, the tuner was able to find an acceptable match on all bands from 10 through 160 meters. Of course, on 160 meters the antenna was quite short, but I was still able to make contact with stations 500 miles distant running just 100 W on CW. The performance on 40 meters and up was impressive and seemed to rival the all-band dipole arrangement I had been using previously.

If you have two supports available, a short Inverted L with a remote tuner might be an option to consider. Even if you have just a single tree, it may be possible to use your house as the support for far end of the horizontal section (see **Figure 3.22**). Don't worry too much about the dimensions. As with most wire antennas the axiom "high as possible and long as possible" applies. Make the vertical section as high as you can get it and the horizontal section as long as your space allows. Also put down as many radials as feasible and make them as long as possible. As you'll learn when we discuss vertical antennas, recent research has shown that you don't need a huge network of radials for acceptable performance. If all you can

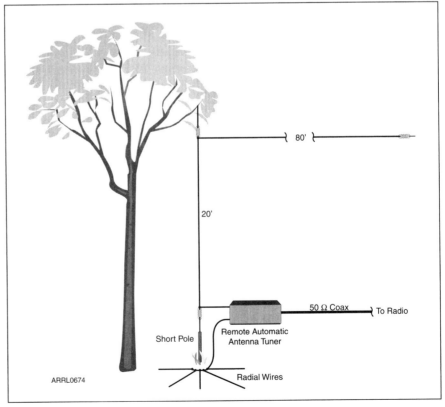

Figure 3.21 — An Inverted L antenna can be fed with a remote automatic antenna tuner at its base.

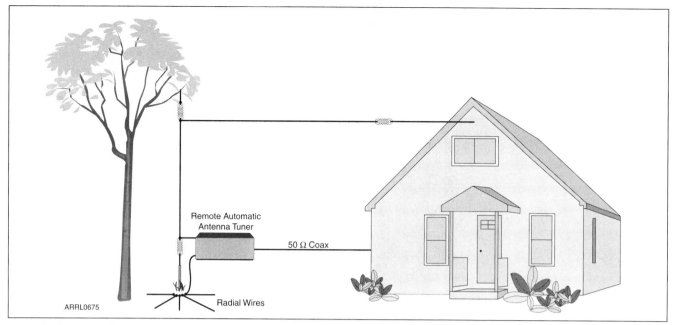

Figure 3.22 — If you have only a single tree to support an Inverted L, your house can function as the support for the "far" end.

do is install just a handful of radials, so be it. You'll likely find that the remote tuner will still find matches on several bands and the antenna will perform in ways that will surprise you.

END-FED WIRE ANTENNAS

End-fed wire antennas have an ancient pedigree going all the way back to the beginning of Amateur Radio itself. They remain in the ham radio antenna arsenal today because they are relatively easy to set up and use in almost any environment. For best performance they require one high support, a ground return system of some sort (radials or a counterpoise wire) and an impedance matching network, typically an antenna tuner.

For amateurs with space limitations, an end-fed wire may offer an attractive solution. For example, I've had good luck using a 70 foot end-fed wire and an ICOM AH-4 remote automatic antenna tuner (see **Fig-ure 3.23**). My automatic tuner was attached to the back of a utility shed. The antenna ran from the branch of a tall oak tree (the branch was about 40 feet from the ground) to the side of the shed. A short wire dropped down to the antenna tuner, connecting to the "hot" terminal on the AH-4. The ground terminal was connected to a network of 20 buried radial wires, each about 40 feet long. With this setup I managed to make a "Clean Sweep" (working all US and Canadian sections) during the 2003 ARRL Phone Sweepstakes contest. Not too shabby for an antenna tuner and a collection of wire.

There was nothing magical about the 70-foot length of my antenna. With an end-fed wire, longer is always better, but if you can only string up, say, 45 feet of wire, you can be reasonably sure it will work on 80 through 10 meters. There is also nothing magical about the ICOM AH-4 antenna tuner. Any good quality tuner will do.

There is a commercial version of this concept available from DX Engineering. At the heart of their DXE-SMBA-2 package (**Figure 3.24**) is a remote automatic antenna tuner in a watertight enclosure. This very low profile unit is easily hidden — even in small bushes or shrubs — and the only thing that shows is the wire antenna element, which can be a very small diameter for a near-zero visual impact. The system sells for $399 and comes complete with the tuner, stainless steel radial plate, radial wires, hardware and even the antenna wire and two insulators.

An end-fed wire can also be a solution for condo and apartment dwellers. See **Figure 3.25**. The "station end" of the wire

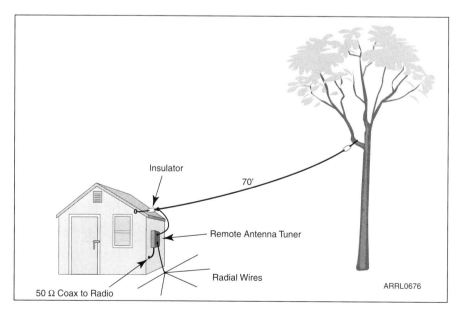

Figure 3.23 — I once used an ICOM AH-4 remote automatic antenna tuner to load an end-fed wire. The wire sloped down from a tree to the tuner, which was mounted on the exterior wall of a shed. The tuner ground was connected to a network of 10 30-foot radial wires. The antenna worked remarkably well from 160 through 10 meters.

Figure 3.24 — DX Engineering offers a commercial version of the end-fed wire configuration depicted in Figure 3.23. Their DXE-SMBA-2 package includes a remote automatic antenna tuner in a watertight enclosure. This very low profile unit is easily hidden — even in small bushes or shrubs — and the only thing that shows is the wire antenna element which can be a very small diameter for a near-zero visual impact.

40 meters, for instance, this would be about 33 feet. This may sound like a lot of wire, but you can run it along the baseboards and behind furniture; it doesn't have to be out in the open. This counterpoise may carry high voltages at times so it must be insulated and be sure to tape the end where the conductor may be exposed.

The problem with using an end-fed wire in this fashion, as you may have guessed, is that you run the risk of introducing a lot of RF into your living environment. If you are generating significant RF power, you can easily end up with "hot" station equipment — complete with sparks and painful "bites." With that in mind, I'd only recommend an installation like this for low power operating at 10 W or less.

You may want to consider a device such as the MFJ-931 "Artificial Ground" manufactured by MFJ Enterprises to essentially "tune" the counterpoise wire. The MFJ-931 (**Figure 3.26**) connects between the antenna tuner ground and the counterpoise wire. By adjusting the unit you can maximize the RF current in the counterpoise and keep it from flowing in the rest of your equipment. You'll also increase the efficiency of your antenna

can attach to a windowsill while the other end is anchored in a tree. To match the wire you'll need an antenna tuner, either manual or automatic. Among manual tuner designs, look for a model that offers a balanced output in addition to its unbalanced outputs. The balanced output typically sports two bind-ing posts that are connected to an internal 4:1 balun. The "hot" post may be red and labeled as the "long wire" connection. Your end-fed wire attaches to this post.

To the other post you'll need to attach a counterpoise wire that is ¼ wavelength at the lowest frequency you intend to use. For

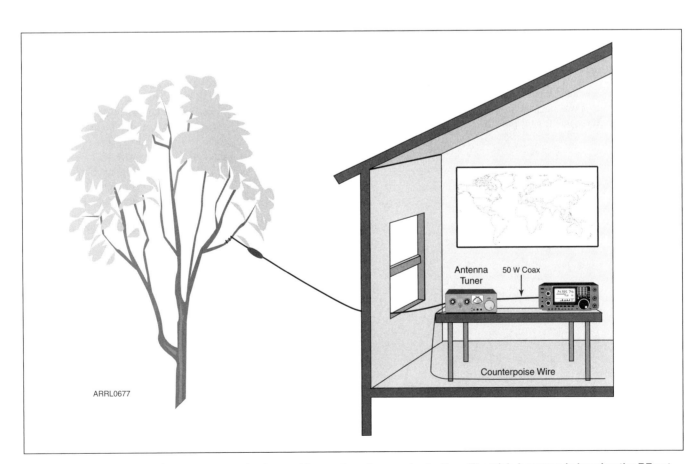

Figure 3.25 — An end-fed wire antenna can also be used by apartment or condo dwellers. The trick, however, is keeping the RF out of your equipment. To help prevent this, you'll need to attach an insulated counterpoise wire that is ¼ wavelength at your lowest frequency. The wire can lie on the floor along the baseboards tucked behind furniture. Considering the RF voltage and exposure issues, it is best to use low power with an antenna of this type.

Figure 3.26 — The MFJ-931 "Artificial Ground" by MFJ Enterprises "tunes" the counterpoise wire in end-fed installations. The MFJ-931 connects between the antenna tuner ground and the counterpoise wire.

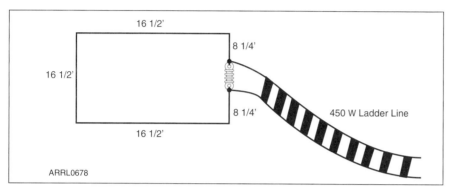

Figure 3.27 — A half-wavelength loop antenna. This one is designed for the 40 meter band.

system. When this book went to press, the MFJ-931 was selling for about $110.

LOOP ANTENNAS

Loop antennas for the HF bands tend to be large, so why are we discussing them in a book devoted to small antennas? The answer is found in the fact that if you can find the room for a loop antenna, it is capable of offering a significant performance advantage compared to some other wire antennas.

The smallest size of a "large" loop is usually one having a conductor length of ½ wavelength. At 40 meters, for example, that would be 66 feet. The conductor is usually formed into a square, as shown in **Figure 3.27**, making each side ⅛ wavelength long. So for our 40 meter square loop example, each side would be 16 ½ feet in length. When fed at the center of one side, the current flows in a closed loop. The current distribution is approximately the same as on a ½ wavelength wire, and so is maximum at the center of the side *opposite* the feed point, and minimum at the feed point itself. This current distribution causes the field strength to be at maximum in the plane of the loop and in the direction looking from the low-current side to the high-current side.

If your property is blessed with two sizeable trees, a ½ wavelength loop could become part of your antenna farm. Looking

back at our 40 meter loop again, such a square antenna could easily fit between two trees about 20 feet apart.

Stepping up in size, you have the *full wave loop*. At 40 meters you'd be talking about a total conductor length on the order of 132 feet. That translates to a square with 33-foot sides.

The directional characteristics of loops of this type in the vertical plane are opposite in sense to those of a small loop. That is, the radiation is maximum perpendicular to the plane of the loop and is at minimum in either direction in the plane containing the loop.

A loop antenna doesn't have to be formed into a square. It can be a circle or a triangle (the venerable *delta loop*). The shape of the loop *will* change its radiation pattern, as will its height above ground and the presence of nearby objects. Even so, in a cramped antenna environment we generally don't care about radiation patterns all that much. We want an antenna that *works* and if you're looking for something that offers a slight overall performance advantage, a loop is something to consider.

Many hams prefer to feed loop antennas with 450-Ω ladder line and, of course, an antenna tuner. This is a good solution since it provides multiband operation and removes the need to tweak the loop to bring it into resonance.

I enjoyed good performance with a delta loop supported by a single tree (see **Figure 3.28**). The lower corners of the triangle were anchored atop an 8-foot tall wood privacy fence. A remote automatic antenna tuner was connected directly to the loop at the middle of the bottom leg.

Another interesting approach that some

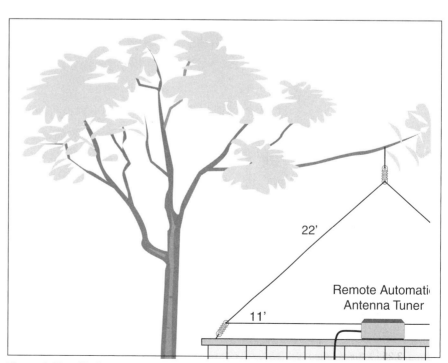

Figure 3.28 — My "stealthy delta" loop took advantage of a cedar privacy fence and a nearby tree. The remote automatic antenna tuner loaded this antenna from 40 through 10 meters.

amateurs use is to "wrap" the loop antenna around their homes using insulated wire and anchoring the corners to their gutters or roofs and feeding the antennas with 450 Ω ladder line. While a loop installation of this type is certainly stealthy (almost invisible), the home is obviously bathed in RF. Depending on the amount of power one is using, this raises RF exposure issues as well as a strong possibility of interference to every piece of electronics in the house.

VERTICAL ANTENNAS

If you are severely cramped for space and still want to erect an HF antenna on your property, it is hard to beat a vertical. Unlike a typical wire dipole that may require tens of feet of horizontal space, a vertical needs only a couple of square feet at its base — unless you count the *radial wires*, although they are usually buried in the soil and out of sight. A vertical antenna relies on these radial wires to create a path for return currents.

In the crudest sense of the word, a vertical antenna is simply a vertically oriented metal tube or wire. The vertical can be a ¼ wavelength long, or it might be ⅝ wavelength, or any other length that can be matched to the feed line. One conductor of the feed line is attached to the vertical radiating element of the antenna and the remaining conductor attached to the ground plane.

Ground Systems

When compared to horizontal antennas, verticals suffer more acutely from two main types of losses: *ground return losses* for currents in the near field, and *far-field ground losses*. Ground losses in the near field can be minimized by using many ground radials. Far-field losses are highly dependent on the conductivity and dielectric constant of the earth around the antenna, extending out as far as 100 wavelengths from the base of the antenna. There is very little that someone can do to change the character of the ground that far away -- other than moving to a small island surrounded by saltwater!

AM radio broadcasters are well aware of the need for efficient ground systems. They often bury hundreds of radial conductors at the bases of their towering vertical antennas. If you ever find yourself taking a train west out of New York City, be sure to look to your right as your train emerges in New Jersey from the Hudson River tunnel. Within minutes you'll see the triple shared antennas of stations WMCA and WNYC standing just above the saltwater in a tidal marsh. The radials of these antennas are as close to

ideal as you are likely to see — hundreds of conductors bathed in saltwater on the bottom of the marsh. This installation has a ground plane that would be the envy of any amateur.

But very few of us have salt marshes on our properties, so if we're considering ground mounted verticals we also must consider the prospect of laying down a number of radial wires as well. This conjures visions of spending hours on your knees, tediously burying dozens of long wires under your lawn. Suddenly the space requirements of a dipole don't seem so bad!

Take heart. Recent research has shown that for Amateur Radio applications it is not necessary to establish giant networks of radials in your soil. In the March 2010 issue of *QST* magazine there is an article by Rudy Severns, N6LF, titled "An Experimental Look at Ground Systems for HF Verticals." In the article Rudy demonstrates that you can enjoy perfectly acceptable vertical antenna performance with a modest number of radials (20 seems to be a good number). This groundbreaking article (no pun intended) is so important that I've included it in the **Appendix** section of this book.

The old saw about radials having to be ¼ wavelength at the lowest operating frequency has also proven to be false. The lengths of the radial wires appear to be less important than the *total number* of wires. Bottom line: put down as many radials as your time and patience allow and make them as long as your space allows. Don't go overboard since you'll reach the point of diminishing returns fairly quickly. If you can only place four 30-foot radial wires, do it. If you can place 20 wires, but they are all only 10 feet in length, that's fine, too. Yes, more radials on the ground will improve your antenna performance, but for casual operating (as opposed to competitive DXing or contesting) the benefits of a large radial network are questionable.

Placing radial wires in a perfect circle on the ground around the base of the antenna is ideal, but if you can't achieve that, don't worry. Lay the wires any way you can — straight, zigzag or whatever. Your antenna's radiation pattern won't be perfectly omnidirectional, but in all likelihood you'll never notice.

Are you reluctant to dig channels in your lawn for the radial wires? I can't blame you. The good news is that you can let Mother Nature do the work for you. The trick is to chop up some very stiff wire into V or U shaped pieces better known as "garden staples." At the time of this writing, you could also purchase these staples from vendors such as Ross Radio at **radialstaple.wordpress.com**. Stretch out your radial wires on the ground

The shared AM antennas of WMCA/WNYC standing in a saltwater tidal marsh in New Jersey. Their massive networks of radial conductors are constantly bathed in saltwater, the ideal environment for a radial ground system.

and place the staples every foot or so to hold the wires in place. Over the coming months, the grass will gradually grow over the radials and bury them for you!

Radial wires can be bare or insulated. Insulated wires will have greater longevity by virtue of reduced corrosion and dissolution from soil chemicals. Hardware cloth and chicken wire are also quite effective, although the galvanizing must be of high-quality to prevent rapid rusting. Steer clear of aluminum wire as this will corrode to powder in most soils.

Also resist the urge to rely on ground rods. This is the ground system of absolute last resort and it is a poor one at that. A single ground rod, or group of them bonded together, is seldom as effective as a collection of random-length radial wires.

The Monoband Vertical

If you are only interested in operating on a single band, a ¼ wavelength monoband vertical may fit the bill. You can use the following equation . . .

Length = 234 / Frequency (MHz)

. . . to calculate the length of the antenna, although keep in mind that the result is an approximation. As they say in automobile commercials, your mileage may vary.

The antenna can be made from metal mast sections (I once made a 20-meter vertical from 16 feet of electrical conduit). Alternatively, you could place a 12-gauge wire inside a tube made from sections of PVC tubing to achieve the same result with the advantage that wire is much easier to trim if you need to adjust for the lowest SWR.

An end-fed metal radiator must be insulated from ground (**Figure 3.29**) unless special matching techniques are used. If you choose to build your antenna from mast sections and you decide to the clamp the antenna to a metal pipe that you've hammered into the soil, make sure the outside of the pipe is covered with an insulating material (wrapping it with electrical tape will do for a while, but a sleeve of PVC pipe is a better long term insulator).

As you plan your vertical consider the fact that the antenna may be vulnerable in high winds. I've seen 43-foot verticals survive 50 MPH sustained winds with little difficulty. For taller antennas you may need to consider guy wires (or just Dacron line) spaced at equidistant points around the base of the antenna (**Figure 3.30**), attaching at the middle with an insulated ring or clamp.

Multiband Verticals

With a little assistance from a remote automatic antenna tuner, a multiband vertical is remarkably easy to build.

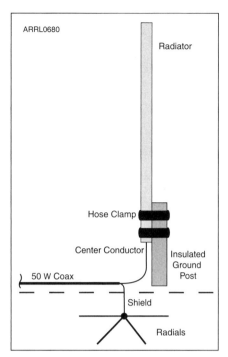

Figure 3.29 — The classic single-band vertical antenna consists of a ¼ wavelength radiator attached to an insulated ground support. The general rule for radial wires is to put down as many as your time and patience will allow. Studies by Rudy Severns, N6LF, have shown that 20 is a reasonable number. In terms of length, the radials should simply fit the space you have available.

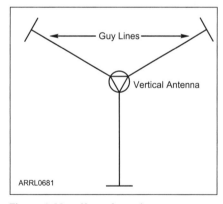

Figure 3.30 — If you intend to erect a particularly tall vertical (taller than about 45 feet), consider attaching Dacron guy lines and anchoring them to the ground at equidistant points around the antenna. You can use metal hose clamps to secure the Dacron lines to the antenna.

The design shown in **Figure 3.31** is based on a 33-foot radiator. This is about ¼ wavelength on 40 meters. The remote antenna tuner is installed at the base of the antenna. If the tuner isn't fully weatherproof, you'll need to provide some sort of watertight en-

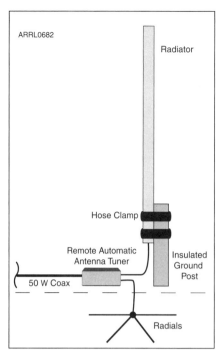

Figure 3.31 — If you can place a remote automatic antenna tuner at the base of a vertical antenna, you'll enjoy multiband operation. In this example, a 33 foot vertical can be used on 40 through 10 meters.

closure. Of course, this antenna will also require a network on radial wires on the ground.

The antenna tuner will have an easy time tuning this antenna on 40 meters since the impedance will already be close to 50 Ω at the base. The tuner will also likely find an acceptable match on 30, 20, 17, 15, 12 and 10 meters. Depending on the design of the tuner you've chosen, it may even match the antenna on 80 meters, although the antenna is only ⅛ wavelength at this frequency.

If a 33-foot radiator is too tall, consider a 16 foot design. With the antenna tuner at the base, you'll likely be able to operate on all bands from 20 through 10 meters. It may function on 40 meters as well, but once again, it will be only ⅛ wavelength at this frequency.

As you comb through the ham literature you'll stumble across references to 43-foot vertical antennas. Forty-three feet may seem like an odd length for a vertical antenna since it isn't a ¼ wavelength on any amateur band except 60 meters. The idea behind the 43-foot vertical is to create an antenna that creates feed point impedances that fall within the ranges of most remote automatic antenna tuners on *every* HF band. This length also provides low angle radiation, good for DX, on 160 through 20 meters where it is the opti-

An S9v vertical by S9 Antennas.
www.s9antennas.com

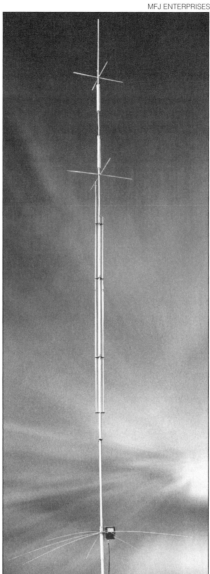

The Cushcraft R8 vertical antenna.
www.mfjenterprises.com

A Bencher Butternut HF9V antenna.
www.bencher.com

mum length. While this approach can certainly work, bear in mind that a 43-foot vertical is electrically short on 80 and 160 meters. A remote tuner will probably be able to find a match, but don't expect barn-burning performance on these bands. Your signal could be as much as 10 dB down from those running "full sized" antennas on 80 and 160 meters.

Commercial Verticals

With so many amateurs living under the burden of antenna restrictions, a number of commercial vendors have brought vertical antennas to market. You'll find 43 foot verticals including "packages" that combine both the antenna and the remote automatic antenna tuner. Remember that you can use a remote tuner with any single-radiator vertical, regardless of its length. For example, at the time of this writing I'm enjoying good performance from a 33-foot S9 Antennas

vertical (a design that includes a radiating wire within a telescoping fiberglass tube) tuned by an MFJ-927 antenna tuner at its base.

You'll also find verticals that dispense with the antenna tuner at the base and instead use a 4:1 UNUN — unbalanced to unbalanced — transformer to convert the impedance values at the antenna input. You still need an antenna tuner, but the tuner can reside indoors next to your radio (or if your radio has a built-in tuner, that may suffice). The downside of this approach is that you must use low-loss coaxial cable such as Belden 9913 or LMR 400 between the antenna and your station. High SWR values will be present on the feed line and without low-loss cable much of your power will effectively disappear.

Other commercial vertical designs rely on traps or cleverly constructed tuning sections to allow multiband operation. These antennas work well and don't require antenna tuners, although your operation will be restricting to the available bands and to the 2:1 SWR frequency ranges within each band. These antennas are also more mechanically complicated and challenging to install. The Cushcraft R8 antenna is a good example of a vertical antenna that incorporates a series of traps for multiband operation (40 through 6 meters).

The R8 also avoids the need for ground radials by providing seven short radials at the base. Note that the base of this antenna must be installed at least 10 feet above the ground. It is debatable how well this small radial system performs compared to tradi-

Is it a tree or an antenna? Actually, it is the Zero Five Stealth Vertical. www.zerofive-antennas.com

Verticals on Roofs

If you don't have enough room for a vertical antenna on the ground, consider your roof. Elevated verticals can actually perform very well, rivaling dipole antennas in many instances, but there are several drawbacks.

The most obvious problem is visibility. A tall vertical antenna on your rooftop will be highly visible to the entire neighborhood. Don't be surprised if it draws questions from your neighbors or even complaints. (People are particularly concerned about anything that appears to harm the "look" of a neighborhood, resulting in reduced property values.)

A rooftop vertical antenna still requires radial wires. If you erect a single-band vertical, you'll need to attach two to four wires and each must be cut to approximately ¼ wavelength for the band in question. As with a dipole antenna, you will need to carefully trim or lengthen the wires until you achieve the lowest SWR at your desired frequency. If you install a multiband vertical, you'll need at least one ¼ wavelength radial wire for each band. As you might imagine, tuning an antenna in this fashion while negotiating a steep roof would be a challenge (to put it mildly). The exception would be an antenna such as the Cushcraft R8 that provides shortened radial rods at its base.

Safely securing an HF vertical antenna to a roof presents another challenge. Do not attempt to use your chimney as a support. Chimneys were never designed to survive the wind loading stress a large vertical antenna would inflict. Instead, use a roof tripod (available at RadioShack and elsewhere) or consider side mounting the antenna at the edge of the roof using brackets that attach to the eaves of the house. You'll find more information on the subject of roof-mounted antennas in Chapter 4.

Finally, there is the problem of increased interference and RF exposure. With the antenna so close to your house, you may find that you'll suffer much more interference to your consumer electronic devices, or much more interference from them. Be sure to do an RF exposure evaluation as discussed in Chapter 1 to make sure that you won't exceed the maximum permissible levels according to the frequencies you'll be using and your anticipated output power.

tional radials. In most instances, verticals with longer in-ground radials offer superior performance. An exception is verticals that operate as an electrical half wave. These act like vertical dipoles and thus don't need a ground as part of the antenna. However, if you are considering a vertical antenna installed on your roof, the R8 and similar designs offer a strong advantage when you contemplate the prospect of spending hours on your roof carefully trimming the radials of a conventional vertical. See the sidebar "Verticals on the Roof."

One of the more unusual vertical antenna designs of recent years debuted with the Fluidmotion SteppIR antenna. This vertical is comprised of a hollow fiberglass tube that contains a long beryllium tape that's perforated on both sides like old fashioned movie film. At the base of the tube is an electric stepping motor that adjusts the length of the copper tape in response to commands from a microprocessor-based controller back in the station. The result is an antenna that literally changes its length according to the band you've chosen!

The SteppIR concept has become quite popular in the amateur community. It has expanded to include SteppIR Yagi antennas that adjust their electrical lengths in similar fashion. Both the Yagis and the vertical antennas seem to hold up well in temperature and wind extremes despite their reliance on moving parts. Because of their mechanical complexity, SteppIR antennas are expensive (at the time this book went to press, the 20 — 6 meter SteppIR "SmallIR" vertical was selling for $640). They also require you

A radial plate at the base of a vertical provides a convenient point to attach radial wires.

to install a multiconductor control cable in addition to the feed line.

TEMPORARY ANTENNAS

As you survey your options you may discover that a permanent antenna is out of the question. Your property may be too small, or your landlord or home association may have outlawed permanent outdoor antennas of any kind. If this is the case, you're still in the game. You might review Chapter 2 and

consider an indoor antenna. Alternatively, you might want to look into a temporary outdoor antenna that you can set up and remove at a moment's notice.

In the **Appendix** of this book you'll find several temporary portable antenna projects. If you want something "dirt cheap" and simple, however, look at **Figure 3.32**. This is a portable vertical antenna for 20 meters and it is nothing more than 16 feet of PVC tubing with a wire dangling inside. The base is made from PVC tubing as well. I

The Fluidmotion SteppIR vertical antenna adjusts its length by using an electric motor at the base to raise or lower a beryllium tape within a fiberglass tube. www.steppir.com

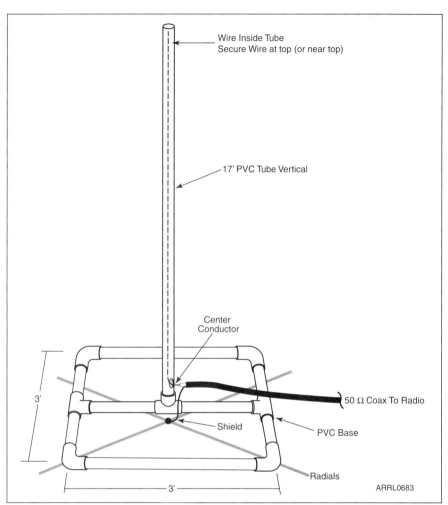

Figure 3.32 — A 20-meter temporary vertical antenna constructed entirely from PVC tubing. The radiator wire is inside the 17 foot vertical tube (you can hang the wire from the top using some fishing line and a hose clamp). The bottom of the radiator wire attaches to the center conductor of the 50 Ω coaxial feed line. The radial wires attach to the coaxial cable shield.

like working with PVC because it is extremely easy to cut with a common hacksaw. With inexpensive tube couplers and some PVC cement, you can slap this antenna together in less than an hour. You'll want to avoid gluing the vertical mast sections together so that you can easily pull the mast apart when it is time to take the antenna down.

For radials all you have to do is toss four 16-foot wires onto the grass around the base. Since this antenna is obviously temporary, you don't have to anchor or bury the wires.

Another design I've used is a temporary vertical antenna made from a single MFJ-1956 telescoping whip. When fully extended, the whip is 12 feet in length. By collapsing or extending the sections as necessary, this antenna will function as a ¼ wavelength vertical on 15, 12 and 10 meters. The whip has a ⅜ × 24 base that will fit into an ordinary mobile antenna bracket. I used the 1956 whip with a triangular "mag mount" mobile

antenna base connected to four 12-foot radial wires. I employed an antenna analyzer to initially help me find the correct whip length for each band and then I marked the whip accordingly with an indelible marker. As a temporary antenna, it performed well.

Speaking of whips, nothing stops you from taking two single-band mobile whip antennas and using them together as a dipole antenna for your favorite band. As we discussed in Chapter 2, a number of manufacturers such as MFJ Enterprises and others sell specially designed brackets for this purpose. I cobbled together a 20 meter dipole in this fashion for a quick bit of vacation operating (see **Figures 3.33** and **3.34**). I had to repeatedly trim the whip elements of the antennas to finally bring the SWR below 1.5:1 at my frequency of choice — 14.100 MHz. The 2:1 SWR bandwidth spanned about 75 kHz either side of the frequency. Since I intended to do mostly digital operating, that range

was perfect. A dipole of this type is far from optimal — it is actually quite lossy — but it *did* work!

Commercial Portables

In Chapter 2 I mentioned the fact that you can use a single or multiband mobile antenna indoors. You can also just as easily use this type of antenna outdoors. So many amateurs are doing this that several HF mobile antenna manufacturers are making accessories to meet the demand. What you'll typically find are tripod stands that allow you to quickly set up a mobile antenna for outdoor operating. A number of these mobile antenna designs use electric motors to adjust the antennas for the lowest SWR on a given frequency. With a small 12 Vdc power supply you can hook up the remote-control panels and tweak the antennas from the comfort of your dining room table (with the coaxial feed line and control wires running out the

Figure 3.33 — A 20-meter temporary dipole antenna made from two Hamstick mobile antennas.

Figure 3.34 — A close-up view of the mount used to attach two mobile antennas in a dipole configuration. This particular mount was purchased from MFJ Enterprises, but is also sold by other manufacturers.

The Super Antennas MP-1.
newsuperantenna.com

door or a nearby window).

As described in Chapter 2, you'll also find antennas designed primarily for amateurs who enjoy hiking and other forms of porta-ble operating. These products can be put to use as temporary outdoor antennas at home as well. The Super Antennas MP-1 lends itself well to this application. You can purchase a tripod mount and within minutes you'll be up and running on bands from low HF through UHF. It is simply a matter of lengthening or shorting the radiator whip and adjusting a metal sleeve over the loading coil at the middle of the antenna. The MP-1 comes with a set of four radial wires that you connect to the base. Like all compromise antennas, the MP-1 can't compare to a full sized antenna, but it will definitely get you on the air. Once you're finished, it disassembles into a tiny box for storage. The MP-1 is available at **newsuperantenna.com**.

A larger portable antenna is the Buddi-Pole. This is a dipole shortened with tapped inductors on both legs. By changing taps and adjusting elements, the BuddiPole operates over a range from 40 meters to 2 meters. In its collapsed form it fits into a package 22 inches in length, but expands to 16 feet when fully assembled. At the time of this writing the BuddiPole sold for $200 at **www. buddipole.com**.

The BuddiPole portable dipole antenna. www.buddipole.com

BILAL COMPANY

The Bilal Isotron antennas can be set up outdoors in either temporary or permanent installations. www.isotronantennas.com

Another antenna first mentioned in Chapter 2 is the Bilal Isotron. This is an extremely compact series of HF antennas. The 40-meter Isotron, for example, is only 22 × 16 × 15 inches. No ground radials are required. Performance is on par with a mobile antenna, which again means not spectacular but good enough to make contacts under restricted conditions. Prices range from about $78 to $200, depending on the model. More information is available online at **www.isotron antennas.com**.

Finally, there are the MFJ-1786 or 1788 loop antennas. This is the same antenna we discussed (and showed) in Chapter 2. The 1786 covers 30 through 10 meters; the 1788 spans 40 through 15 meters. Despite the small size of these antennas (only about 3 feet in diameter), they seem to do a credible job on the air. Both loops use large tuning capacitors driven by electric motors. You must tune carefully because the low-SWR point for any frequency is very narrow. If you become impatient with the tuning control, you'll skip right past the "sweet spot." For this reason it can be a bit of a pain to change frequencies with these antennas. Both models sell at prices between $420 and $470. You can learn more at **www.mfjenterprises.com**.

Regardless of what type of temporary antenna you choose, take care to prevent people or animals from coming into contact with it. If you are operating at low power levels (less than 5 W), the risk of injury is essentially zero, but at 100 W there are substantial voltages present — more than enough to give someone a serious burn! When setting up a

temporary antenna choose a spot that reduces the likelihood of someone getting near it. Pick an operating position that allows you to keep the antenna in view at all times and tell your family members not to touch the antenna. It may also be a good idea to place a HIGH VOLTAGE warning placard near the antenna as well.

OUTDOOR IDEAS

A Stealthy Fence Antenna

Many homes these days have vinyl or wooden "privacy fences" that usually define all or part of a property line. They are particularly common in tightly packed housing developments. If you are blessed with such a fence, the odds are good that you can put the fence to work as a means to get on at least one HF band.

The type of antenna I'm about to describe might seem a little counterintuitive. When

we think of HF antennas, the old maxim "put up as much wire as possible, as high as possible" comes to mind. Privacy fences are not very high (typically 7 or 8 feet tall), so it is reasonable to wonder how well an antenna could perform if it depends on a privacy fence for its entire support structure.

Back in the 1970s, there was considerable discussion about an antenna design known as a *DDRR*, or Direction Discontinuity Ring Radiator. Credited to J. M. Boyer, the DDRR was designed as a ¼ wavelength horizontal ring of metal tubing grounded at one end and elevated a short distance above a metal plate. The intent was to create a low-profile antenna that could be installed on ships above steel decks and other metallic surfaces.

There was nothing magical about the DDRR. It was really just a very short top-loaded vertical antenna. However, it *did* work — not extremely well, but not horribly either.

You might call the privacy fence antenna

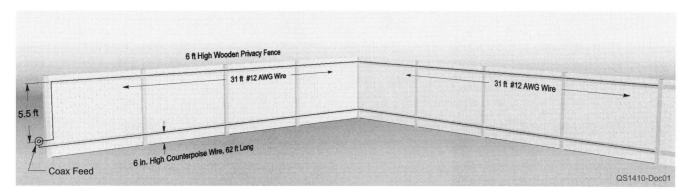

Figure 3.35 — The 80 meter version of the pseudo-DDRR antenna. In this installation, the top radiator wire is a total of 67 ½ feet in length, which is about ¼ wavelength at 3.5 MHz. The bottom wire functions as a counterpoise and runs directly beneath the radiator along its entire length.

shown in **Figure 3.35** is an offspring of the DDRR concept. The top wire is the radiating wire. It is connected to the center conductor of your coaxial cable. From that connecting point, the radiator goes upward to the top of the fence, or close to it. The wire then goes horizontal and snakes along the top of the fence line, turning corners as necessary.

From the feed point, another wire runs horizontally, directly beneath the top wire, at a distance of about 6 inches above the soil. This wire connects to the outer braid of your coaxial cable and functions somewhat like a counterpoise. In this antenna it is important to maintain a consistent vertical separation between the radiator and counterpoise wires.

In the diagram you'll see that the radiator is a total of 67 ½ feet in length (5 ½ feet vertically and 62 feet horizontally). This is roughly a quarter wavelength at 3.5 MHz. If you don't have that much fence at your disposal and don't mind being limited to a higher-frequency band, use a shorter length for the radiator, but make sure that the total length is ¼ wavelength for your desired frequency. For example, if you want to try this antenna on 20 meters, make the total length of the radiator 16 ½ feet: 5 ½ feet vertically plus 11 feet horizontally. The length of the bottom counterpoise wire isn't critical, but for best performance it should equal the length of the horizontal portion of the radiator.

Speaking of wire, a thicker gauge is best to minimize loss, but if you're in a situation where stealth is your primary concern, you can use something as thin as AWG #22 wire. The wire does not have to be insulated, but for safety sake, insulation may be best. Besides, it is much easier to buy insulated wire to match the color of your fence. At the very least, you can paint the insulation to match.

This type of antenna is not likely to yield a perfect 1:1 SWR at the feed point. If you can get your hands on an antenna analyzer, I'd recommend using it to find the low SWR

point and then lengthening or trimming the wires equally to "move" that point to your chosen frequency.

Don't be surprised if the low SWR point is only 3:1 or 5:1. High as that SWR may seem, it is still within the range of most antenna tuners, including the one in your transceiver (if it has such a feature). If your antenna tuner is at your station, I'd recommend using low-loss coaxial cable such as LMR 400 between the tuner and the antenna feed point. That way, you will minimize any loss due to the elevated SWR.

And, of course, you can always choose to place an antenna tuner at the feed point for even less loss. A remote automatic antenna tuner would do the job, as would a manual tuner in a weatherproof enclosure. If you're willing to experiment, you could dispense with complex tuners entirely and simply try a 20 pF variable capacitor at the feed point in series with the radiating wire. You may find that by adjusting this capacitor you can obtain a lower SWR.

This pseudo-DDRR antenna won't blow anyone's doors off. In most cases your signal will be about 1.5 to 2 dB weaker at the receiving end compared to a traditional vertical antenna. But when you consider the visual impact of having a ¼ wavelength vertical pole planted in your yard, and the hassle of laying out a network of radial wires in the soil, this fence antenna is a perfectly acceptable compromise.

The KE4PT Off-Center End-Fed Dipole

In the March 2015 issue of *QST*, Kai Siwiak, KE4PT, discussed an interesting approach to an antenna originally intended for portable applications. His novel design is an antenna that is physically fed at the end, but electrically it is off-center fed. Therefore, we can call it an OCEF — an *Off-Center End-Fed* dipole.

If you live on the upper floors of an apartment or condominium, you can easily deploy this antenna with a 20-foot telescoping Fiberglass tent pole (see **Figure 3.36**). The antenna can be extended in a matter of minutes, and then removed just as quickly. For a permanent installation, you can anchor the far end of the antenna on any convenient support.

The OCEF dipole consists of two dipole legs and an optional droop wire (see **Figure 3.37**). For the longest portion, I suggest using 30 feet of insulated AWG #20 wire connecting to a plastic or ceramic insulator. Solder the other end of this wire to the center conductor of 11 ½ feet of miniature RG-174 coaxial cable. The second radiating part of the antenna — the "other half" of the dipole — is the outer braid of the RG-174 cable.

Make sure you start with enough RG-174 (at least 13 feet) so that you can wind three turns around each of the two ferrite chokes and terminate the coax in a BNC connector. The ferrite chokes are used to attenuate the radiating currents and keep them from flowing back into your home.

If you don't have access to RG-174 cable, there is no reason why you could not use something bigger such as RG-58 coax. Larger coax would also allow you to terminate in a standard PL-259 connector rather than BNC. However, you'll also have to use larger ferrite chokes to accommodate wrapping the thicker cable.

Look at Figure 3.37 again. Point C is where you can attach the optional 2-foot droop wire. It isn't necessary *per se*, but it may help reduce the high impedance that may exist at the end of the antenna.

Overall, this OCEF dipole is 41.5 feet long when you measure from A to C in Figure 3.37, or 42.4 feet when measured from A to D. The wire between the end insulator and the end of the optional droop wire acts like a dipole radiator. However, this antenna is most definitely a non-self-resonant design,

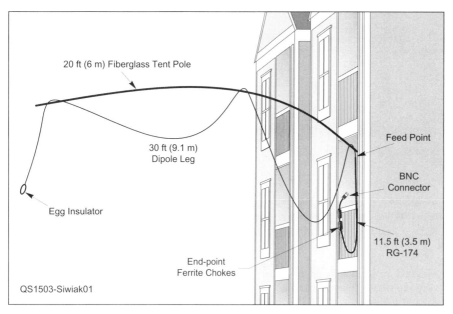

Figure 3.36 — The portable version of the OCEF dipole deployed with a 20 foot tent pole.

which means that you will need to use an antenna tuner. The tuner can be an external type, or the type of tuner built-in to a transceiver. Either way, the tuner doesn't need to have a wide impedance matching range.

The OCEF dipole can work surprisingly well, especially if you can elevate the end significantly above ground. In my tests with this antenna, I was able to use a small antenna tuner to feed the OCEF on every band from 40 to 6 meters. Despite the use of ferrite chokes to limit the presence of RF on the feed line, I'd still recommend using this antenna at reduced power levels. I enjoyed good performance with just 5 W output, but if you run 100 W you may find some RF making its way into your station.

A Self-Supporting Inverted V

Here is a single-band antenna that can be permanent or temporary. It is great for limited-space environments because the

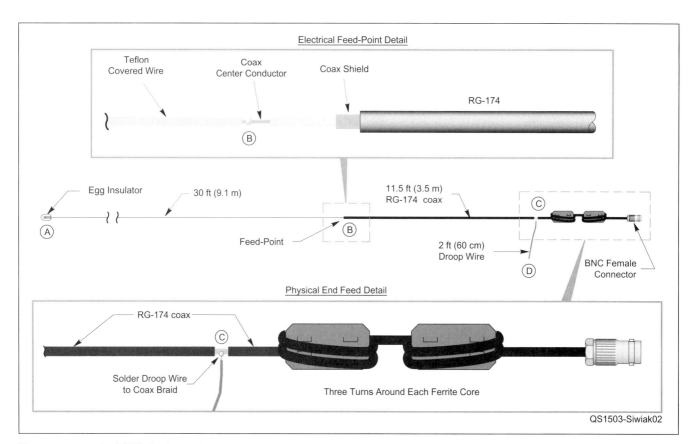

Figure 3.37 — This OCEF dipole detail shows radiating portions A — D, the details of the electrical feed point, and the common-mode chokes at the end of the antenna. You need about 32 feet of insulated copper wire, 13 feet of RG-175 coaxial cable, two snap-on ¼ inch Mix-31 split ferrites (www.Palomar-Engineers.com) and a BNC connector (either male or female).

Table 3.1
Self-Supporting Inverted V

(Lengths are in inches)

Band (Meters)	A	B	Height C	Base D
40	390	390	276	552
20	198	198	140	280
17	156	156	110	221
15	132	132	93	187
12	113	113	80	160
10	98	98	69	139

support is "built in." That is to say, you don't have to worry about finding a strategically located pole or tree for this antenna. Best of all, you can build it from thick-walled PVC pipe; all you need is PVC cement and possibly a saw.

Joseph Littlepage, WE5Y, was among the first to publish this design for a lightweight, rotatable inverted V antenna. See **Figure 3.38**. A photograph of his antenna in a portable application is shown in **Figure 3.39**. Joseph used a telescoping push-up mast for the center support, but for a permanent installation you could replace this with single or multiple lengths of PVC pipe. A wood support can also be used. If you choose PVC and want to paint it to blend into the background, be sure to use paint designed for PVC. Ordinary paint will flake off over time.

In his original design, Joseph used thin spreaders for the base of the antenna, so he needed to add short lengths of PVC at the base to support the spreaders. The idea here is to avoid "droop" as much as possible while making the antenna easy to disassemble. In a permanent installation, however, if you can source stronger materials for the base, such as wood or thick-walled PVC, the ad-

ditional supports should not be necessary.

Table 3.1 shows the wire lengths for 40 through 10 meters. For this antenna to function properly, you'll need to make sure that the wires slope downward to form a triangle with 90 degree corners. Try to elevate to base of the antenna as much as possible. Ideally, the ends of the wires should be at least 6 feet above the soil.

A 40-meter version of this antenna puts the apex at 23 feet (276 inches). In addition, the base is 46 feet in length. If you decide to build this version you'll need to use something strong for the center support. Thick-wall PVC may be adequate, but a thick wood support may be better. The antenna wires will provide tension and support for the base, so the PVC or wood used for this part of the structure does not have to be as robust.

As with all inverted V antennas, this antenna is fed at the top. You can use a standard dipole center insulator here, or even just an SO-239 coaxial connector. Dress the coaxial cable down along the center support, using cable ties or electrical tape to hold it in place.

This antenna will require trimming to obtain the lowest SWR at your desired fre-

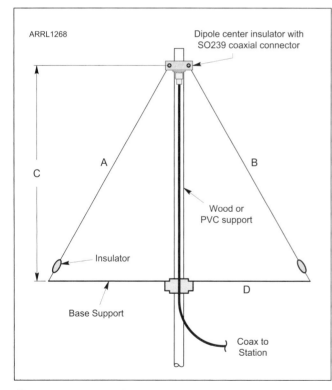

Figure 3.38 — The self-supporting inverted V dipole. See Table 3.1 for dimensions for A, B, C, and D.

Figure 3.39 — The self-supporting inverted V in a portable application.

quency. (An antenna analyzer comes in very handy for this part of the process.) You'll likely find that you have to trim the lengths of the wires to bring the low-SWR point to the frequency you need. The good news, however, is that this antenna is fairly "broad," which means that you should enjoy a reasonably low SWR through much of the band. If you build the 40 meter version, don't be surprised to find that you have a low SWR point on the 15 meter band as well.

Although this is intended as a single-band antenna, there is nothing to prevent you from using a remote antenna tuner at the base and turning this into a multiband antenna. You can use a remote antenna tuner designed for outdoor use, or take an indoor tuner and place it in a weatherproof enclosure as described later in this chapter.

Fun with MFJ Whips

Earlier in this chapter we briefly discussed the idea of using two mobile antennas in a dipole configuration to create an easy-to-assemble temporary antenna. It is as simple as screwing two Hamstick-style (MFJ calls them "HF Stick") antennas into an MFJ-347 Double T Pipe Mount (turn back to Figure 3.34 to refresh your memory). The mounts cost only $19.95, so the majority of the cost is in the mobile whip antennas themselves.

As I pointed out, however, mobile antennas are not the best performers on the HF bands, even when fed in pairs as dipoles. They are essentially loading coils with short radiators and, as such, they tend to be highly inefficient.

But consider *full size* telescoping whip antennas. MFJ Enterprises (**www.mfjenterprises.com**) sells several models according to their maximum lengths:

MFJ-1974 — 8.2 feet, $34. 95
MFJ-1976 — 10 feet, $39.95
MFJ-1977 — 12 feet, $44.95
MFJ-1979 — 17 feet, $59.95

If you do the math you'll quickly discover that these antennas can be extended or retracted to ¼ wavelengths on a number of HF bands . . .

MFJ-1974 = 10 meters
MFJ-1976 = 12 and 10 meters
MFJ-1977 = 15, 12 and 10 meters
MFJ-1979 = 20, 17, 15, 12 and 10 meters

The whips are stainless steel with 3/8 — 24 mounting stubs. Two whips can be mounted back to back as dipole antennas with the MFJ-347 mount, or a single whip can be used as a vertical antenna with an MFJ-342T or MFJ-344 mount.

In practice, I've found that using the whips as horizontal dipoles can be effective, although as the lengths exceed 10 feet the whips droop considerably. With the pos-

Figure 3.40 — Two MFJ-1977 antennas used as a 10 meter semi-stealthy dipole. If you look closely, you can see the coaxial balun. This antenna performed remarkably well, especially considering that it was only about 15 feet off the ground.

Figure 3.41 — An MFJ-1979 as a 20 meter vertical antenna.

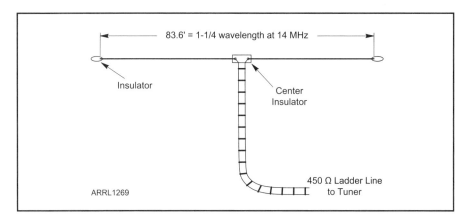

83.6' = 1-1/4 wavelength at 14 MHz

Insulator

Center
Insulator

450 Ω Ladder Line
to Tuner

ARRL1269

Figure 3.42 — An 83.6-foot extended double zepp dipole fed with 450 Ω ladder line. This design is 1.5 wavelengths at 14 MHz and offers significant gain on that band, plus good performance on other HF bands. If is shown here in a horizontal configuration, but it can be bent as needed for smaller spaces.

sibility of wind damage in mind, I couldn't recommend using MFJ-1979 whips as full sized 20 meter dipoles.

That said, I have used a pair of MFJ-1977s as a ½ wavelength dipole on 10 meters with excellent results. See **Figure 3.40**. I operated this antenna as my "stealth" antenna in the trees behind my house at an altitude of only 15 feet. It soon became one of my favorite antennas for 10 meters.

I began by attaching the whips to the mount and then extending them to the lengths I had calculated to yield a total ½ wavelength at 28.300 MHz (16 feet, 6 inches). Of course, my measurements were off, so I had to adjust the lengths again until I had achieved a 1.3:1 SWR.

It is worth noting that I had some initial problems with what seemed like a "variable" SWR. I'd measure it once and get 1.3:1 at the antenna, only to connect the rest of the feed line to the station and see the SWR jump to almost 3:1 on the meter at my transceiver. It turned out that the antenna was causing some common-mode currents to flow in the feed line. Fortunately, the cure was easy. All I had to do was create a choke balun near the antenna feed point by coiling six turns of the coaxial cable into a circle about 5 inches in diameter. If you look closely at Figure 3.40, you can see the balun.

You can also put a single whip to work as an effective vertical antenna. When fully extended, the MFJ-1979 can function well as a 20 meter ¼ wavelength antenna. During Field Day 2014 I screwed an MFJ-1979 into an MFJ-344 mount and attached the mount to a length of PVC pipe I had hammered into the soil. I strung eight 16-foot radial wires in various directions along the ground and then made slight adjustments in the length of the whip until I achieved a 1:1 SWR. See **Figure 3.41**.

Even with just eight radials, the whip worked surprisingly well on 20 meters. It was a rather breezy day, which kept the antenna in constant motion, but the whip seemed to tolerate the motion well.

Whether as dipoles or verticals, these telescoping whip antennas are good performers. The advantage of the whip approach is twofold: (1) The antennas require only a single support, either at the dipole center or on the ground and (2) the antennas can be easily adjusted when you want to change bands or frequencies.

MFJ whips also have potential as temporary HF verticals if you live in an antenna restricted environment. You could permanently install the MFJ-344 or MFJ-342T mount at ground level and bury a network of radial wires in the soil (the more wires the better). Then, whenever you wanted to operate, it would be a matter of walking outside, screwing the whip into the mount and extending it to whatever length you need.

The Extended Double Zepp Dipole

A ½ wavelength dipole, is a dipole, is a dipole. Right?

Generally, the answer is "yes." If you cut a wire dipole antenna to ½ wavelength at a given frequency, you can expect a certain behavior. If you get it high enough off the ground and away from sizeable metal objects, you can be reasonably sure of seeing something close to a 1.5:1 SWR at the feed point.

However, if you increase the length beyond ½ wavelength, and feed it with 450 Ω ladder line, some interesting things happen. See **Figure 3.42**.

When the antenna becomes one wavelength long at a given frequency, for example, it may offer about 1.5 dB gain relative to

a standard half wavelength dipole. If you increase the length of the antenna yet again to about 1¼ wavelength, you'll realize significantly more gain, depending on the frequency, of course. These antennas are often called Extended Double Zepps.

Assuming one can hang the antenna horizontally at least 35 feet above ground, antenna modeling software suggests significant directivity on 20 meters, which is the result you'd expect on that band. The models also suggested decent performance on 40, 15 and 10 meters.

This is a book about small antennas and, at almost 84 feet in length, the antenna I've just described isn't necessarily small. Even so, as we've discussed before, size (length) only becomes an issue if you insist on hanging this antenna in a straight horizontal line. The good news is the extended double zepp doesn't have to be perfectly horizontal. In fact, if you can find a single support for the center, this antenna can be installed as a classic inverted V. Chances are good that a wide range antenna tuner with a 4:1 balun can load the antenna in an inverted V configuration on a number of bands.

In the August 2015 issue of *QST* magazine I reviewed MFJ's version of this antenna, the model 1742. In my installation, the antenna was hung as an inverted V at an apex of about 30 feet (**Figure 3.43**) with the legs drooping until they reached a privacy fence about 8 feet off the ground. The run of 450 Ω ladder line connected to a remote

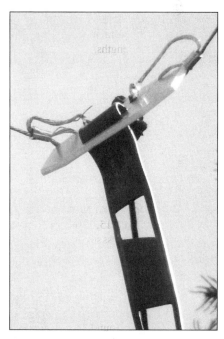

Figure 3.43 — The rugged center insulator of the MFJ-1742 extended double zepp dipole.

antenna tuner about 40 feet away.

The remote tuner was able to load the antenna on every HF band, including 160 meters. I suspected that there would be substantial voltage in the tuner if I attempted to run 100 W on 160, so I decided not to press my luck.

The point is, if you have the room to accommodate the extended double zepp at this length, even if you have to become "creative" in the installation, you may reap some worthwhile benefits. And if you can bring the ladder line all the way back to your station and use an antenna tuner with a balanced output, you won't need the remote tuner approach that I used.

Take Your Indoor Antenna Tuner Outdoors

In Chapter 1 we discussed how placing an antenna tuner at or near the feed point of an antenna can provide a low SWR on the coaxial cable that runs back to your station. The advantage of this technique is that it allows you to enjoy the convenience of using coaxial cable, especially inexpensive cable such as RG-58, while not having to worry about SWR-induced losses in the cable.

You can purchase weatherproof remote automatic tuners from a number of companies such as MFJ and LDG. But what about the tuner you already own, or maybe the affordable indoor auto tuner you've seen advertised in *QST* magazine? With the right enclosure to protect the device, there is no reason why you can't take an indoor antenna tuner outdoors.

Earlier in this chapter I showed you an example of a crude antenna tuner enclosure at the base of a vertical antenna. It was essentially a large Tupperware container. Although that enclosure did the job, we can most definitely do better!

In **Figure 3.44** you'll see an antenna tuner enclosure I created from a BUD Industries NBB-15243 NEMA box. The box is 11-$^{17}/_{64}$ inches long, 5½ inches tall and 7-$^{15}/_{32}$ inches wide. The lid is hinged, offers two snap locks, and includes a rubber gasket that makes a waterproof seal when the lid is closed.

The box is made from tough ABS plastic that almost feels like metal. When this book was written, the NBB-15243 sold on Amazon.com for $42. That may seem like a lot to pay for a box, but considering the rugged construction and weatherproof design, the NBB-15243 is well worth the price.

The NBB-15243 isn't the only box I would consider; there are other similar models. But whichever box you choose, go for durability and a weatherproof specification. Your tuner enclosure could be sitting outdoors for a number of years, so you want something that will withstand whatever Mother Nature can dish out.

For my tuner box I needed one port to attach the coaxial cable from my station (the enclosure's **TX** port), and another port (the **ANT** port) for a short coax jumper that connects to a weatherproof 4:1 balun. I was using a balun because I was feeding RF power to a dipole antenna via a 40 foot length of 450-Ω ladder line. Otherwise, the **ANT** port

would connect directly to the antenna feed point, which would presumably be a short distance away.

For the coaxial ports you could use two SO239 female bulkhead connectors with washers to keep out moisture. However, I decided upon a more elegant solution with two back-to-back SO-239 panel connectors. They are somewhat difficult to find, but I located them on Amazon for $6.50 each.

The back-to-back SO239 connectors (**Figure 3.45**) not only supply secure connections to the external coaxial cables, they offer equally secure internal connections for short coaxial jumper cables inside the tuner box.

My tuner box presently holds an LDG indoor automatic antenna tuner. This particular model, the Z11 Pro 2, is an *RF-sensing* design, which is ideal for this application. An RF-sensing antenna tuner will automatically begin tuning whenever it senses RF energy at its input.

Like most automatic tuners, the Z11 Pro 2 includes microprocessor memories. Each time the tuner finds an acceptable match, it stores the information in a memory slot. If you tend to operate at or near certain frequencies much of the time, the tuner will be able to retrieve the information from its memory and tune much faster than it might otherwise.

Thanks to its sophisticated design, an indoor RF-sensing automatic antenna tuner does not require human interaction. You never need to push buttons or twist knobs.

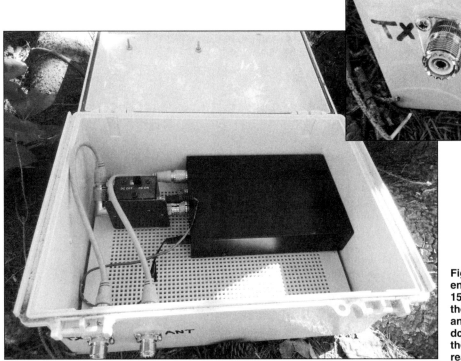

Figure 3.45 — A view of the back-to-back female SO239 panel connectors I use as ports for coaxial cables coming from my station and going to my antenna.

Figure 3.44 — My remote antenna tuner is enclosed in a rugged BUD Industries NBB-15243 NEMA box. In this photo you can see the LDG Z11 Pro 2 automatic antenna tuner and an MFJ-4116 Bias T. The Bias T removes dc power from the coaxial cable to power the tuner while still allowing RF energy to reach the tuner input.

This is exactly the type of tuner you need for your remote antenna tuner box. You want a model that will function autonomously at a considerable distance from your operating position. All you have to do is transmit and the tuner takes care of the rest.

But what about dc power? Ah, there's the rub! You must get dc power to your tuner in its remote location. There are several ways to tackle this problem.

The most straightforward method is to run a separate two-conductor wire between the dc power supply at your station and the remote antenna tuner. It is a simple solution, but it comes with its own problems. You have the hassle of running yet another cable out of your home and you will have to drill another hole in your remote box (a hole you will also have to seal) to accommodate the cable. You may also find that you'll have to use heavy gauge wire for the dc cable if the distance is more than 30 feet. Otherwise, you'll encounter a substantial voltage drop due to resistive loss.

Another solution is to place a battery in the remote box to power the tuner. Automatic antenna tuners don't require much power, so they tend to draw relatively small amounts of current when operating. I once used this method to power a remote tuner and my battery choice was a 4 Ah (Amp Hour) 12 V gel cell. The gel cell ran the remote tuner for more than a year — even at below-zero temperatures — before I finally had to recharge it — and that is the primary drawback. At some point you will be forced to remove the battery from the tuner box (which may be in an inconvenient location) and recharge it. What if the tuner box happens to be under several feet of snow when the battery chooses to die? You could find that you're off the air for some time!

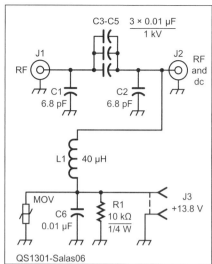

Figure 3.46 — A Bias T designed by Phil Salas, AD5X. Mouser Electronics part numbers shown where applicable.
C1, C2 — 6.8 pF, 1 kV ceramic disk capacitors
C3, C4, C5, C6 — 0.01 µF, 1 kV ceramic disk capacitors
J1, J2 — SO239 female coaxial connectors
J3 — Chassis connector for dc power
L1 — 40 µH, 3 A inductor (Mouser 542-5240-RC)
MOV — 18 V Metal Oxide Varistor. (Mouser 667-ERZ-V10D220)
R1 — 10 kΩ, ¼ W resistor

My favorite solution is the one that I believe is the most elegant: powering the antenna tuner with a dc voltage sent down the coaxial cable itself. To do this, you'll need two dc power injectors, often called "Bias Ts." One unit in your station injects dc power into the coax; the second unit inside the remote tuner box removes the dc power from the coax and makes it available to the antenna tuner.

Bias Ts are simple devices. They work their magic through the use of an inductor that passes dc while it blocks RF energy from getting into your power supply. At the same time, ceramic capacitors are used to prevent the dc power from going where it shouldn't — into your radio or the RF input of the remote antenna tuner. **Figure 3.46** shows the schematic diagram of a Bias T designed by Phil Salas, AD5X. You can also purchase Bias Ts from several sources. MFJ Enterprises (**www.mfjenterprises.com**) sells their MFJ-4116 Bias T for $29.95. Remember that you'll need to purchase two of these.

Throughout this discussion we've been talking about automatic antenna tuners in remote applications, but are they strictly necessary? Rather than housing an auto tuner and the necessary dc power connections, what if your remote box held nothing more than a manual antenna tuner — one of the small, inexpensive kind? As odd as this may sound, this type of remote tuner makes perfect sense if your goal is to operate your antenna on just one band. You can install the tuner and then adjust it for the best match at your favorite frequency — done! Or, you may not mind strolling over the to the remote box and making a couple of tweaks — twisting the knobs according to homemade labels you've added to the antenna tuner — whenever you want to switch bands.

Either way, investing in a well-built, weather-tight enclosure for your antenna tuner will allow you to locate the device to where it will do the most good and protect it there for years to come.

Outdoor Antennas for VHF+

Compared to their HF and MF cousins, antennas for the bands above 50 MHz are much easier to accommodate in a limited space environment. Generally speaking, the higher the frequency the smaller the antenna. This doesn't mean that all VHF+ antennas qualify as "small." As you'll see later, some of these antennas can actually be quite large.

Despite their relative size differences vs HF antennas, VHF+ antenna systems come with their own unique challenges.

THE IMPORTANCE OF HEIGHT

In our discussions of HF antennas, you may recall that we weren't overly concerned about height. Yes, horizontal HF antennas benefit from being elevated as high as possible above ground (within reason), but for casual operating an HF antenna at almost any height will do. The primary job of an HF antenna is to radiate your signal to the ionosphere where it will be diffracted and returned to earth a substantial distance away. If your HF antenna can send a large portion of your signal at a shallow angle to the ionosphere, the signal may return to *terra firma* thousands of miles from where it originated.

On the other hand, an HF antenna installed very low to the ground may send most of your energy nearly straight up. When it reaches the ionosphere it will bounce right back down, resulting in a signal that covers only a couple of hundred miles. Some HF antennas are intentionally designed to behave this way. They are called Near Vertical Incidence Skywave (NVIS) antennas and they are ideal when you need reliable HF communication within a confined area. (Communication within a large disaster zone comes to mind.)

But when it comes to VHF+, we can't always rely on the ionosphere to relay our signals. In fact, for frequencies higher than 50 MHz, we usually can't rely on the ionosphere at all. When a VHF+ signal reaches the ionosphere, it usually goes straight through and out into space, which is one of the reasons VHF, UHF and microwave frequencies are ideal for satellite communications.

There are exceptions, of course. As we discussed briefly in Chapter 2, a type of propagation known as *Sporadic E* is capable of sending 6 and 2 meter signals over large distances. We're talking thousands of miles in some instances. But as its name implies, Sporadic E is … well … "sporadic." It is

an uncommon phenomenon that comes and goes with little warning. For reasons not fully understood, Sporadic E is limited to the late spring and summer months, with a weaker appearance in late December into January.

At the peak of a particularly active Solar Cycle, 6 meters can occasionally behave like an HF band. The ionosphere becomes so intensely ionized that the high "F" layer will diffract 6 meter energy, sending it bouncing around the globe. Under those conditions even the proverbial "wet string" antenna is capable of worldwide communication.

But if some form of ionospheric propagation isn't in play, you are mostly limited to line-of-sight communication at 50 MHz and above. This doesn't necessarily mean that you can only communicate with stations you can see. On the contrary, VHF+ signals can reflect off objects ranging from mountains to meteors and end up traveling quite far. Certain weather conditions in the lower atmosphere — the *troposphere* — can also reflect signals over several hundred miles or more. This is the "tropo ducting" phenomena you may encounter on 2 meters and above. But in all of these examples we're talking about signals traveling in straight lines; they are not diffracted by the ionosphere as HF and low VHF signals can be.

Line-of-sight communication is the *norm* above 50 MHz; the other "propagation enhancements" are much less common in the grand scheme of things. So, to make the most of this situation your antennas need to be as high as possible so that your signals can travel as far as possible without being blocked by buildings, hills or mountains. Also, especially above 222 MHz moisture absorption becomes a serious issue. Trees and other vegetation are filled with copious amounts of water that will severely attenuate your signals at these frequencies. Once again, the cure is to elevate your antennas as much as possible above nearby trees.

The single exception to the line-of-sight rule, at least from an operational standpoint, occurs when you're operating FM voice or digital and live within the coverage area of a repeater or digipeater. These relaying devices will usually compensate for your lack of clear line-of-sight pathways. As you may recall from Chapter 2, with a repeater to help you, a VHF antenna can be placed just about anywhere and you'll still be able to communicate.

Many VHF+ enthusiasts rely on towers to gain the necessary height for their antennas, but in a limited-space environment it is safe to assume that towers are out of the question. If you had the ability to erect a tower on your property, I strongly doubt that you'd be reading this book! The good news is that there are other options available, such as putting your home to work as a "tower."

POLARIZATION

Another important factor to consider with VHF+ antennas is polarization. All antennas are polarized, including HF antennas. In Amateur Radio applications we commonly deal with either horizontal or vertical polarization (or occasionally circular polarization, particularly with satellite work). For most antennas it is very easy to determine the polarization — it is simply in the same plane as the elements of the antenna relative to their positions above the earth (**Figure 4.1**). Vertical and horizontal are the simplest forms of antenna polarization and they both fall into a category known as *linear* polarization.

For normal HF operating we don't care very much about antenna polarization. When our signals are diffracted by the ionosphere, their polarizations "rotate." Whatever polarization the signal had when it left the HF antenna will be different when it arrives at its destination. We obviously have little control over this, so we don't attempt to design our antennas accordingly. The impact on signal strength is minimal.

At VHF+ it is a very different story. Unless you're dealing with ionospheric propagation such as Sporadic E, the polarization of your antenna can be critical. With line-of-sight propagation the polarization of the signal that leaves your antenna will remain largely unchanged at its destination. So, if your antenna is vertically polarized and the other guy's antenna is horizontally polarized, a substantial portion of your signal will not be received at his end. The same will be true for his signal at your station. The resulting loss can be as much as 20 dB, which is enough to make communication impossible under many circumstances.

How do you know which antenna polarizations other stations are using? You don't. However, hams long ago established a convention that everyone follows to this day. If you operate FM, you use vertically polarized antennas, thanks to the fact that vehicles, which do the lion's share of FM operating, have vertically polarized antennas. If you operate SSB or CW, you use horizontal polarization. Most digital communications such as APRS and D-STAR use vertical polarization, but "weak signal" digital modes such as WSJT use horizontal polarization.

FEED LINES

Throughout this book I've expended a great deal of ink talking about the importance of feed lines. At frequencies above 50 MHz, minimizing feed line loss becomes extremely important. *Do not* attempt to save money by scrimping on the quality of your feed lines. You'll regret it.

Otherwise excellent antennas and transceivers can be rendered worthless if you link them with poor feed lines. Typically found in the form of coaxial cable in VHF+ applications, the feed line is the critical pipeline between the radio and the antenna. It is responsible for delivering RF power to your antenna and received signals back to your radio.

The chief issue with feed lines is *loss*. Every feed line has some degree of loss. If you insert 100 W of RF at the station end of the line, you will always have something less than 100 W at the antenna. The same concept works in reverse — the received signal at the antenna will always be somewhat weaker by the time it reaches your radio. Feed line loss increases with frequency and length. It also increases when the antenna impedance is mismatched to the feed line, resulting in an elevated Standing Wave Ratio (SWR).

Although feed line loss can never be eliminated, it *can* be reduced to acceptable levels by…

▪ Choosing the lowest-loss feed line for the application

▪ Keeping the feed line as short as possible

▪ Adjusting the antenna for the lowest possible SWR

Go back to Chapter 1 and look at Table 1.1. Let's take the Chapter 1 loss example and apply it to a VHF+ station.

Consider the Belden 8240 brand of RG-58 coaxial cable and assume that we're using 100 feet of it to feed a 2 meter/70 cm Yagi antenna combo. At 100 MHz (close enough to 2 meters for this discussion), the matched loss is 3.8 dB. Since we're talking about loss, 3 dB represents a halving of power, so you will stand to lose *more than half* your RF in this feed line between the radio and the Yagi. *Ouch!* At 70 cm it will be even worse, possibly a *quadruple* loss or more. It's obvious that this cable would be a poor choice in this application!

How about RG-213 (Belden 8267)? Now the loss at 2 meters drops to 1.9 dB. That may be acceptable at 2 meters, but at 70 cm we're still talking about something on the order of 3 dB. Not good.

Now consider the TMS (Times Microwave Systems) LMR400 brand of RG-8 coax. At 2 meters the loss is only 1.3 dB, rising to 4.1 dB at 1000 MHz. This is an acceptable loss at 2 meters and at 70 cm it is an equally acceptable 2 dB. If the feed line turned out to be less than 100 feet long, the losses would be lower still.

When considering microwave signals, loss becomes excessive among the types of cables hams are likely to purchase. Consider LDF6-50A Heliax in Table 1.1. The matched loss at 1000 MHz is outstanding, even at microwave frequencies, but this cable is very expensive and difficult to work with, so much so that it is impractical for most ham stations. The cost-effective solution for a microwave ground station is to operate the radio at a much lower frequency and convert to or from microwave at the antenna with devices such as *transverters* and *downconverters*.

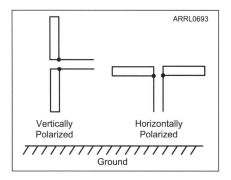

Figure 4.1 — **Vertical or horizontal polarization largely depends on an antenna's orientation in reference to ground, as shown here.**

OMNIDIRECTIONAL ANTENNAS

A powerful clue to the nature of an omnidirectional antenna is found in its prefix: *omni*, meaning "all," or in this context, "everywhere." An ideal omnidirectional antenna receives and transmits in all directions. Its radiation pattern looks like a smooth bubble. In the real world, however, many omnidirectional antennas exhibit radiation patterns that are far from uniform (see **Figure 4.2**). Even so, there is enough uniformity to consider them omnidirectional for all intents and purposes.

The benefit of an omnidirectional antenna is found in the fact that you don't need to rotate it. You simply install the antenna and start operating; you don't need to be concerned about which way it is pointing. On the other hand, its omnidirectional nature is also its weakness. An omnidirectional antenna can't focus signal energy to bridge the communications gaps between distant points.

The Ground Plane

The ground plane is one of *the* classic omnidirectional antennas for FM use. It's vertically polarized, lightweight, easy to assemble and has the virtue of being somewhat difficult to see. If you have a sensitive repeater reasonably close by, you can put this antenna on a short mast in your yard and it will perform admirably. However, if you can get this ground plane to a higher elevation, on your roof perhaps, you'll notice a world of difference. Increase the altitude of the antenna from, say, seven feet to 15 or 20 feet, and you'll be pleasantly surprised at the improvement.

In Chapter 2 I showed you a design for the classic ground plane antenna. Let's consider it here as well (see **Figure 4.3**). This design has a broad 2:1 SWR bandwidth, so it is pretty forgiving when it is time to cut the wires and assemble the antenna. The "ground plane" portion of the ground plane antenna is formed by the four radial wires extending

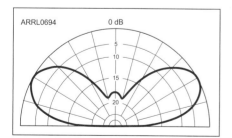

Figure 4.2 — The radiation pattern of a typical ground plane antenna is not necessarily omnidirectional in the strict sense of the word (notice the overhead null), but it is close enough to being uniform for practical purposes.

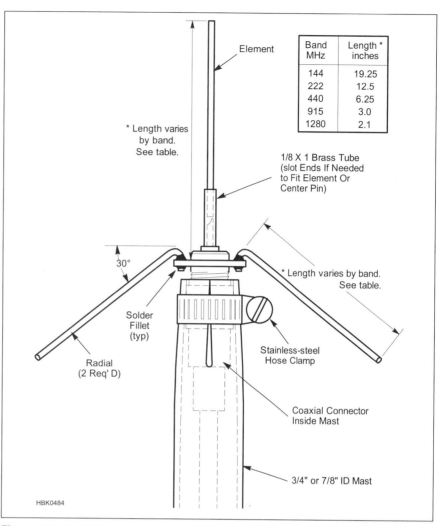

Band MHz	Length * inches
144	19.25
222	12.5
440	6.25
915	3.0
1280	2.1

Element

* Length varies by band. See table.

1/8 X 1 Brass Tube (slot Ends If Needed to Fit Element Or Center Pin)

30°

* Length varies by band. See table.

Solder Fillet (typ)

Stainless-steel Hose Clamp

Radial (2 Req' D)

Coaxial Connector Inside Mast

3/4" or 7/8" ID Mast

HBK0484

Figure 4.3 — A simple ground-plane antenna for the 144, 222 or 440-MHz bands. The feed line and connector are inside the PVC mast, and a hose clamp squeezes the slotted mast end to tightly grip the plug body. Vertical element and radial dimensions given in the drawing are good for the entire band.

Figure 4.4 — A J-Pole antenna for 2 meters perched on a balcony in Hungary.

from the base. These should slope downward at about a 30° angle. Feel free to adjust this angle if necessary to improve the SWR.

The J-Pole

Here is another refugee from Chapter 2 — the ever-popular J-Pole. In case you haven't browsed Chapter 2, let me repeat that the J-Pole is an end-fed omnidirectional dipole matched to the feed line by a quarter wavelength "stub." That's what gives the antenna its name since it looks like the letter **J** (see **Figure 4.4).**

FM enthusiasts seem endlessly infatuated with J-Pole antennas. They are second only to ground planes in terms of sheer popularity. Hams love making J-Poles out of everything from copper tubing to 300-Ω TV twinlead. In fact, Edison Fong, WB6IQN, designed a dual band (2 meter and 70-cm) J-pole made from 300 Ω twinlead. You'll find his article titled "The DBJ-2 A Portable VHF-UHF Roll-up J-pole Antenna for Public Service" in the **Appendix** of this book.

As you look at a J-Pole you'll notice right away that unlike the radials of a ground plane antenna, the J-Pole seems to lack any sort of ground return for RF currents. There is nothing magical going on here, nor does the J-Pole violate fundamental physics, which states that the current flowing into the end of the antenna must equal the same amount of current flowing into a ground system or counterpoise. In the case of the J-Pole the feed line shield usually ends up carrying common-mode currents away from the antenna. The result can be an antenna that is tricky to tune for lowest SWR, and one that tends to be sensitive to surrounding objects.

Despite this shortcoming, the J-Pole can be an attractive solution if you're looking for a low-profile antenna for FM work. A J-Pole exhibits some gain compared to an ordinary ground plane antenna, so that is an incentive as well.

Discones

The *discone* is a highly popular antenna among scanner enthusiasts. The reason is that this antenna can exhibit an extremely broad frequency response, offering a decent match to 50 Ω coaxial cable from low VHF all the way to low microwave frequencies, depending on the design.

A discone antenna is really a variation of what is known as a *biconical* antenna (**Figure 4.5**). In its classic design a biconical antenna consists of two cones. These cones can be made of solid metal, or they can be comprised of individual wires arranged in a cone shape (when placed close together, the individual wires behave like a single piece of metal at lower VHF frequencies, electrically

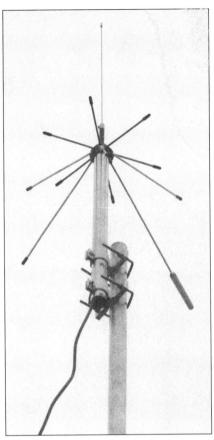

Figure 4.5 — A discone antenna with a vertical radiator.

speaking). The cones are fed as the two legs of a dipole antenna.

With the discone we're removing one of the biconical cones and replacing it with a disc, either solid or comprised of individual rods and, in some designs, a single vertical

radiator. A discone is mounted vertically with the disk at the top and the cone beneath. The discone antenna is vertically polarized.

Discones are available from a number of commercial sources, including RadioShack (model 20-043; $75). Sometimes they are marketed as "receiving antennas" or "scanner antennas," but any discone can be a transmitting antenna as well.

A discone antenna typically has at least three major components: the disc, the cone and the insulator. The disc should have an overall diameter of 0.7 times a quarter wavelength at the antenna's lowest frequency. So for a discone with a "bottom" frequency of 50 MHz, the disc would have a diameter of about 3 feet, 4 inches. The antenna's feed point is at the center where the disc and cone meet, so you'd connect the center conductor to the disc and the outer conductor to the cone.

The cone should have a length equal to ¼ wavelength at the lowest operating frequency. In the case of our discone example above, that would be approximately 4 ½ feet. The cone angle is generally between 25 to 40 degrees. The disc and cone must be separated by an insulator (just like the center insulator of a wire dipole antenna). The reason many commercial discones include a vertical wire is to extend the low frequency response.

Here is a homebrew approach to a discone antenna for 144 through 450 MHz. The cone is made of 16 wires (I used #12 copper clad steel; the stiffer the wire, the better), each 20 ½ inches in length. Make sure all the wires are of equal length. The wires are soldered to a small copper plate 4 inches in diameter. I accomplished this by drilling 16

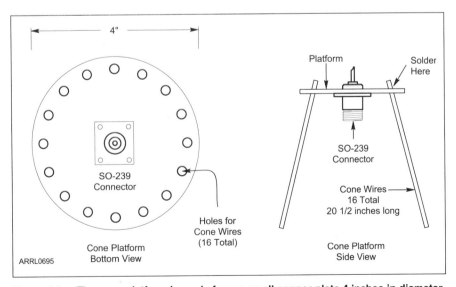

Figure 4.6 — The cone platform is made from a small copper plate 4 inches in diameter with 16 holes spaced equally around the center. The individual wires are pushed slightly through the holes and soldered with a torch. In the center of the plate attach an SO-239 coaxial connector.

holes spaced equally around the center. I pushed the ends of the wires slightly through the holes and soldered with a torch. In the center of the plate attach an SO-239 coaxial connector. See **Figure 4.6**.

The disc of this discone is another solid copper circle, this one 13 ¾ inches in diameter. A hole about ⅛ inches in diameter is drilled in the center of the disk. About 1 inch from the center hole drill another hole just wide enough to accommodate a short stainless machine screw. Attach the screw tightly with a stainless steel nut and star washer, and include a solder lug (**Figure 4.7**).

The next trick is to attach this disc to the center of the SO-239 connector without shorting the disc to the cone platform below. One option is to use a 2-inch length of PVC tubing 1 inch in diameter. Attach a 6-inch length of insulated wire to the center conductor of the SO-239 connector and pass the wire through the inside of the PVC tube. The PVC tube sits over the hole in the cone platform where the center conductor of the SO-239 connector protrudes. Glue the PVC to the cone platform with a high strength adhesive such as Devcon Plastic Steel. Bring the wire through the hole in the center of the disc and then glue the disc to the top of the short PVC tube (**Figure 4.8**).

Once the glue has dried, cut the wire so that it will just reach the solder lug when the insulation is peeled back. Solder the wire to the lug.

The final challenge is supporting the antenna. My technique was to run a length

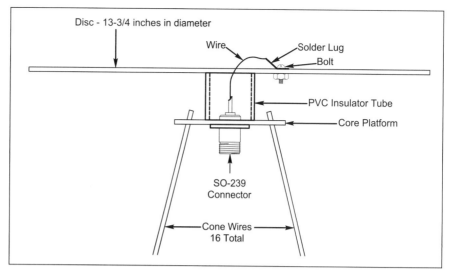

Figure 4.8 — The discone center insulator is a 2 inch length of PVC tubing 1 inch in diameter. Attach a 6-inch length of insulated wire to the center conductor of the SO-239 connector and pass the wire through the inside of the PVC tube. The PVC tube sits over the hole in the cone platform where the center conductor of the SO-239 connector protrudes. Glue the PVC to the cone platform with a high strength adhesive such as Devcon Plastic Steel. Bring the wire through the hole in the center of the disc and then glue the disc to the top of the short PVC tube

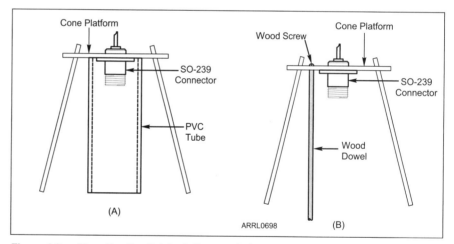

Figure 4.9 — Mounting the finished discone. At (A) we use a 3-foot length of rigid PVC tubing glued over the PL-259/SO-239 connection. At (B) we have an alternative approach -- attaching a varnished wood dowel next to the SO-239 connector and securing it in place with a stainless steel screw.

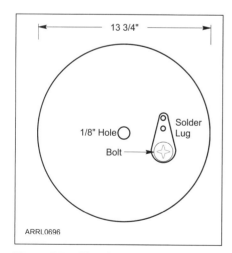

Figure 4.7 — The disc of the discone is another solid copper circle, this one 13 ¾ inches in diameter. A hole about ⅛ inch in diameter is drilled in the center of the disk. Abou 1 inch from the center hole drill another hole just wide enough to accommodate a short stainless machine screw. Attach the screw tightly with a stainless steel nut and star washer, and include a solder lug

of coaxial cable (with a PL-259 connector) through a 3-foot length of rigid PVC tubing, connect the PL-259 to the SO-239 connector and then glue the PVC over the connection. Plastic Steel creates a bond that can withstand more than 300 lbs of lateral force, so it has held up well outdoors. You might wish to try a different approach such as attaching a varnished wood dowel next to the SO-239 connector and securing it in place with a stainless steel screw (see **Figure 4.9**).

Arrange the cone wires so that they hang at roughly a 30 to 40° angle. The finished antenna should not require much tuning,

although you can change the angles of the cone wires to touch up the SWR.

Loop Antennas

Loop antennas for VHF+ can be effective, depending on the application, and they fit within fairly small spaces. At 50 MHz and up, ½ wavelength loops are most common, although you may also encounter full wavelength varieties. At 6 meters, this type of "square loop" is only about 31 inches across (see **Figure 4.10**). The 2:1 SWR bandwidth of a typical ½ wavelength loop at 6 meters is about 1 MHz.

Figure 4.10 — A 6-meter square loop antenna.

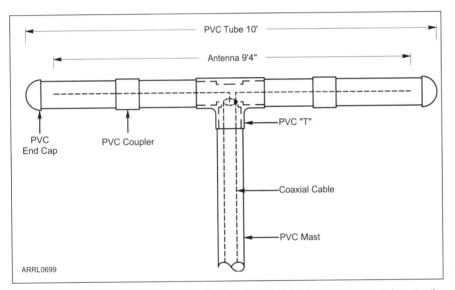

Figure 4.11 — Here is an easy 6-meter dipole using PVC tubing as a support (see text).

In the **Appendix** you'll find two interesting projects: a loop for 450 MHz and, one of my favorites, a 2-meter loop antenna disguised as a rooftop weathervane. Most loops are designed for horizontal polarization and used for SSB/CW work. Interestingly enough, the way the weathervane loop is fed actually creates a vertically polarized signal.

A 6-Meter PVC Dipole

If you can't install a directional antenna for 6 meters, consider the freestanding dipole shown in **Figure 4.11**. This antenna is only 10 feet in length and easy to assemble. The dipole antenna itself is just stiff #12 wire within PVC tubing. The tubing exists only to provide support.

For the PVC tubing I recommend a rigid variety with thick walls so it has a reasonable chance of making it through a blustery day. You'll notice that I built my antenna using PVC couplers about midway in each leg. The reason for doing this was so that I would easily take apart the antenna and get at the wire to trim the dipole for the lowest SWR. Once I was satisfied that the antenna was tuned properly, I used PVC cement to permanently connect all the pieces.

Construction is simple. Bring the coaxial feed line through the PVC "T". Strip the end of the cable to expose the center conductor and the shield. Solder the center conductor to a wire 56 inches in length. Solder the shield to another 56-inch wire. "Dry fit" the tubing by inserting the wires into the PVC sections

nearest the "T", attaching the couplers and then feeding the wire through the couplers and into the remaining PVC sections. Attach the PVC end caps.

With the antenna at least 8 feet off the ground, measure the SWR. If you need to trim the wire, open the tubes and do so. Once you've reached an acceptable SWR (below 2:1), you're done. Use PVC cement to permanently connect all the sections of the antenna. If you want the antenna to blend in visually consider painting it green, gray or any other color that will make it less obvious to your neighbors.

With this dipole on your roof or other elevated position you'll be surprised to discover that you can work quite a few distant stations when Sporadic E propagation makes an appearance. When Sporadic E is absent, the antenna is still worthwhile for local communication.

DIRECTIONAL ANTENNAS

Omnidirectional antennas are fine for local or regional communication, but if you want to extend your effective range at VHF+, the directional antenna is the only way to go. A directional antenna focuses your transmitted signal in a particular direction and it is equally selective when it comes to received signals.

For "weak signal" SSB/CW work, directional antennas are almost mandatory. Among weak signal VHF operators you'll hear of routine communication over hundreds of miles. During band openings the range can extend to a thousand miles or more. Virtually all of these operators are using directional antennas, often installed atop tall towers. You don't need a tower to get in on the fun — a rooftop will do — but you *do* need directional antennas.

As we discussed earlier, directional antennas at VHF+ aren't always small. Some 6-meter directional antennas are more than 12 feet in length and 10 feet wide. Yes, the antennas become smaller at higher frequencies, but in some instances they can still be quite long. The reason, as you'll see shortly, has to do with the antenna's ability to focus the signal.

And since directional antennas create such focused signal patterns, you need to be able to rotate them toward the stations you hope to reach. This means the addition of an electric antenna rotator, which we'll discuss later.

Yagi

The Yagi antenna is, by far, the most popular directional antenna at VHF+. At minimum, it consists of a single ½ wavelength dipole element — the *driven element* — and a parasitic element, typically 5% longer,

A pair of 2-meter Yagi antennas mounted on the same cross boom.

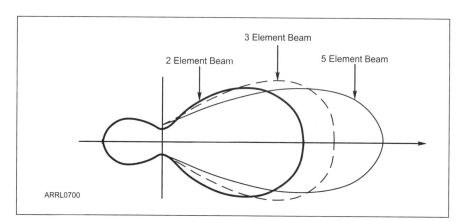

Figure 4.12 — An approximate radiation pattern for a Yagi antenna. Notice how the pattern narrows and becomes more focused as the number of elements increases.

A dual-band Yagi antenna with cross-polarized elements.

positioned "behind" the dipole. This element is known as the *reflector*. In a high-gain Yagi there are one or more parasitic elements in front of the dipole known as *directors*.

Without going into a lengthy treatise on antenna theory, the short explanation of how a Yagi works is that the reflector is designed to cancel the RF energy being emitted from the driven element toward the *rear* of the antenna and redirect it toward the front. On the other hand, the directors are designed to reinforce the energy traveling from the driven element in the *forward* direction. The result is a focused radiation pattern extending from the front of the antenna (**Figure 4.12**). A Yagi usually has only one reflector, but it can have many directors. More directors equal a more concentrated signal, which means higher gain. More directors, however, also means a longer antenna.

Speaking of gain, this is typically expressed in dBi, or gain relative to an ideal isotropic dipole antenna. The gain of an antenna is best measured on an antenna test range using sensitive, precisely calibrated instruments. You can also calculate the gain of an antenna using antenna modeling software such as *EZNEC*. A well-designed multi-element Yagi can boast a gain on the order of 10 to 15 dBi.

If you browse the advertising pages of *QST* magazine you'll often note that most antenna advertisements lack gain figures. *QST* requires antenna manufacturers to submit modeling or measurement results if they want to include this data in their advertisements. A number of manufacturers do not do this, but a large part of the reason is economic. Most manufacturers don't have access to antenna test ranges. It is possible to pay engineering companies to test your antennas on their ranges, but this can be costly.

In addition to single-band Yagis you'll find multiband designs as well. For satellite operating, for example, dual-band 2-meter/70-cm Yagis are common. The antenna elements are arranged on the support boom in such a way as to "cross" their signal polarities.

Most amateurs purchase commercial Yagis, but it is possible to build these antennas as well. In the **Appendix** of this book you'll find Yagi projects for 6 meters, 2 meters and 70 cm.

Moxon

One interesting variation on the Yagi is the Moxon antenna. It is a simple two-element directional antenna with one driven element and one reflector. The design is rectangular, with roughly half of the rectangle being the driven element and the other half being the reflector. It is fair to consider a Moxon an-

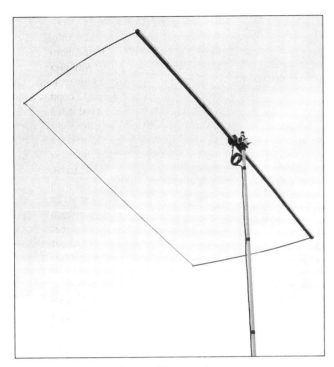

The PAR Electronics 6-meter Moxon antenna.

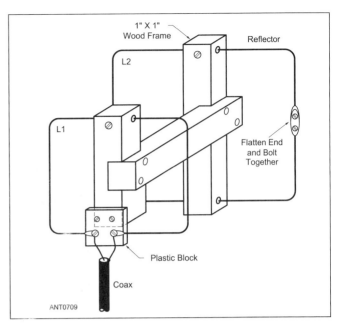

Figure 4.13 — Mechanical details of a 2-element quad antenna for 2 meters. The driven element, L1, is one wavelength long; reflector L2 is 5% longer. With the feed line connection shown here, the resulting radiation pattern is horizontally polarized.

tenna as a Yagi with bent elements.

The main selling point of the Moxon for many amateurs is that it provides substantial gain in a relatively small space. Alan Baker, KG4JJH, designed a 6-meter Moxon that's only about 7 feet long and 2½ feet wide. You'll find this project in the **Appendix**. By re-scaling the dimensions, this same design could also be used at 2 meters.

If you'd prefer to buy a VHF Moxon off the shelf, one product to consider is the SM-50 6-meter Moxon by PAR Electronics at **www. parelectronics.com/stress-moxon.php**. This antenna packs 5.8 dBi gain into a compact design.

Quad

The quad antenna has been a favorite in the Amateur Radio since its inception nearly 70 years ago. Like a Yagi, a quad has a driven element, a reflector and, in some versions, several directors. The difference is that rather than using elements crafted from straight, open-ended wires or tubing, a quad's elements are *loops*.

Ever since I can remember, hams have been debating the benefits of quads vs Yagis. Quad boosters generally cite the following:

■ **Higher gain in a smaller space.** A 2-element quad has about the same gain as a 3-element Yagi in about half the space.

■ **Broader bandwidth**. Some quad designs have considerably broader 2:1 SWR

bandwidths compared to Yagis for the same bands.

A 2-METER, 2-ELEMENT QUAD

If you'd like to try your hand at building a quad for VHF, consider the basic 2-element quad array for 144 MHz shown in **Figure 4.13**. The supporting frame is 1 × 1-inch varnished wood. The elements are #8 aluminum wire. The driven element is 83 inches long, and the reflector five percent longer at 87 inches. The dimensions are not critical, as the quad is relatively broad in frequency response.

The driven element is open at the bottom, its ends fastened to a plastic block. The block is mounted at the bottom of the forward vertical support. The top portion of the element goes through the support and is held firmly by a screw running into the wood and then bearing on the aluminum wire. You can feed the driven element with 50-Ω coax soldered directly. The reflector is a closed loop, its top and bottom portions running through the rear vertical support. It is held in position with screws at the top and bottom. The loop can be closed by fitting a length of tubing over the element ends, or by hammering them flat and bolting them together as shown in the diagram.

The elements in this model are not adjustable, though this can easily be done by the use of stubs. It would then be desirable to

make the loops slightly smaller to compensate for the wire in the adjusting stubs. The driven element stub would be trimmed for length and the point of connection for the coax would be adjustable for best match. The reflector stub can then be adjusted for maximum gain.

In the model shown only the spacing is adjusted, and this is not particularly critical. If the wooden supports are made as shown, the spacing between the elements can be adjusted for the lowest SWR. The spacing has little effect on the gain, so the variation in impedance with spacing can be used for matching.

The Quagi

The Quagi is a hybrid antenna for VHF+. It is a combination of Yagi and quad designs. The Quagi antenna was designed by Wayne Overbeck, N6NB. He first published information on this antenna in 1977. There are a few tricks to Quagi building, but nothing very difficult or complicated is involved.

Tables 4.1 and 4.2 give the dimensions for Quagis for various frequencies up to 446 MHz. For the designs of Tables 4.1 and 4.2, the boom is *wood* or any other nonconductor (such as, fiberglass or Plexiglas). Many amateurs dislike wood booms, but in a salt air environment they outlast aluminum (and cost less). Varnish the boom for added protection.

The 144-MHz version is usually built on a 14 foot, ⅓ inch boom, with the boom tapered to 1 inch at both ends. Clear pine is best because of its light weight, but construction grade Douglas fir works well. At 222 MHz the boom is less than 10 feet long, and most builders use ½ or (preferably) ¾ or 1¼ inch pine molding stock. At 432 MHz, except for long-boom versions, the boom should be ½ inch thick or less. Most builders use strips of ½-inch exterior plywood for 432 MHz.

The quad elements are supported at the current maxima (the top and bottom, the latter beside the feed point) with Plexiglas or small strips of wood. See **Figure 4.14**. The quad elements are made of #12 copper wire, the same type commonly used in house wiring. Some builders may elect to use #10 wire on 144 MHz and #14 on 432 MHz, although this changes the resonant frequency slightly.

Solder a type N connector (an SO-239 is often used at 144 MHz) at the midpoint of the driven element bottom side, and close the reflector loop. The directors are mounted through the boom. They can be made of almost any metal rod or wire of about ⅛-inch diameter. Welding rod or aluminum clothesline wire works well if straight.

A TV type U bolt mounts the antenna on a mast. A single machine screw, washers and a nut are used to secure the spreaders to the boom so the antenna can be quickly "flattened" for travel. In permanent installations two screws are recommended.

ANTENNA ROTATORS

Rotators (some hams incorrectly refer to them as "rotors") are little more than high-torque electrical motors controlled remotely through a multiconductor cable (**Figure 4.15**). Making the correct decision as to how much capacity the rotator must have is very important to ensure trouble-free operation.

Rotator manufacturers generally provide antenna surface area ratings to help you choose a suitable model. The maximum antenna area is linked to the rotator's torque capability. Some rotator manufacturers provide additional information to help you select the right size of rotator for the antennas you plan to use. Hy-Gain provides an *Effective Moment* value. Yaesu calls theirs a *K-Factor*. Both of these ratings are torque values in

Table 4.1
432MHz, 15-Element, Long Boom Quagi

Element Lengths (inches)	Interelement Spacing (inches)
Reflector—28	Reflector to Driven Element—7
Driven Element—26⅝	Driven Element to Director 1—5¼
Director 1—11¾	Director 1 to Director 2—11
Director 2—11¹¹⁄₁₆	Director 2 to Director 3—5⅞
Director 3—11⅝	Director 3 to Director 4—8¾
Director 4—11⁹⁄₁₆	Director 4 to Director 5—8¾
Director 5—11½	Director 5 to Director 6—8¾
Director 6—11⁷⁄₁₆	Director 6 to Director 7—12
Director 7—11⅜	Director 7 to Director 8—12
Director 8—11⁵⁄₁₆	Director 8 to Director 9—11¼
Director 9—11⁵⁄₁₆	Director 9 to Director 10—11½
Director 10—11¼	Director 10 to Director 11—9⁹⁄₁₆
Director 11—11³⁄₁₆	Director 11 to Director 12—12⅜
Director 12—11⅛	Director 12 to Director 13—13¾
Director 13—11¹⁄₁₆	

Boom: 1 × 2 inch × 12 foot Douglas fir, tapered to ⅝ inches at both ends.
Driven element: #12 TW copper wire loop in square configuration, fed at bottom center with type N connector and 50-Ω coax.
Reflector: #12 TW copper wire loop, closed at bottom.
Directors: ⅛ inch rods passing through boom

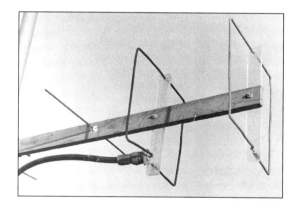

Figure 4.14 — A close-up view of the feed method used on a 432 MHz Quagi.

Table 4.2
Dimensions, Eight-Element Quagi

Element Lengths	144.5 MHz	147 MHz	222 MHz	432 MHz	46 MHz
Reflector	86⅝"	85"	56⅜"	28"	27⅛"
Driven Element	82"	80"	53½"	26⅝"	25⅞"
Directors	35¹⁵⁄₁₆" to 35" in ³⁄₁₆" steps	35⁵⁄₁₆" to 34⅜" in ³⁄₁₆" steps	23⅜" to 23¾" in ⅛" steps	11¾" to 11⁷⁄₁₆" in ¹⁄₁₆" steps	11⅜" to 11¹⁄₁₆" in ¹⁄₁₆" steps
Spacing					
R-DE	21"	20½"	13⅝"	7"	6⅞"
DE-D1	15¾"	15⅜"	10¼"	5¼"	5⅛"
D1-D2	33"	32½"	21½"	11"	10¾"
D2-D3	17½"	17⅛"	11⅜"	5⅞"	5⅝"
D3-D4	26⅛"	25⅝"	17"	8¾"	8½"
D4-D5	26⅛"	25⅝"	17"	8¾"	8½"
D5-D6	26⅛"	25⅝"	17"	8¾"	8½"

Figure 4.15 — A light duty antenna rotator like this one is sufficient for smaller antennas such as 3-element 2-meter Yagis.

force of the wind can move the gear train and motor of the rotator, while the indicator remains fixed. Such rotator systems have mechanical stops to prevent continuous rotation during operation, and a provision is usually included to realign the indicator against the mechanical stop from inside the shack. Of course, the antenna and mechanical stop position must be oriented correctly during installation. In most cases the proper direction is true north.

In larger rotator systems with adequate brakes, indicator misalignment is caused by mechanical slippage in the antenna boom-to-mast hardware. Many texts suggest that the boom be pinned to the mast with a heavy duty bolt and the rotator be similarly pinned to the mast to stop slippage. But in high winds the slippage may, in fact, act as a clutch release, preventing serious damage to the rotator. On the other hand, you might not want to climb to the roof and realign the system after each heavy windstorm!

ROOF MOUNTING

As we discussed at the beginning of the chapter, height is critical when it comes to successful operating above 50 MHz. Assuming you can't install a small tower or guyed mast, the one option remaining may be directly above you — *your roof.*

As you examine your roof, resist the urge to imagine the vents and chimney as your new antenna supports. Chimneys and vents were never intended to have objects attached to them, especially antennas. As thin as an antenna may appear to be, you'd

foot-pounds. You can compute the Effective Moment of your antenna by multiplying the antenna turning radius by its weight. So long as the effective moment rating of the rotator is greater than or equal to the antenna value, the rotator can be expected to provide a useful service life.

There are several rotator grades available to amateurs. The lightest-duty rotator is the type typically used to turn TV antennas. These rotators will handle small VHF and UHF antennas. The problem with TV rotators is that they lack braking or holding capability. High winds can turn the rotator motor via the gear train in a reverse fashion. Broken gears sometimes result.

The next grade up from the TV class of rotator usually includes a braking arrangement, whereby the antenna is held in place when power is not applied to the rotator. Generally speaking, the brake prevents gear damage on windy days. If adequate precautions are taken, this type of rotator is capable of holding and turning a stack of satellite antennas, including a parabolic dish which, by its nature, presents considerable wind loading. Keep in mind that as rotators increase in power, they become more expensive.

Regardless of which type you choose, proper installation of the antenna rotator can provide many years of dependable service. Sloppy installation can cause problems such as a burned out motor, slippage, binding and even breakage of the rotator's internal gear and shaft castings and outer housing. Most rotators are capable of accepting mast sizes of different diameters, and suitable precautions must be taken to shim an undersized

mast to ensure dead-center rotation.

Don't forget to provide a loop of coax to allow your antenna to rotate properly. Also, make sure you position the rotator loop so that it doesn't snag on anything.

A problem often encountered in amateur installations is that of misalignment between the direction indicator in the rotator control box and the heading of the antenna. With a light duty TV antenna rotator, this happens frequently when the wind blows the antenna to a different heading. With no brake, the

Figure 4.16 — Placing too many antennas and too much wind loading on a chimney can produce catastrophic results!

be surprised at how much wind loading it can exert on whatever it is attached to. Directional antennas in particular can create large loads in a stiff breeze. And if you live in northern climes, there is the added stress of ice loading.

When a chimney or vent fails because of wind or ice loading, it will often do so in catastrophic fashion (**Figure 4.16**). The result will be an expensive home repair, or even an injury if chimney bricks tumble toward the sidewalks and become anti-personnel missiles. This isn't to say that you can never mount an antenna on a vent or chimney. A single small ground plane, loop or J-Pole should be able to safely attach to these structures. But anything larger requires its own solution.

The safest approach to rooftop antenna installations is the roof tripod. You can purchase these at home centers and, at the time of this writing, at RadioShack. Perhaps the biggest problem with a tripod is determining how to fasten it securely to the roof. For best results, follow manufacturer's installation instructions. One method of mounting a tripod on a roof is to nail 2 × 6 boards to the undersides of the rafters. Bolts can be extended from the leg mounts through the roof and the 2 × 6s. To avoid exerting too much pressure on the area of the roof between rafters, place another set of 2 × 6s on top of the roof (a mirror image of the ones in the attic). Installation details are shown in **Figures 4.17** through **4.20**. The 2 × 6s are cut 4 inches longer than the outside distance between two rafters. Nails are used to hold the boards in place during installation, and roofing tar or heavy duty caulk is used to seal the area to prevent leaks.

Start by finding a location on the roof that will allow the antenna to turn without obstruction from such things as trees, TV antennas and chimneys. Determine the rafter locations below. (Chimneys and vent pipes make good reference points.) Set the tripod in place atop three 2 × 6s. You can use an improvised plumb line dangling from the top center of the tripod to center it on the peak of the roof and ensure that the center

Figure 4.18 — The strengthened anchoring for the tripod mount. Bolts are placed through two 2 × 6s on the underside of the roof and through the 2 × 6s on the top of the roof, as shown in Figure 4.17.

Figure 4.19 — Three lengths of 2 × 6 wood mounted on the outside of the roof and reinforced under the roof by three identical pieces provide a durable means for anchoring the tripod.

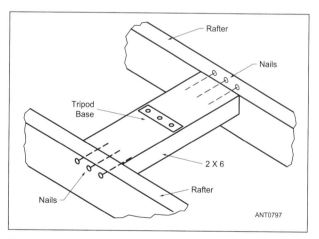

Figure 4.20 — This cutaway view illustrates how the tripod mount is secured to the roof rafters. The leg to be secured to the cross piece is placed on the outside of the roof. Another cross member is fastened to the underside of the rafters. Bolts, inserted through the roof and the two cross pieces, hold the inner cross member in place.

Figure 4.17 — This tripod tower can support one or more VHF antennas. A ground lead fastened to the lower part of the frame is for lightning protection.

of the tripod is perfectly straight. With the tripod centered, mark the mounting holes and start drilling.

Before proceeding, the bottoms of the 2 × 6s and the area of the roof under them should be given a coat of roofing tar or a heavy duty waterproof caulk. Leave about ⅛ inch of clear area around the holes to ensure easy passage of the bolts. Put the tripod back in place, insert the bolts and tighten them from below (in the attic). Now apply tar or caulk to the bottom of the legs and the wooden supports, including the bolts. For larger antenna systems, plan on bracing the structure *beneath* the roof as well, per manufacturer's instructions.

Allow 24 hours for the tar or caulk to completely set before you begin installing your rotator and antenna. You can use the same tar or caulk to seal the holes where your feed line and rotator cables enter the roof.

Appendix

Antenna Projects and Useful Information

Folded Skeleton Sleeve 40 and 20 Meter Dipole

This design provides a matched coax-fed antenna with performance similar to a full size dipole on two bands, 40 and 20 meters. The mechanical and electrical design is such that it can be fabricated from a single piece of nominal 450 Ω window line.

By Joel Hallas, W1ZR

There have been many approaches to multiband operation — traps, parallel dipoles and others. This antenna is somewhat different in two regards:

■ It uses the parasitic *skeleton sleeve* coupling from a single driven 40 meter dipole to a single higher frequency element to provide the second band — rather than the more common parallel connection.

■ The ends of the lower frequency dipole are bent back to almost reach the higher frequency one. This results in an antenna about 10 feet shorter than the usual 40 meter dipole. This is independent of the sleeve coupling method.

The first change eliminates the narrow bandwidth usually encountered in closely spaced parallel wired dipoles. The close spacing employed allows the whole antenna to be constructed from a single piece of nominal 450 Ω window line. Additional structural integrity is provided because the

20 meter section is continuous across the center feed point, as shown in Figure 1.

Construction

Any of the usual antenna construction techniques can be used. To provide strength at the ends and the connection point, I suggest a the use of standard antenna insulators or other mechanically sturdy fixtures. For my prototype, as shown in the lead photo, I just tied the halyards through "windows" near the ends and it has held up so far — but for long term use, I'd do something better. The connection of the coax to the driven dipole should be reinforced so that the hanging coax is not supported by the connections. The open end of the coax must be sealed so that water cannot penetrate into the cable structure.

While good practice, but not essential in most installations, to insure accurate SWR readings, I formed a common mode choke

by temporarily wrapping eight turns of the coax feed line through an FT-240-43 ferrite toroid. A better approach, particularly if foam coax is used, would be to use five 43 mix ferrite beads, with inner diameter selected to fit snugly on your coax just below the feed point. They could be secured with shrink tubing or PVC pipe, if desired. A *QST* author described the use of five Palomar FB 56-43 beads over RG-58C coax. His measured results should prove satisfactory here.[1,2]

This design should be adaptable to any of the various parallel window lines. The line I used was marked "JSC WIRE & CABLE #1317 18 AWG 19 STRAND MADE IN USA."[3] The conductors were stranded copper plated steel — a good choice for both flexibility and strength. If a different type of cable is selected, I would expect that dif-

[1]Notes appear on page 3.

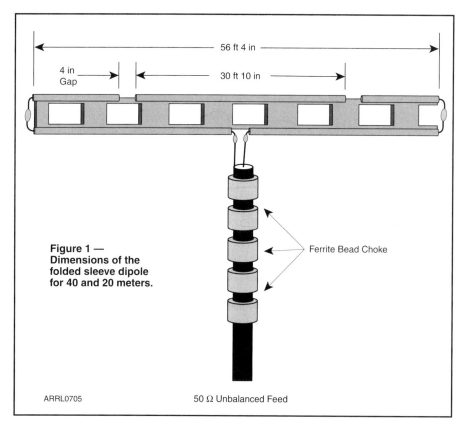

Figure 1 —
Dimensions of the
folded sleeve dipole
for 40 and 20 meters.

56 ft 4 in

4 in
Gap

30 ft 10 in

Ferrite Bead Choke

ARRL0705

50 Ω Unbalanced Feed

all length of the antenna by 1 inch moves the 40 meter resonance about 130 kHz — keep in mind that, because it is folded on 40, it changes more rapidly than might be expected. The same adjustment in overall length makes a change to the 20 meter resonance by only about 10 kHz. Changing the length of the 20 meter dipole by 1 inch (by making a change in the 4 inch gap) results in a change of about 50 kHz with virtually no change to the 40 meter resonance — so start with the 40 meter adjustment, if needed. As expected, making either portion shorter results in higher resonant frequencies.

Performance

This antenna provides gain and directivity comparable to a full size dipole on both 40 and 20 meters. See Figures 2 and 3 for the *EZNEC* elevation patterns.[4] Note that on 20 meters, *EZNEC* predicts about a 1.5 dB gain over a half-wave dipole, as a result of narrowing the main beams by 4-5°. This is likely the effect of radiation from each side of the 40 meter antenna acting as 20 meter half waves in phase — a small bonus at no extra cost.

At its design height of 30 feet, the SWR across both bands is 2:1 or less to 50 Ω coax as shown in Figures 4 and 5. There is a small variation in resonance predicted at heights from 20 through 50 feet, however, at the end of 100 feet of RG-8X coax it is still within a 2:1 SWR across both bands at any height within the range.

On the Air

I used the antenna to make multiple contacts on each band with good results compared to my other antennas. With the

ferences in wire dimensions and dielectric properties would necessitate a change in the lengths shown in order to achieve resonance on each band.

One assembly caution should be noted. It is critical that the fed wire be connected to the longer 40 meter wire. There is a mode in which it can be made to work the other way, feeding the shorter dipole instead, however,

the dimensions will be different and the system will not match 50 Ω.

I performed some sensitivity analysis using *EZNEC*, in case your antenna needs trimming to make it resonant within the band or desired segment. The good news is that unlike the case with close spaced parallel dipoles, there is almost no interaction between the bands. Changing the over-

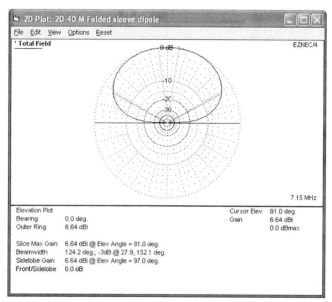

Figure 2 — *EZNEC* predicted elevation pattern of two-band dipole on 40 meters at a height of 30 feet.

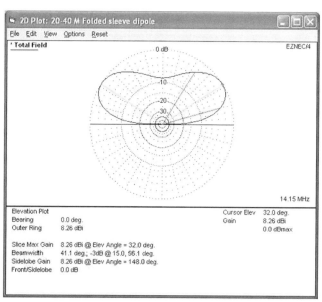

Figure 3 — *EZNEC* predicted elevation pattern of two-band dipole on 20 meters at a height of 30 feet.

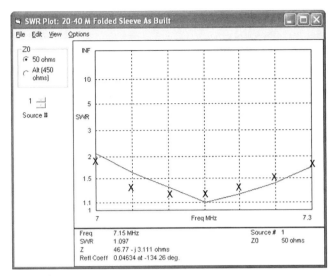

Figure 4 — *EZNEC* predicted SWR sweep of the two-band dipole on 40 meters. The Xs indicate measured SWR at the end of 45 feet of RG-8X with a height of 25 feet.

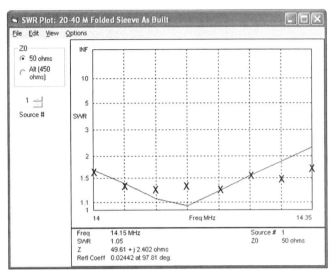

Figure 5 — *EZNEC* predicted SWR sweep of the two-band dipole on 20 meters. The Xs indicate measured SWR at the end of 45 feet of RG-8X with a height of 25 feet.

antenna just below my second story roofline, I was surprised to find that my first contact on 20 meters in a late afternoon was from Connecticut to Australia with 100 W on 20 meter CW. The station was stronger on this dipole than on a one element rotary about 10 feet higher, in the clear and pointed at VK. On 40 meters stations were just a bit lower in level than on my 100 foot center fed dipole fed with window line. This was expected since my 100 foot dipole is about twice as high, and it also provides some gain over a full size half wave dipole on 40.

ARRL Test Engineer Bob Allison, WB1GCM, tried the antenna from his house, just to keep me honest. He found that it was more effective on 40 than his inverted L, with much less noise pickup. 20 meters was also quieter, with similar signals levels from most directions compared to his ground plane at the same height. His first contact on 20 meter SSB was with Perth, Australia — not sure if VK contacts can be guaranteed, but it certainly seems to work well! Bob plans to make one of his own soon.

Notes
[1]L. Burke, W7JI, "An Easy to Build 500 W Mini Balun," *QST*, Mar 2009, p 74.
[2]Available from Palomar Engineers, PO Box 462222, Escondido, CA 92046, tel 760-747-3343, part number FB 56-43.
[3]Mine came from Davis RF, their part number LL450-553. See **www.davisrf.com/ladder. php**.
[4]Several versions of *EZNEC* antenna modeling software are available from developer Roy Lewallen, W7EL, at **www.eznec.com**.

Joel Hallas, W1ZR, is the ARRL Technical Editor. You can contact Joel at **w1zr@arrl.org**.

Six Band Loaded Dipole Antenna

*W8NX's unique design technique makes trap look-alikes do double duty.
Here's a wire antenna that covers 160/80/40/30/17/12 meters!*

Al Buxton, W8NX

Introduction

This article presents a new loaded wire dipole antenna. It covers the classic 160, 80 and 40 meter bands, plus 30, 17 and 12 meters. I call it the *W8NX Special*. Any amateur who installs this antenna and who has a triband beam for 20, 15 and 10 meters has a very good antenna system for working all the amateur high frequency bands from 160 through 10 meters. I installed my W8NX Special as an inverted V, using the tower holding up my triband Yagi as the center support. See Figure 1.

This antenna is based on the highly efficient *dominant element principle*, requiring only two pairs of load elements to give six bands of operation.[1] The radiation patterns have a single pair of broadside lobes on the classic 160, 80 and 40 meters bands but are similar to those of long wire antennas on the 30, 17 and 12 meter bands.

Radiation takes place along the entire length of the antenna on all bands, providing small but useful antenna gains. Good bandwidth is provided on all bands when used in conjunction with an antenna tuner. With the exception of the 160 meter band, full band coverage is provided on all bands. On 160 meters the effective working bandwidth is typically limited by the size of the capacitors in the antenna tuner. The built-in antenna tuner in my FT-1000MP Mark V transceiver can cover 55 kHz on 160 meters using this antenna.

The antenna length is 134 feet, suitable for installation on most city lots. Mine is installed as a "droopy" inverted V dipole, with the apex at 47 feet on the beam tower and drooping to a height of 20 feet at each end. There is little mutual coupling between the triband beam and the six band dipole, since the working frequencies of the two antennas are sufficiently separated to prevent interaction. Some bending and folding at the ends of the dipole antenna is permissible to accommodate installation on a short city lot.

Figure 1 — W8NX Special antenna mounted at 47 feet on tower used to hold triband Yagi. This is an efficient antenna system that covers 160/80/40/30/17/12 meters with the dipole and 20/15/10 meters with the triband Yagi.

Antenna Performance

Figure 2 shows the schematic diagram of the antenna. The schematic looks the same as that of a standard three band trap dipole. However, the loads do not use the truncating capability of tuned parallel resonant traps. This new type of load acts as either a pair of inductors or capacitors to supply the necessary reactance to bring the antenna into resonance with a low feed-point impedance, on both fundamental and odd-order harmonic modes. This makes the antenna suitable for feeding via a 1:1 current balun with either 50 or 75 Ω coaxial cable.

I advise that you use 75 Ω cable because it makes a typical antenna tuner more effective, especially on 160 meters where the size and cost of the large high voltage tuner capacitors is the limiting factor in the

effectiveness of a tuner. The innermost pairs of loads create fundamental resonance on both 160 meters and 80 meters. The outermost pairs create fundamental resonance on 40 meters and third harmonic resonance on 30 meters. The overall antenna gives fifth harmonic resonance on 17 meters and seventh harmonic resonance on 12 meters.

The loads are large physically, with significant stray capacitance. They exhibit a parasitic series resonance at approximately 45 MHz (not shown in the Figure 2 schematic). These parasitic stray effects make small increases in the electrical length of the antenna, slightly lowering the antenna operating frequencies. The loads are necessarily large to achieve high Q, low loss performance. Wide air gaps between turns of the load windings and the use of thin walled

[1] A. Buxton, "Dominant-Element-Principle Loaded Dipoles," *QEX*, Mar/Apr 2004, pp 20-30.

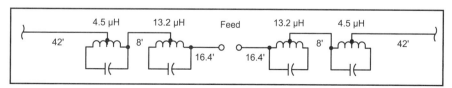

Figure 2 — Schematic for six band W8NX Special using dominant element principle dipole.

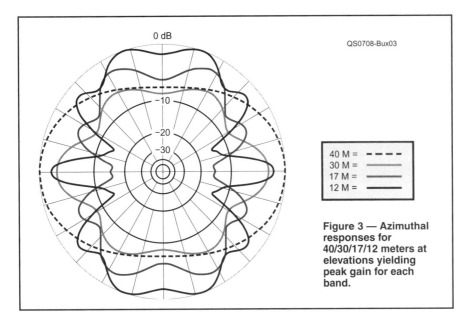

0 dB

QS0708-Bux03

-10
-20
-30

40 M =
30 M =
17 M =
12 M =

Figure 3 — Azimuthal responses for 40/30/17/12 meters at elevations yielding peak gain for each band.

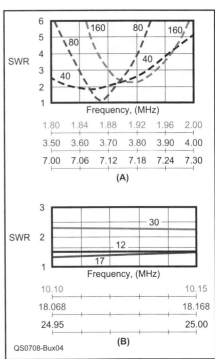

Figure 4 — At A, SWR curves for 160/80/40 meters. At B, SWR curves for 10/17/12 meters.

PVC coil forms minimize dielectric losses in the load elements. The use of RG-8U coax cable with large diameter stranded wire center conductors minimizes skin effect I^2R losses.

The Q of each 160/80 meter load is 260, and the Q of the 40/30 meter loads is 325. Load losses on 80 through 12 meters are less than 0.5 dB, but on 160 meters the loss approaches 3 dB. On 160 meters the radiation resistance of the antenna is low because of the relatively short length of the antenna, reducing the overall radiation efficiency to about 50%.

The radiation patterns have a single pair of broadside lobes on 160, 80 and 40 meters. Figure 3 compares the azimuthal patterns for 40 through 12 meters, at the peak elevation angles for each band. The patterns on the higher frequencies display numerous lobes, characteristic of long wire types of antennas. The peak gain on 40 meters is 1.5 dB above

an ordinary dipole. As is the case with an ordinary dipole this has only two lobes. The gain on 12 meters is about the same as on 40 meters but the pattern has 10 lobes.

The measured SWR curves for the 160, 80 and 40 meter bands are shown in Figure 4A; those for the 30, 17 and 12 meter bands are shown in Figure 4B. The SWR curves are those measured at the rig end of an 80 foot long, 75 Ω RG-59 feed line. The curves pretty much speak for themselves.

Those of you interested in getting as much effective working bandwidth as possible on 160 meters can employ the trick of extending the feed line length when operating on 160 to that of a quarter-wave impedance inverter. The length of the extension must bring the total length of the RG-59 feed line to about 100 feet. This maximizes the effectiveness of the antenna tuner, reducing the required size of the tuner capacitors. The tuner now has an easier matching job of keeping your

rig or linear amplifier happy. However, you have increased your feed line losses and even though your rig is happy over a broader bandwidth you have somewhat degraded the radiation efficiency of your antenna system. If you carry this trick to extreme measures under high power linear amplifier operation, you could conceivably incur current or voltage breakdown in your antenna feed line. The safe upper limit on 160 meters for SWR for RG-59 feed line is about 6:1 at maximum legal power operation corresponding to a maximum usable bandwidth of 130 kHz.

Remember your rig or linear amplifier never sees this SWR — the antenna tuner shields it from this level of mismatch. Your

Figure 5 — At left, construction techniques for 160/80 meter load element. At right, construction techniques for 40/30 meter load element.

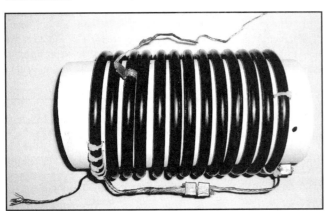

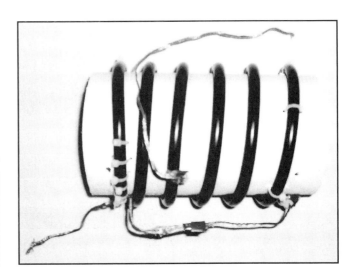

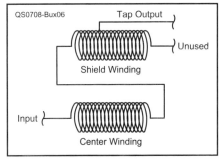

Figure 6 — RG-8U load element schematic.

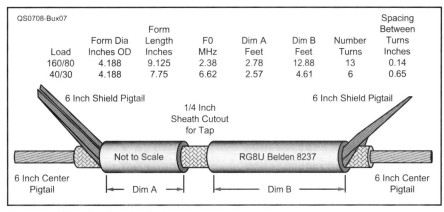

Load	Form Dia Inches OD	Form Length Inches	F0 MHz	Dim A Feet	Dim B Feet	Number Turns	Spacing Between Turns Inches
160/80	4.188	9.125	2.38	2.78	12.88	13	0.14
40/30	4.188	7.75	6.62	2.57	4.61	6	0.65

Figure 7 — Details of the load element coax.

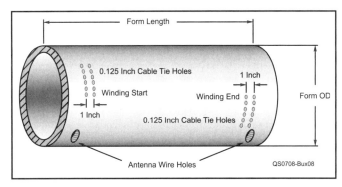

Figure 8 — Details of coil form.

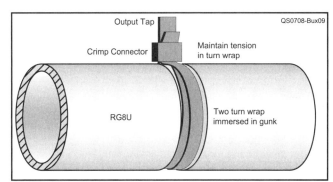

Figure 9 — Output tap detail.

Construction

antenna tuner does not reduce the SWR on the feed line. While some amateurs frown upon using this trick, it does give considerably more effective working bandwidth for 160 meter operation.

Construction

The toughest part of constructing this antenna is making the load elements. Figure 5A shows the 160/80 and 40/30 meter load elements. The load element schematic is in Figure 6. Note how the pigtail at the output end of the center winding is fed backward to the pigtail of the input end of the shield winding. The loads are made of RG-8U coaxial cable (Belden 8237) wound on a form made of 4.188 inch outside diameter PVC drain pipe.

Figure 7 shows details of the coax used for the loads. Figure 8 shows the load forms, the critical ones being the lengths and diameters of the forms and the 1 inch edge margins of the windings on the forms. Dimensions A and B fix the output tap location, with the RG-8U laid out flat and straight on a table. The tap is a 15 inch length of silvered braided shield wire cannibalized from RG-58 coax cable. The tap requires two turns tightly wrapped around the RG-8U wire at the ¼ inch break cut in the PVC sheath. Cover this break with anti corrosion gunk (Burndy Products, Penetrox A will do) to prevent

resistance developing at the tap.

Care is required in making the output tap to hold the two turn wrap around the RG-8U permanently in tension using a crimp connector. Figure 9 shows the details of the 15 inch output tap of the loads. Unfortunately, soldering at the tap would weaken the electrical properties of the RG-8U coax cable so a mechanical-only connection is necessary.

The input terminal of any load is the near end (nearest the feed line) of the center conductor winding of the coax cable. The far end of the center conductor is fed back to the near end of the shield winding. The output of the load is taken at the tap on the outer shield winding. The output tap acts as an auto transformer, giving the needed L/C ratio for the load. You should fine tune the loads to within 1% of the specified frequency. I used a dip meter and an accurately calibrated receiver for fine tuning the loads.

Air gap spacing between the turns of each load reduces dielectric load losses and permits fine tuning of the load resonant frequency. Expanding the air gap increases the load resonant frequency; reducing the gap lowers the frequency. Do not hesitate to increase the gap between turns as much as necessary to achieve the resonant frequency of the load, even though you may distort the appearance of the load. After completion of the fine tuning, the location of the turns must be

stabilized by cable ties, as shown in Figure 5. More cable ties are actually required than are shown, especially around the first and last turns of the load winding. Stabilizing the interior turns is not as critical, as they have less effect on the load's resonant frequency than the outermost first and last turns.

Although making the loads for this antenna may seem like a challenging task, your efforts will be well rewarded. There is nothing as satisfying in ham radio as the successful completion of a good, hands-on homebrew project.

I wish to thank my friend and colleague, Mel Vye, W8MV, whose help and constructive comments are greatly appreciated. I also wish to thank Jeremy (KB8QVF) and Angie Holland for their help with the photography of the antenna and the load elements.

*Al Buxton, W8NX, has been a radio amateur since he was first licensed as W7GLC in 1937. A registered professional engineer, Al holds BSEE and MSEE degrees from Tulane University. His career spans industry and academia: 26 years in the defense industry with Goodyear Aerospace, six years with Tulane University and 11 years with the University of Akron. He's an Associate Professor Emeritus of Akron University. In industry, Al worked on the development of computers, automatic controls, radar, aircraft guidance, and navigation and space antennas. You can reach Al at 2225 Woodpark Rd, Akron, OH 44333 or **buxtonw8nx@aol.com**.*

The DBJ-2: A Portable VHF-UHF Roll-Up J-pole Antenna for Public Service

WB6IQN reviews the theory of the dual band 2 meter / 70 cm J-pole antenna and then makes detailed measurements of a practical, easy to replicate, "roll-up" portable antenna.

Edison Fong, WB6IQN

It has now been more than three years since my article on the dual band J-pole (DBJ-1) appeared in the February 2003 issue of *QST*.[1] I have had over 500 inquires regarding that antenna. Users have reported good results, and a few individuals even built the antenna and confirmed the reported measurements. Several major cities are using this antenna for their schools, churches and emergency operations center. When asked why they choose the DBJ-1, the most common answer was value. When budgets are tight and you want a good performance-to-price ratio, the DBJ-1 (*Dual Band J-pole–1*) is an excellent choice.

In quantity, the materials cost about $5 per antenna and what you get is a VHF/UHF base station antenna with λ/2 vertical performance on both VHF and UHF bands. If a small city builds a dozen of these antennas for schools, public buildings, etc it would cost about $60. Not for one, but the entire dozen!

Since it is constructed using PVC pipe, it is UV protected and it is waterproof. To date I have personally constructed over 400 of these antennas for various groups and individuals and have had excellent results. One has withstood harsh winter conditions in the mountains of McCall, Idaho for four years.

The most common request from users is for a portable "roll-up" version of this antenna for backpacking or emergency use. To address this request, I will describe how the principles of the DBJ-1 can be extended to a portable roll-up antenna. Since it is the second version of this antenna, I call it the DBJ-2.

Principles of the DBJ-1

The earlier DBJ-1 is based on the J-pole,[2] shown in Figure 1. Unlike the popular ground plane antenna, it doesn't need ground

[1]Notes appear on page 157.

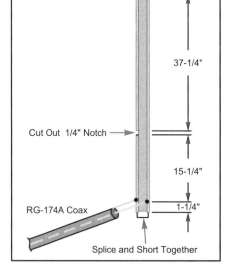

Figure 1 — The original 2 meter ribbon J-pole antenna.

radials. The DBJ-1 is easy to construct using inexpensive materials from your local hardware store. For its simplicity and small size, the DBJ-1 offers excellent performance and consistently outperforms a ground plane antenna.

Its radiation pattern is close to that of an ideal vertical dipole because it is end-fed, with virtually no distortion of the radiation pattern due to the feed line. A vertically polarized, center-fed dipole will always have some distortion of its pattern because the feed line comes out at its center, even when a balun is used. A vertically polarized, center-fed antenna is also physically more difficult to construct because of that feed line coming out horizontally from the center.

The basic J-pole antenna is a half-wave vertical configuration. Unlike a vertical dipole, which because of its center feed is usually mounted alongside a tower or some kind of metal supporting structure, the radia-

tion pattern of an end-fed J-pole mounted at the top of a tower is not distorted.

The J-pole works by matching a low impedance (50 Ω) feed line to the high impedance at the end of a λ/2 vertical dipole. This is accomplished with a λ/4 matching stub shorted at one end and open at the other. The impedance repeats every λ/2, or every 360° around the Smith Chart. Between the shorted end and the high impedance end of the λ/4 shorted stub, there is a point that is close to 50 Ω and this is where the 50 Ω coax is connected.

By experimenting, this point is found to be about 1¼ inches from the shorted end on 2 meters. This makes intuitive sense since 50 Ω is closer to a short than to an open circuit. Although the Smith Chart shows that this point is slightly inductive, it is still an excellent match to 50 Ω coax. At resonance the SWR is below 1.2:1. Figure 1 shows the dimensions for a 2-meter J-pole. The 15¼ inch λ/4 section serves as the quarter wave matching transformer.

A commonly asked question is, "Why 15¼ inches?" Isn't a λ/4 at 2 meters about 18½ inches? Yes, but twinlead has a reduced velocity factor (about 0.8) compared to air and must thus be shortened by about 20%.

A conventional J-pole configuration works well because there is decoupling of the feed line from the λ/2 radiator element since the feed line is in line with the radiating λ/2 element. Thus, pattern distortion is minimized. But this only describes a single band VHF J-pole. How do we make this into a dual band J-pole?

Adding a Second Band to the J-pole

To incorporate UHF coverage into a VHF J-pole requires some explanation. (A more detailed explanation is given in my February 2003 *QST* article.) First, a 2 meter antenna does resonate at UHF. The key word here is

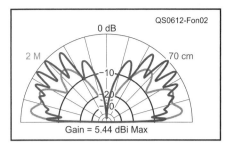

Figure 2 — Elevation plane pattern comparing 2 meter J-pole on fundamental and on third harmonic frequency (70 cm), with the antenna mounted 8 feet above ground. Most of the energy at the third harmonic is launched at 44°.

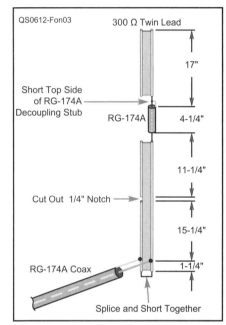

Figure 3 — The original DBJ-1 dual-band J-pole. The dimensions given assume that the antenna is inserted into a ¾ inch Class 200 PVC pipe.

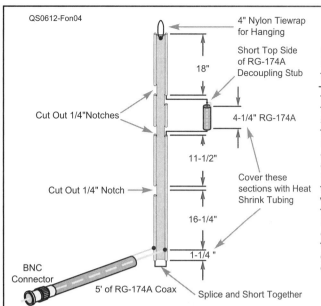

Figure 4 — The dual-band J-pole modified for portable operation — thus becoming the DBJ-2. Note that the dimensions are slightly longer than those in Figure 3 because it is not enclosed in a PVC dielectric tube. Please remember that the exact dimensions vary with the manufacturer of the 300 Ω line, especially the exact tap point where the RG-174A feed coax for the radio is connected.

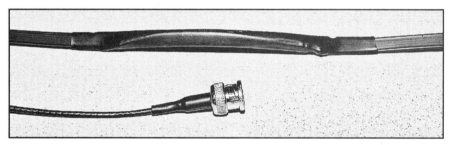

Figure 5 — The λ/4 UHF decoupling stub made of RG-174A, covered with heat shrink tubing. This is shown next to the BNC connector that goes to the transceiver.

resonate. For example, any LC circuit can be resonant, but that does not imply that it works well as an antenna. Resonating is one thing; working well as an antenna is another. You should understand that a λ/4 146 MHz matching stub works as a 3λ/4 matching stub at 450 MHz, except for the small amount of extra transmission line losses of the extra λ/2 at UHF. The UHF signal is simply taking one more revolution around the Smith Chart.

The uniqueness of the DBJ-1 concept is that it not only resonates on both bands but also actually performs as a λ/2 radiator on both bands. An interesting fact to note is that almost all antennas will resonate at their third harmonic (it will resonate on any odd harmonic 3, 5, 7, etc). This is why a 40 meter dipole can be used on 15 meters. The difference is that the performance at the third harmonic is poor when the antenna is

used in a vertical configuration, as in the J pole shown in Figure 1. This can be best explained by a 19 inch 2 meter vertical over an ideal ground plane. At 2 meters, it is a λ/4 length vertical (approximately 18 inches). At UHF (450 MHz) it is a 3λ/4 vertical. Unfortunately, the additional λ/2 at UHF is out of phase with the bottom λ/4. This means cancellation occurs in the radiation pattern and the majority of the energy is launched at a takeoff angle of 45°. This results in about a 4 to 6 dB loss in the horizontal plane compared to a conventional λ/4 vertical placed over a ground plane. A horizontal radiation pattern obtained from *EZNEC* is shown in Figure 2. Notice that the 3λ/4 radiator has most of its energy at 45°.

Thus, although an antenna can be made to work at its third harmonic, its performance is poor. What we need is a simple, reliable method to decouple the remaining λ/2 at UHF of a 2 meter radiator, but have it remain electrically unaffected at VHF. We want independent λ/2 radiators at both VHF and UHF frequencies. The original DBJ-1 used a combination of coaxial stubs and 300 Ω twinlead cable, as shown in Figure 3.

Refer to Figure 3, and start from the left hand bottom. Proceed vertically to the RG-174A lead in cable. To connect to the antenna, about 5 feet of RG-174A was used with a BNC connector on the other end. The λ/4 VHF impedance transformer is made from 300 Ω twin lead. Its approximate length is 15 inches due to the velocity factor of the 300 Ω material. The λ/4 piece is shorted at the bottom and thus is an open circuit (high impedance) at the end of the λ/4 section. This matches well to the λ/2 radiator for VHF. The 50 Ω tap is about 1¼ inches from the short, as mentioned before.

For UHF operation, the λ/4 matching stub at VHF is now a 3λ/4 matching stub. This is electrically a λ/4 stub with an additional λ/2 in series. Since the purpose of the matching stub is for impedance matching and not for radiation, it does not directly affect the radiation efficiency of the antenna. It does, however, suffer some transmission loss from the additional λ/2, which would not be needed if it were not for the dual band operation. I estimate this loss at about 0.1 dB. Next comes the λ/2 radiating element for UHF, which is about 12 inches. To

Table 1

Measured Relative Performance of the Dual-band Antenna at 146 MHz

VHF λ/4 GP 4 radials	VHF Flexible Antenna	Standard VHF J-Pole	Dual-Band J-Pole
0 dB reference	–5.9 dB	+1.2 dB	+1.2 dB

Table 2

Measured Relative Performance of the Dual-band Antenna at 445 MHz

UHF λ/4 GP 4 radials	UHF Fexible Antenna	Standard VHF J-Pole	Dual-Band J-Pole
0 dB reference	–2.0 dB	–5.5 dB	0.5 dB

make it electrically terminate at 12 inches, a λ/4 shorted stub at UHF is constructed using RG-174A. The open end is then connected to the end of the 12 inches of 300 Ω twin-lead. The open circuit of this λ/4 coax is only valid at UHF. Also, notice that it is 4½ inches and not 6 inches due to the velocity factor of RG-174A, which is about 0.6.

At the shorted end of the 4½ inch RG-174A is the final 18 inches of 300 Ω twinlead. Thus the 12 inches for the UHF λ/2, the 4½ inches of RG-174A for the decoupling stub at UHF, and the 18 inches of twinlead provide for the λ/2 at 2 meters. The total does not add up to a full 36 inches that you might think. This is because the λ/4 UHF RG-174A shorted stub is inductive at 2 meters, thus slightly shortening the antenna.

Making it Portable

The single most common question that people asked regarding the DBJ-1 is how it could be made portable. The original DBJ-1 had the antenna inserted into Class 200 PVC pipe that was 6 feet long. This was fine for fixed operation but would hardly be suitable for portable use. Basically the new antenna had to have the ability to be rolled up when not in use and had to be durable enough for use in emergency communications.

The challenge was to transfer the concepts developed for the DBJ-1 and apply them to a durable roll-up portable antenna. After much thought and experimenting, I adopted the configuration shown in Figure 4.

The major challenge was keeping the electrical characteristics the same as the original DBJ-1 but physically constructing it from a continuous piece of 300 Ω twin-lead. Any full splices on the twinlead would compromise the durability, so to electrically disconnect sections of the twinlead, I cut small ¼ inch notches to achieve the proper resonances. I left the insulating backbone of the 300 Ω twinlead fully intact. I determined the two notches close to the λ/4 UHF decoupling stub by experiment to give the best SWR and bandwidth.

Because this antenna does not sit inside a dielectric PVC tube, the dimensions are about 5% longer than the original DBJ-1.

I used heat shrink tubing to cover and protect the UHF λ/4 decoupling stub and the four ¼ inch notches. Similarly, I protected with heat shrink tubing the RG-174A coax interface to the 300 Ω twinlead. I also attached a small Teflon tie strap to the top of the antenna so that it may be conveniently attached to a nonconductive support string.

Figure 5 shows a picture of the λ/4 UHF matching stub inside the heat shrink tubing. The DBJ-2 can easily fit inside a pouch or a large pocket. It is far less complex than what would be needed for a single band ground plane, yet this antenna will consistently outperform a ground plane using 3 or 4 radials. Setup time is less than a minute.

I've constructed more than a hundred of these antennas. The top of the DBJ-2 is a high impedance point, so objects (even if they are nonmetallic) must be as far away as possible for best performance. The other sensitive points are the open end of the λ/4 VHF matching section and the open end of the λ/4 UHF decoupling stub.

As with any antenna, it works best as high as possible and in the clear. To hoist the antenna, use non-conducting string. Fishing line also works well.

Measured Results

I measured the DBJ-2 in an open field using an Advantest R3361 Spectrum Analyzer. The results are shown in Table 1. The antenna gives a 7 dB improvement over a flexible antenna at VHF. In actual practice, since the antenna can be mounted higher than the flexible antenna at the end of your handheld, results of +10 dB are not uncommon. This is the electrical equivalent of giving a 4 W handheld a boost to 40 W.

The DBJ-2 performs as predicted on 2 meters. It basically has the same performance as a single band J-pole, which gives about a 1 dB improvement over a λ/4 ground plane antenna. There is no measurable degradation in performance by incorporating the UHF capability into a conventional J-pole.

The DBJ-2's improved performance is apparent at UHF, where it outperforms the single band 2 meter J-pole operating at UHF by about 6 dB. See Table 2. This

is *significant*. I have confidence in these measurements since the flexible antenna is about –6 dB from that of the λ/4 ground plane antenna, which agrees well with the literature.

Also notice that at UHF, the loss for the flex antenna is only 2.0 dB, compared to the ground plane. This is because the flexible antenna at UHF is already 6 inches long, which is a quarter wave. So the major difference for the flexible antenna at UHF is the lack of ground radials.

Summary

I presented how to construct a portable, roll-up dual-band J-pole. I've discussed its basic theory of operation, and have presented experimental results comparing the DBJ-2 to a standard ground plane, a traditional 2 meter J-pole and a flexible antenna. The DBJ-2 antenna is easy to construct, is low cost and is very compact. It should be an asset for ARES applications. It offers significant improvement in both the VHF and UHF bands compared to the stock flexible antenna antenna included with a handheld transceiver.

If you do not have the equipment to construct or tune this antenna at both VHF and UHF, the antenna is available from the author tuned to your desired frequency. Cost is $20. E-mail him for details.

Notes
[1] E. Fong, "The DBJ-1: A VHF-UHF Dual-Band J-Pole," QST, Feb 2003, pp 38-40.
[2] J. Reynante, "An Easy Dual-Band VHF/UHF Antenna," QST, Sep 1994, pp 61-62.

Ed Fong was first licensed in 1968 as WN6IQN. He later upgraded to Amateur Extra class with his present call of WB6IQN. He obtained BSEE and MSEE degrees from the University of California at Berkeley and his PhD from the University of San Francisco. A Senior Member of the IEEE, he has 8 patents, 24 published papers and a book in the area of communications and integrated circuit design. Presently, he is employed by the University of California at Berkeley teaching graduate classes in RF design and is a Principal Engineer at National Semiconductor, Santa Clara, California working with CMOS analog circuits. You can reach the author at **edison_fong@hotmail.com**. 🔲ST🔲

A Weather Vane Antenna for 2 Meters

VHF incognito! Here's a 2 meter antenna your neighbors won't recognize.

**John Portune, W6NBC, and
Fred Adams, WD6ACJ**

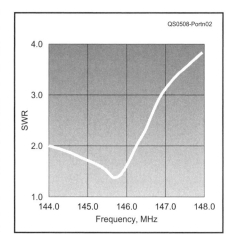

Figure 1—The completed weather vane antenna. Can you find the loop?

Keeping a homeowners' association happy isn't easy. Many hams burdened with CC&Rs often live with badly compromised antennas. Why not combine a compact magnetic loop with a functional weather vane and put high-performance right out in full view? A neighbor even asked me where I got mine, so she could get one, too.

Compact loops, often called magnetic loops, have been around for years. They're tiny open-ended ring radiators, always less than roughly $1/10$ wavelength in diameter. Recently we've seen them mostly on HF where their small size is of great appeal. But they work very well on other bands too; here on 2 meters. Remarkably, this VHF version achieves an efficiency of 93%, yet radiates as if it were a full-sized dipole or a J-pole, but from a space only 7 inches square. What's best, it is disguised as a nice-looking weather vane. Your neighbors won't guess that your rooster has a call sign.

What makes a magnetic loop so easy to camouflage besides its size is its radiation pattern. It may surprise you, but a horizontal compact loop radiates as if it were a full-sized half-wave dipole on the vertical axis of the loop. Yet, here it looks like nothing more than the support for the weather vane's direction letters (Figure 1).

There is a restriction, however. Compact loops require low conductor resistance as compared to full-sized dipoles. (See the technical discussion later in this article.) This requires that we use copper water pipe for construction. Also, compact loops have narrow bandwidth (BW)—in this case, a theoretical BW of 600-700 kHz. Practically, however, the BW is wider. Figure 2 shows an actual SWR plot of my loop.

On the positive side, a magnetic loop's narrow bandwidth increases the received signal-to-noise ratio (SNR). In a noisy environment a compact loop will better discriminate than a dipole or J-pole. [While horizontal loops do better in noisy situations because that local noise tends to be mainly E-field oriented, the perceived SNR improvement of a narrow-band antenna is principally due to the reduction in out-of-band signals that cause IMD, rather than any reduction of the receiver noise floor.—*Ed.*] They also tend to work better close to the ground or near other objects.

Construction

All materials (Figures 3A and 3B) are common hardware store items. I recommend a tubing cutter for cutting the pipe, copper and PVC. Also, a different brand of copper fittings may require slight adjustments to the cutting dimensions shown. But, don't worry; high precision isn't required. The loop will tune up easily if you are roughly within $1/8$ inch of these dimensions.

The only part of this design that requires special attention is the $3/4$-$1/2$ inch reducer that acts as a tuning capacitor across the open ends of the loop. Drill or file the inside so that it will slide freely on the pipe ($21/32$ inch, roughly). Otherwise you will not be able to tune the antenna easily. As purchased, stock pipe fittings are too tight. Also, cut the slot shown for a securing screw.

Important Note: Do not cut the two end pieces at first. Instead, cut just one piece the same size as the opposite side. Later, after soldering, you'll cut a gap in center. This assures good alignment of the tuning capacitor.

For soldering, clean all joints thoroughly and apply a little flux. Use a propane torch and common solder, not silver solder (Figure 4). Also, solder sparingly. It isn't necessary to make watertight

Figure 2—An SWR plot of the completed loop. A 1:1 match at the resonant frequency is possible by compressing or expanding the feed loop.

SWR				QS0508-Portn02

SWR plot: x-axis Frequency, MHz (144.0 to 148.0); y-axis SWR (1.0 to 4.0)

Table 1
Relative Room Temperature Conductivity of Common Metals

Metal	Conductivity
Silver	100
Copper	95.2
Gold	68.3
Aluminum	60.3
Steel	9.5
Stainless Steel	2.4

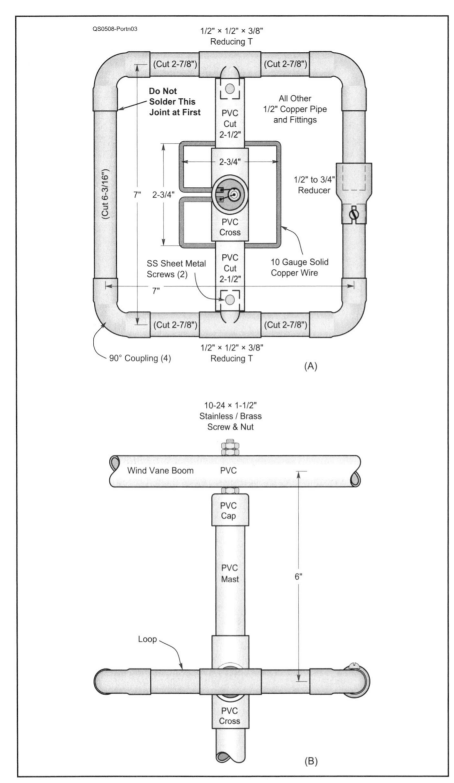

QS0508-Portn03

1/2" × 1/2" × 3/8"
Reducing T

(Cut 2-7/8")   (Cut 2-7/8")

**Do Not
Solder This
Joint at First**

PVC
Cut
2-1/2"

All Other
1/2" Copper Pipe
and Fittings

2-3/4"

2-3/4"

7"   2-3/4"

1/2" to 3/4"
Reducer

PVC
Cross

(Cut 6-3/16")

PVC
Cut
2-1/2"

10 Gauge Solid
Copper Wire

SS Sheet Metal
Screws (2)

7"

(Cut 2-7/8")   (Cut 2-7/8")

90° Coupling (4)

1/2" × 1/2" × 3/8"
Reducing T

(A)

10-24 × 1-1/2"
Stainless / Brass
Screw & Nut

Wind Vane Boom   PVC

PVC
Cap

PVC
Mast   6"

Loop

PVC
Cross

(B)

Figure 3—Parts and assembly details for the 2 meter loop are shown in (A). Note that most material is ¹/₂ inch copper pipe and fittings, except as noted. The inductive feed loop is made of 10 gauge solid copper wire. Basic details of the PVC weather vane support are shown in (B).

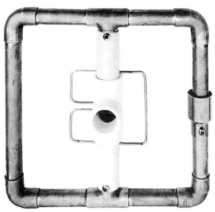

Figure 4—The copper pipe 2 meter loop. Note the inductive feed loop at the center.

the center of the copper pipe on the tuning capacitor side of the loop. Also, make a hole for a sheet metal screw to secure the tuning capacitor. Then cut the two short PVC center support arms. Note that the copper T-fittings are of the reducer type. The arms of both are ¹/₂ inch, but the necks are ³/₈ inch. Also, add two more sheet metal screws (Figure 3A) to keep the loop from rotating.

Next, install the tuning capacitor, glue the PVC support arms to the center PVC cross, put all the parts together, and then finally solder the one remaining copper joint, again keeping the loop flat. For the final solder joint, wrap wet rags around the T-fittings and PVC pipe to prevent damage to the PVC.

The Feed Loop

For matching to the coax, I prefer an inductive loop, as shown. To me, this is the easiest technique for feeding a compact loop. Other methods also work, such as a gamma match, but are generally more difficult to fabricate. I only had to make a couple of trial loops during the prototype stage to find the correct size. Loops seem to normally need a coupling loop that is roughly ¹/₃ the size of the main loop. The dimensions will yield a good match without any further experimenting.

You can, however, after final tuning, make minor adjustment to SWR by squeezing or stretching the feed loop. Fabricate the feed loop from bare 10 gauge or 12 gauge solid copper wire. Drill holes in the PVC pipe, then thread the coupling loop through, progressively bending the corners as you go.

For weather protection, solder the coax to the coupling loop inside the PVC cross fitting. Ideally, the loop should have a balun. In practice, however, I have experienced no discernable difference with or without it. But if you prefer, heatshrink several small VHF RF toroidal

connections—tack soldering is fine. At RF frequencies, skin effect makes low dc resistance at the joints completely unnecessary. Keep the loop flat on a heat-resistant surface while soldering.

Important Note: Do not have the tuning capacitor installed while soldering. You will put it on later. Also, be very careful not to solder the one joint indicated (Figure 3A). Otherwise you will not be able to assemble the antenna.

After soldering, cut a ¹/₂ inch gap in

Figure 5—(A) The weather vane "head" and "tail" cutouts and compass points. (B) The rooster cutout. These examples are not to scale—use your imagination!

cores over the coax, inside the PVC cross, to form a feed line choke.

The Weather Vane

I cut the decorative parts of the vane (Figure 4) with tin snips from an inexpensive heavy-duty plastic storage tub. The Web contains a wealth of wonderful weather vane designs, or you may use the one shown. You are obviously free to be innovative here. Do *not*, however, use metal for any of the pieces. This will detune the antenna.

For the rotating arm, keep two things in mind. First, the tail end must have more wind surface than the head end so that the vane will point into the wind. Therefore, the head end must be weighted. I used six-ounce fishing sinkers, silicone glued inside the boom. To hold the head and tailpieces on the arm, cut slots in the ends and use a little more silicone glue. Second, the pivot hole must be drilled at the balance point. Otherwise the arm will not rotate easily. The length of the vane is not critical. Mine is roughly 16 inches long.

Attach the rooster (Figure 5), or whatever "critter" you choose, with plas-

tic cable clamps and some additional glue. Punch two small appropriately located holes in the direction letters and attached them with wire ties. Finally, give the entire structure a coat of black outdoor spray paint. This will give the impression that your weather vane is made of wrought iron, a final touch for the disguise.

Tuning

For tuning, you'll need no special tools, only a VHF SWR bridge and a 2 meter transceiver. In the design phase, I did use a FET dip oscillator to get the prototype in the ballpark. Subsequently I've only needed an SWR bridge and a handheld transceiver to tune up a new vane.

The basic tuning technique is simple. Begin with the tuning capacitor as far away from the $1/2$ inch end gap as the securing screw will permit. Apply low power with your transceiver and measure the SWR at the top and again at the bottom of the 2 meter band. Write down the difference. With the capacitor all the way out, the SWR should be worse at the low end. That's because the loop is tuned too high in frequency. Remember, always keep the securing screw tight when making the SWR measurements. Also, at first, both SWR readings will be poor. Only the difference between high and low matters.

Progressively move the tuning capacitor inward, in small increments, again taking high/low readings. As you reach the desired operating frequency, high and low readings should become equal. Still, they won't necessarily be low. If you go too far, the SWR will become better at the low end, the reverse of above. Your objective is to find the position where both readings are equal and lowest. To obtain a final 1:1 match you may need to squeeze or stretch the feed loop a little. Generally, I have not had to bother with the dimensions given. Adjusting the tuning capacitor alone has yielded an adequate SWR.

A Technical Discussion

Theoretically, a compact/magnetic loop antenna is a parallel-tuned LC "tank" circuit. The variable capacitor across the ends ($1/2$-$3/4$ inch reducer) resonates the inductance of the loop to the frequency of operation. A multi-turn inductor can't radiate because of its small size. But, with a large single-turn inductor, such as a compact loop, good radiation characteristics can be achieved.

A compact loop, however, *must* be smaller than about 0.1 wavelength in diameter and 0.35 wavelength in circum-

ference. This causes it to radiate in a unique way. The classical RF bible, *Electronic and Radio Engineering* by F. Terman, states that: "The directional pattern of a small loop is identical with that of an elementary doublet (dipole). The only difference is that *the electric and magnetic fields are interchanged.*" A small horizontal loop, therefore, radiates as if it were a vertical dipole.

If we make the loop larger than 0.1 wavelength in diameter, the radiation pattern will slowly take on the more familiar form. A full half wavelength dipole, for example, folded into a loop, radiates horizontally. This is the popular "halo" antenna, once common during the early days of 2 meter mobile.

On the other hand, within limits, a compact loop may be made much smaller. A tiny loop compared to wavelength is easily implemented by merely increasing the capacitor across the loop's ends. In this way, lower frequencies or even multiple bands can be achieved. This technique is often used on HF, for example, and several good small multi-band HF compact loops are currently on the market for hams with limited space.

Radiation Resistance

There is, however, a practical limit to how small a loop can be made, due to another important characteristic of all small antennas—radiation resistance. Radiation resistance is not resistance in the usual sense. It is a kind of virtual resistance created by the actual loading of space on an antenna. Said another way, radiation resistance is a measure of how well an antenna couples to space.

But, as far as your transmitter is concerned, radiation resistance looks just like an ordinary resistor at the end of the coax. But instead of converting transmitter power into heat, which an actual resistor would do, radiation resistance does what we want, and converts RF power into a radio signal. Therefore, radiation resistance is the kind of resistance we want in an antenna. And, here's why.

In free space, a full-sized dipole has moderately high radiation resistance, roughly 72 Ω. Smaller antennas like compact loops have a radiation resistance that is much lower. The bigger the antenna, the larger a piece of space it captures, and the higher the radiation resistance. Specifically, as the size of an antenna decreases, the radiation resistance decreases —roughly as the square of size. Our weather vane is less than $1/10$ wavelength in diameter. It has an actual radiation resistance of only 1.7 Ω.

But, as long as we correctly match the transmitter's output impedance (normally 50 Ω) to the radiation resistance of the antenna, efficient radiation will take place. Hence, a compact loop with a very low radiation resistance can theoretically radiate just as well as dipole or a J antenna with a much higher radiation resistance.

There is a fly in the ointment, however—conductor resistance. That's because conductor resistance is in series with radiation resistance. And both forms of resistance must share the power from the transmitter. The power the conductor resistance (a real resistance) receives is wasted as heat. The power the radiation resistance (a virtual resistance) receives makes useful radio waves.

Therefore, in a dipole, with a relatively high radiation resistance of 72 Ω, conductor resistance isn't of much concern. Even for a thin wire of poor conductance, conductor resistance is only a small fraction of the radiation resistance. Thus it shares very little of the transmitter's power. But for a compact loop, where the radiation resistance may be very low, conductor resistance can easily waste significant power. That's why we should construct small antennas with large diameter conductors, not thin wire. This is also one of the reasons why mobile HF whip antennas are characteristically low in efficiency.

Metal Conductivity

Also for a small antenna, the kind of metal can be important. Table 1 illustrates how poorly conductive some common metals are, and why copper is really the only good choice for a compact loop. Two interesting points to note are that gold is a poorer conductor than either silver or copper. Gold is used on electronic connectors not because it is the best conductor, but because it does not corrode. Also, notice that stainless steel is 40 times poorer than copper, and that aluminum is about 60% as good.

Bandwidth

The final theoretical limitation of a small antenna, as mentioned earlier, is its low bandwidth. Bandwidth is a function of an antenna's natural LC ratio. In a dipole, this ratio is low. That is, the native self-inductance of a straight wire is relatively small compared to its self-capacitance. Q, therefore, is low, and bandwidth high. For a compact loop the opposite is true. A one-turn coil has high L compared to C. Hence, Q is high and bandwidth low. This is equally true for a loaded mobile HF whip. The large loading coil is very inductive, giving the antenna high Q and low bandwidth.

So, as an overall guideline, if we use large copper conductors and can live with a small bandwidth, a compact loop is a high efficiency choice for a small space. It is also easier to camouflage. My 40 meter rose trellis loop is also rarely noticed.

Designing a Loop

And, in case you would like to try your hand at a compact loop on another band, I have placed on **www.w6nbc.com/loop. html** the loop design equations and an excellent little Basic program that quickly calculates all parameters, including efficiency, of compact loops of almost any size and frequency. It is one of the many freeware programs for compact loop design available on the Web. It is a simple DOS program, but emulates well on a modern computer running *Windows XP*.

My Operating Experience

I have had two of the weather vane loops in service for several months now, one on my mobile home and the other at a friend's house. At my location I also have a comparison J-pole antenna (basically a full-sized dipole) at the same height, and I can detect little difference. Also, the weather vanes have experienced

significant wind and weather exposure during that time and show no tendency to detune. Give one a try. They've been an "undercover" winner for me.

Photos by the authors.

John Portune, W6NBC, first received his Advanced class amateur license in 1965, but has held an FCC First Class General Radiotelephone commercial license since 1961. He spent the first five years in Amateur Radio in England, as G5AJH. John upgraded to Amateur Extra in 1985. He is active on all bands through 440 MHz and has written articles for various ham and electronics journals. John is a retired TV broadcast engineer (KNBC, Burbank, California) and technical instructor (Sony Electronics, San Jose, California). He is currently an active VE team leader and participates in Central California ARES/RACES activities. You can reach him at 1095 W McCoy Ln, #99, Santa Maria, CA 93455 or jportune@aol.com.

Fred Adams, WD6ACJ, was first licensed as WN6AIH in 1961. Fred says that he was interested in CB radio prior to that time and that his career has mainly been in the mechanical engineering area. He advised and collaborated with W6NBC on this antenna—principally in the area of construction. Fred says he's built many antennas, but this design was a new concept to him. You can reach him at fredeadams@verizon.net. QST~

Lowe's Loop for 432 MHz

Your brand-new rig covers 432 MHz, but you don't have an outside antenna for that band? Here's an easily constructed antenna that will get you on 70 cm.

Ben Lowe, K4QF

Introduction

Many of the small modern transceivers on the market today are supplied with 432 MHz capabilities, but often operation on this band is not utilized due to the lack of a suitable antenna. This can be a great band for local contacts, and when propagation is good almost any simple antenna with the right characteristics — horizontal polarization and a low SWR — will permit some long-range contacts.

The purpose of this article is to present an antenna that is easy to construct in a couple of hours and is easy to match. It uses inexpensive material readily available at Lowe's Home Improvement, Home Depot or your local hardware store.[1] After all, putting up a 432 MHz antenna and generating some activity on this band would have to be considered a "home improvement" by any true-blue ham! The antenna described in this article is a *halo* loop with a matching scheme that is easy to implement.

Construction

I fabricated this loop with an emphasis on ease of construction and low cost. To that end, I used standard ¾ inch diameter copper water pipe, 5 or 10 feet long for the mast and ¼ inch copper tubing, normally used for ice makers on refrigerators, as the radiating element. Icemaker tubing normally comes in a 10 foot roll at Lowe's, but I only use about 1 foot unless I construct a multi-element array. One roll of tubing will be plenty for you and several of your friends to construct antennas.

This project also requires some #6 brass wood screws, some #8 brass wood screws both ½ inches long, and a ¼ inch nylon spacer 1 inch long. These parts are also available at Lowe's. Table 1 lists the parts needed.

Fabricating the Pipe

The basic approach to construction is straightforward. Use a tubing cutter to cut the radiating element from the ¼ inch tubing

**Figure 1 —
Completed 432 MHz
"Lowe's Loop."**

for a length of 13 inches. Center punch all holes before drilling so that the drill bit does not "walk off" the desired location. Exactly at the center of the element, 6.5 inches from each end, drill a small tap hole using a drill bit of ³⁄₃₂ inches. The precise size of this hole isn't critical, since a screw will hold the element in place until it is soldered. Once you've drilled the center hole, the element is bent around a 4 inch form to create the *halo* loop. Keep the tap hole on the inside portion of the circle. That is, place the hole directly against the circular form facing in toward the surface of the form instead of facing out.

The precise diameter of the halo isn't too critical, since the element diameter can later be adjusted by slightly bending it. I shaped the element into a circular form using a piece of 4 inch diameter PVC pipe obtained from

Lowe's and wrapped the 13 inch long, ¼ inch diameter, ice maker tubing around the pipe. However, any 4 inch diameter circular form can be used. Figure 1 shows the loop element.

You will be drilling a total of six holes in the ¾ inch mast. Using a sharp felt tip pen or a pencil, at a distance of 2 inches from one end of the ¾ inch pipe, mark the position of the first hole to be drilled. At this point along the pipe you will gauge the precise circumference using a piece of masking tape. See Figure 2C. Wrap the masking tape around the pipe, offsetting the edge as you wrap just enough so you can see the starting point. Mark the beginning and end points on the tape.

Inserting the Elements

Remove the masking tape and temporarily stick it to a flat surface. Use a ruler to measure

[1]The author is not related to, nor does he represent, Lowe's Building Supply.

**Table 1
Parts List**

Description	Lowe's Part Number
Round slotted brass wood screw, #6, ½" long.	490120
Round slotted brass wood screw, #8, ½" long.	491257
Nylon spacer, ¼" × 0.140" × 1".	491257
Copper pipe, ¾" × 10' long.	23791
Copper ice maker pipe, ¼" × 5' long.	22100004

the distance along the masking tape. Calculate ¼ of the total circumference distance. Mark points along the tape, each spaced ¼ of the circumference around the pipe. Mark the center point in between two marks. This mark will be used to line up with the tap hole you've already marked on the pipe. (The tap hole is for the #6 element screw that will be used to temporarily hold the radiating element in place while it is soldered.) Rewrap the masking tape on the pipe just below the 2 inch circle previously marked on the pipe using the tap center hole as a reference.

On each side of the center hole, at 90° to each other, you will drill two other holes for the radiator to pass through the mast. Mark the positions for these holes on the pipe, along with the holes 1 inch farther down the pipe used for the nylon insulating spacer, and ¼ inch farther from that down the pipe for the #6 ground tap screw. See Figure 2 again.

Drill the two mounting holes for the radiator, starting with a small starter bit, following with larger diameter bits. You will need to use a rattail file to open up the holes to the shape of ovals to allow the radiating element to pass through the pipe.

Insert the radiating element through the oblong holes and fasten it temporarily in place with a #6 brass set screw. Then, solder the element into place using a high wattage iron or small propane torch. After the element cools to the touch, the element can be bent to make it exactly horizontal when the mast is vertical.

Insert a ¼ inch diameter, 1 inch long, nylon spacer, available from Lowe's, into the spacer hole. This spacer extends approximately ⅛ inch out each side of the pipe mast, forming a standoff insulator for the balun center conductors that make up the antenna feed system. The matching scheme itself is taken from a well known technique for the delta match using the "plumber's delight" approach. It got this name because the radiating element does not require insulation from the mast and thus can be fabricated from plumbing fixtures.

Wiring it Up

Next, construct the 4:1 balun from RG-58 coax cable that is ½λ long as shown in Figure 3. While coax with foam insulation exhibits slightly lower loss, the foam can also act like a sponge for water, changing the characteristics of the dielectric and corroding the shield. Therefore, be sure to use RG-58 coax with solid polyethylene insulation, which isn't nearly so susceptible to water. Even though the loss is slightly higher, the length is so short that the difference is negligible.

The RG-58 coax is rated at 70 W at 432 MHz. With SSB or CW operation, the duty cycle is well below 50%, so I wouldn't

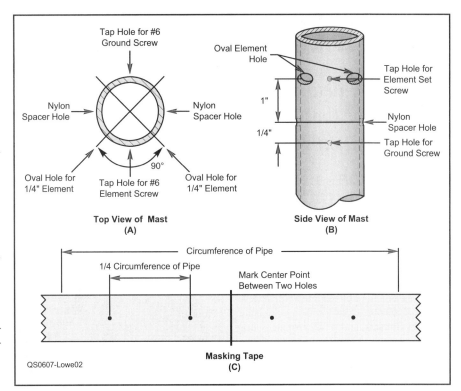

Figure 2 — Hole placement for Lowe's Loop mast. At A, top view of mast. At B, side view of mast. At C, masking tape used to measure exact circumference of mast, and then to mark off four equally spaced hole positions.

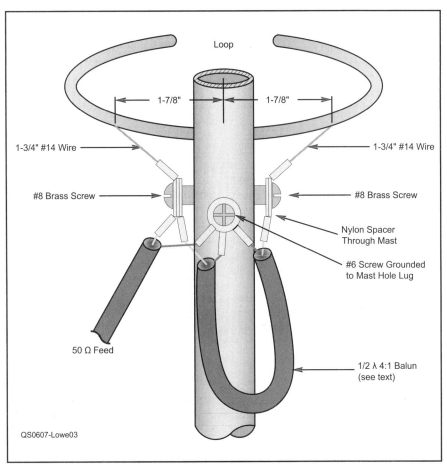

Figure 3 — Feed system, including coaxial 200 to 50 Ω coax balun.

hesitate to run as much as 100 W of RF into this antenna. If you plan to run more than 100 W to the antenna, a larger, higher power coax should be used. Also, with a typical station installation using a nondirectional antenna such as this, most setups will probably have something in the order of 3 dB feed line loss from the shack to the antenna. Therefore, even a transmitter with a couple of hundred watts of output can supply only 100 W to the antenna. As described later, a four-bay array of loops, each at 70 W capability, could take 280 W of average power, or 560 W peak power supplied to the antenna array.

The delta match feed is constructed from the 4:1 balun, two 1¾ inch lengths of 14 gauge copper house wiring and four solder lug terminals. The purpose of the 4:1 balun is to transform the 200 Ω balanced line of the delta match feed point to a 50 Ω unbalanced coax line.

You should mark the elements at the proper distance with a felt tip pen before soldering the delta wires to the element. Attach the 50 Ω feed line's center conductor to one of the lugs at the #8 brass screw that is inserted into the nylon insulator and its shield to the common ground point with the two shield connections from the balun.

The balun uses a piece of RG–58 coax that is 11⅞ inches long. Carefully remove ¾ inches of the black outside covering from each end of the coax, leaving the black covering on the coax 9⅝ inches long. Using a scribe or small sharp object, spread the braided shield on each end of the coax, tightly twisting the shield to form a solid conductor, and then carefully remove one half of the polyethylene insulation remaining on each end of the coax. Solder a small terminal lug suitable for a #6 brass wood screw on the twisted shields on each end of the coax. On the center conductor of each end of the coax, solder terminal lugs suitable for a #8 brass wood screw, along with the two 1¾ inch lengths of #14 copper house wiring as shown. Soldering is done before later attaching the lugs to the nylon spacer in order to not melt the nylon spacer. The final coax balun is shown in Figure 3.

After you've completed the coax balun and bent it into a loop, pass #8 brass wood screws through the solder lugs on the center conductors into each end of the nylon spacer on each side of the mast. If the holes for the nylon spacer barely have clearance, the #8 screws spread the nylon spacer just enough to hold the spacer securely in place. This may require a screwdriver on both ends of the nylon spacer at the same time. Then attach the #6 ground lugs on the shields to the tap hole located ¼ inch below the nylon spacer with a screw. The final step is to solder the #14 buss wires to the bottom side of the

element. These wires are attached to the element at a distance of 1⅞ inch from the brass set screw used to hold the element in place.

Final Test

If the loop and balun dimensions have been followed precisely, very little tuning should be necessary to obtain a low SWR for the antenna. One factor that could require tuning, however, is a variation in the velocity factor of the particular run of coax used to construct the balun. If this is the case, one way to compensate is to make slight adjustments in the length of the balun. This is easier said than done since it requires cutting and soldering the balun each time an adjustment is made. An easier way to make slight adjustments is to vary the spacing between the ends of the loop. You can make slight tweaks in the resonant frequency of the antenna by slightly changing the diameter of the loop. If the SWR is no more than 1.6:1 or 1.7:1, change this spacing by simply holding both sides of the loop and spreading or squeezing the spacing. This should allow the SWR to be brought down to an acceptable level.

For the test antenna and subsequent models, I easily adjusted the SWR to 1.2:1. Most of the models fabricated did not require any adjustments to achieve this SWR. One model required that the spacing be adjusted to 2 inches to obtain an acceptable SWR.

Quick Fix Four-Bay Array

One useful feature of the Lowe's Loop is the ability to stack these loops vertically to narrow the elevation beamwidth and achieve omnidirectional gain in the azimuth plane. Stacking four of the loops separated by ⅝ λ, or 16 inches between loops at 432 MHz, yields a total height of 48 inches for the four loops shown in Figure 4 and should yield about 6 dB gain, minus any losses in the power divider. While you can fabricate one loop on a ¾ inch copper mast, it isn't much more effort to prepare the mast and cut the elements for three more of the loops. If you pay careful attention during the construction, you can achieve a low SWR for all of the loops. Then, it is necessary to provide four equal-amplitude and in-phase drive signals to the four elements.

If all four loops in the array are fed with equal length feed lines, then each element receives the same amplitude and in-phase signal provided by the four way divider.

Tying four identical 50 Ω feed points in parallel results in a feed impedance of 12.5 Ω. I fed the four loops in my array with equal lengths of 50 Ω, RG-58 coax, each with a BNC connector on its end. This provided an easy mechanism to check each antenna individually before combining them into the four bay array. I drilled four holes

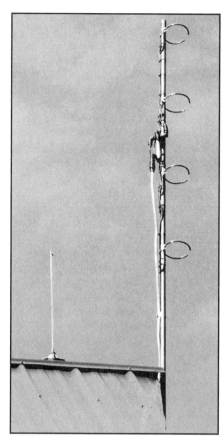

Figure 4 — Four Lowe's Loops mounted in a stacked array for additional horizontally polarized gain.

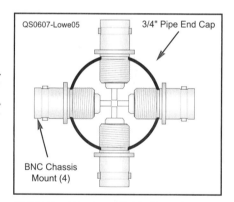

Figure 5 — Four way divider/transformer to feed stacked array of four Lowe's Loops.

in the side walls of a ¾ inch cooper end pipe cap to permit insertion of BNC female chassis mount connectors into the pipe cap, as the divider in Figure 5 shows. I sweat soldered the BNC connectors to the copper end cap.

For the particular version of the BNC connectors used, the center conductor pins had to be cut off a slight amount to allow all four connectors to join together at the center point and still have the ground rings of the connectors seat against the sides of the pipe cap. I did this easily with a pair of wire cutters on the soft metal center pins.

I needed to transform the 12.5 Ω impedance back up to 50 Ω. I decided to use a λ/4 Q section, which requires a 25 Ω characteristic impedance line. You can make a line with this impedance simply by paralleling the center conductors and the shields of two λ/4 lengths of 50 Ω coax. The photo in Figure 6 shows four BNCs mounted through the bottom pipe end cap, together with the two paralleled Q section coaxes before inserting them into the ¾ inch copper pipe and top end cap to finish the final assembly.

I started out by cutting two 5¼ inch lengths of RG-58. I removed ¾ inches of the outside jacket from each end of each coax. I then removed half of the center insulation at each end to expose the bare center conductors and soldered these center conductors together. After some experimentation, the final length of the paralleled cables was 3¾ inches, as shown Figure 7. The difference in length from the calculated value was likely due to the end sections, which act like additional short transmission lines with a different Z_0.

Incidentally, the same approach should be applicable for building two way dividers using paralleled pieces of 72 Ω coax. The paralleled coax characteristic impedance should be 35 Ω to transform the 25 Ω impedance of two 50 Ω antennas in parallel to 50 Ω. The required 35 Ω is very close to two paralleled pieces of 72 Ω coax cut to λ/4 in length.

Once I cut the Q section coax lines to length, I soldered their center conductors to the junction of the BNC center pins, and then soldered the four short ground lead pigtails onto the ground of each BNC connector. I soldered another BNC connector to the top end of the transformer at 90° to the coax to

minimize lead lengths.

It was now time to test the divider/transformer assembly. I connected a 50 Ω termination to each of the four BNC connectors and measured the SWR, which was 1.2:1. After testing, I placed the entire Q section inside a 3 inch long, ¾ inch diameter copper water pipe, together with an end cap with a hole in its side for the top BNC connector. Figure 8 shows a photo of the completed divider/transformer assembly.

Conclusion

This antenna is relatively easy to construct and to put into service. The materials are available at almost any building supply or hardware store. While one antenna provides omnidirectional coverage, the four bay array should approach 6 dB gain over a single element in all azimuth directions. This gain comes from compressing the elevation pattern, the same way that TV transmitting stations obtain gain in their omnidirectional antennas.

I've taken the same approach for a 2 meter halo simply by multiplying all dimensions by three. I've also constructed a 6 meter version, but that required capacitive loading to keep the dimensions of the antenna from getting too large. So far, my best DX on 70 cm has been Texas from Alabama. I've used the 2 meter Squalo to log Toronto to the northeast and Houston to the southwest, among the 42 grids that I've worked since putting it into operation a year ago.

I want to express my appreciation to Dieter Schliemann, KX4Y, for the use of his antenna analyzer and SWR meter, and to George Hall, W4BUW, for review of this manuscript.

Ben Lowe, K4QF, was licensed as KN4VOW in 1958 at the age of 14. He holds an MS degree from Southern Methodist University in Dallas and a BS degree from The University of Tennessee at Knoxville, both in Electrical Engineering. He is a registered Professional Engineer in the states of Alabama and Texas. Ben designs and implements microwave systems, assists the military with GPS applications and wireless architecture development, and conducts RF environmental analysis and measurements for Engineering Systems & Planning of Huntsville, Alabama.

In addition to Amateur Radio, he is a licensed pilot, has an advanced SCUBA certification, and is an avid bicyclist. His primary ham radio interests are in weak signal VHF/UHF operation. He has written numerous articles for QST, CQ, Ham Radio and The ARRL Handbook. Previous call signs include K4VOW, WA5UVM, ZL1AQC, G5EPZ, K4QF/HB/DL/HB0 and ZF2BL. He has two adult children, a daughter who is a research scientist in genetics and a son who is a computer engineer. You can reach Ben at 848 County Rd #138, Scottsboro, AL 35768, or at K4QF@arrl.net. QSTₓ

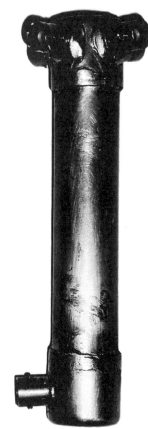

Figure 6 — Photo of four way divider/transformer before mounting in ¾ inch copper pipe with end cap.

Figure 8 — Completed four way combiner/transformer assembly.

3-3/4"

RG-58 Coax

RG-58 Coax

QS0607-Lowe07

Figure 7 — Making a 25 Ω, λ/4 transmission line by paralleling two RG-58 lines.

A Short Boom, Wideband 3 Element Yagi for 6 Meters

L. B. shows us how to craft an easy to reproduce 6 meter Yagi that covers the whole band.

L. B. Cebik, W4RNL

Although there are many 2 and 3 element Yagi designs for 6 meters, few do justice to the needs of the FM operator who requires some gain and directivity from 51 to 54 MHz. The 3 element design described here will actually cover the entire 6 meter band (a bandwidth of about 7.7%) with reasonable performance and a 50 Ω SWR of less than 2:1. The short 3 foot boom is a further attraction. Figure 1 is a photograph of a completed Yagi mounted on a PVC test mast.

Beam Design and User Expectations

Evaluating a beam design requires an appreciation of three ingredients: your needs on a particular band, general beam antenna behavior and reasonable expectations to have of a beam once installed. Your requirements for a beam on 6 meters change depending on your operating goals. If you only use CW, SSB or digital modes, then you tend to operate in the lowest MHz of the band and can use a beam with a narrow operating bandwidth. If you wish to use FM and want some directivity, however, then you need a wideband design with good performance from 51 to 54 MHz.

Moreover, the beam should be vertically polarized, which normally translates into a beam with vertically oriented elements. FM activity generally relies on point-to-point signal paths. Cross polarization of the send-ing and receiving antennas may result in weak signals or no signals at all. As shown in Figure 1, the present antenna is designed for broadband 6 meter service using vertically oriented elements.

Older designs for a truly wideband Yagi depend on the spacing between the driver and the reflector elements to obtain their broad coverage. The wider spacing produces a beneficial side effect — it raises the feed-point impedance to about 50 Ω so that the user can make a direct connection between the feed line and the antenna without needing to add a matching network. However, these designs carry a penalty. The lower gain 2 element driver-reflector Yagi needs a 3.5 foot boom, while the higher gain 3 element Yagi's boom is over 6 feet long. The design here has three elements, but uses a boom less than 36 inches long. Figure 2 shows its outline, while Figure 3 is a photo of the prototype beam.

To obtain higher gain and a shorter boom, you might turn to a driver-director Yagi design. Unfortunately, these designs have quite low feed-point impedances and very narrow operating bandwidths. Broadening the operating bandwidth of a driver-director design involves redesigning the driver, using two elements with a simple phase line between them.

Figure 1 — The prototype 3 element wideband phase-fed Yagi on the test mast. Note that this mast is nonconductive to avoid interactions with the nearby driver elements.

Now you have a beam that competes with the 3 element standard Yagi, but does so on a much shorter boom.

A driver-director design (in fact, any Yagi with one or more directors) has another advantage over the 2 element driver-reflector Yagi if you consider your needs on the band. A driver-reflector Yagi shows its highest gain

Figure 2 — General outline of the 3 element wideband short-boom Yagi for 6 meters.

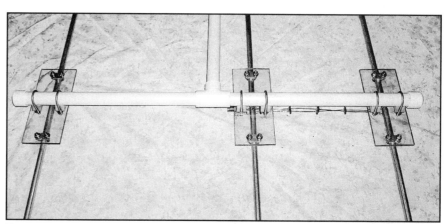

Figure 3 — Photo of the entire central beam structure, including the PVC boom and mast stub.

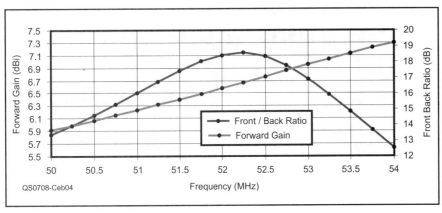

Figure 4 — Modeled free space gain and 180° front-to-back ratio of the 3 element wideband short-boom Yagi for 6 meters.

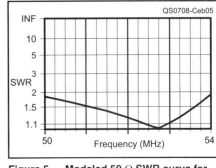

Figure 5 — Modeled 50 Ω SWR curve for the prototype 3 element wideband short-boom Yagi for 6 meters. The array requires no matching network and uses ⅝-½ inch elements with bare wire phase line. The measured SWR was identical to the modeled SWR.

Table 1
Dimensions of the Yagi for Different Construction Methods

Tapered-Element Version Using 0.625"/0.5" Elements; 250 Ω (Open Wire) Parallel Phase Line

0.625" Inner Sections = 24" Each Side of Center or 48" Total; Add 2" to Tip Lengths for Insertion

Element	Total Length	Tip (0.5") Length	Spacing from Rear Element
Rear Driver	110"	31"	—
Forward Driver	103.5"	27.75"	13.75"
Director	101"	26.5"	34.75"

Tapered-Element Version Using 0.625"/0.5" Elements; 250 Ω RG-63 Phase Line

0.625" Inner Sections = 24" Each Side of Center or 48" Total; Add 2" to Tip Lengths for Insertion

Element	Total Length	Tip (0.5") Length	Spacing from Rear Element
Rear Driver	108.5"	30.25"	—
Forward Driver	104"	28"	13.75"
Director	101"	27"	34.75"

Uniform-Element Version Using 0.5" Elements; 250 Ω (Open Wire) Parallel Phase Line

Element	Total Length	Spacing from Rear Element
Rear Driver	108.9"	—
Forward Driver	102.6"	13.6"
Director	99.8"	34.75"

Tapered-Element Version Using 0.5"/0.375" Elements; 250 Ω (Open Wire) Parallel Phase Line

0.5" Inner Sections = 24" Each Side of Center or 48" Total; Add 2" to Tip Lengths for Insertion

Element	Total Length	Tip (0.375") Length	Spacing from Rear Element
Rear Driver	111"	31.5"	—
Forward Driver	104.6"	28.3"	13.6"
Director	102"	27"	34.75"

Tapered-Element Version Using 0.5"/0.375" Elements; 250 Ω RG-63 Phase Line

0.5" Inner Sections = 24" Each Side of Center or 48" Total; Add 2" to Tip Lengths for Insertion

Element	Total Length	Tip (0.375") Length	Spacing from Rear Element
Rear Driver	109"	30.5"	—
Forward Driver	105"	28.5"	13.6"
Director	102"	27"	34.75"

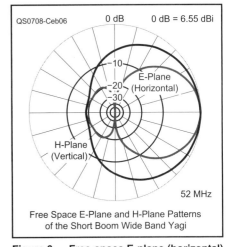

Free Space E-Plane and H-Plane Patterns of the Short Boom Wide Band Yagi

Figure 6 — Free-space E-plane (horizontal) and H-plane (vertical) patterns for the 3 element wideband short-boom Yagi at 52 MHz.

at the low end of the band, with decreasing gain as you increase the frequency. Figure 4 shows the modeled performance of the prototype antenna from 50 to 54 MHz. Like a longer standard 3 element Yagi, the gain shows a rising curve so that we have maximum gain in the FM section of the band. The graph also shows the anticipated front-to-back performance, which varies from nearly 13 dB at the band edges to a peak value of over 18 dB.

The final critical operating parameter is the 50 Ω SWR across the band. The present design requires no additional matching network. Instead, it connects directly to a 50 Ω transmission line (although I always recommend the use of a common-mode current attenuator, such as a ferrite bead choke or a 1:1 balun at the feed-point). Figure 5 shows the modeled SWR curve for the entire 6 meter band. (The test antenna curve overlaps the modeled curve too closely to justify a second line on the graph.)

Newer amateurs who read *QST* often get a wrong impression of Yagi patterns, because almost all beam patterns for HF appear with the elements horizontal (or in the E-plane). E-plane patterns differ from H-plane patterns (when the elements are vertical). Figure 6 overlays the E-plane and H-plane free-space patterns of the phased-driver design at 52 MHz to show the difference. The E-plane pattern shows a limited beamwidth and very deep nulls 90° from the axis of maximum forward gain. The H-plane pattern has the same forward and rearward gain maximums, but has a much broader beamwidth and no side nulls at all. The H-plane pattern generally represents the azimuth pattern that we should expect from a vertically oriented Yagi. Because the beamwidth is so great, the forward gain of a vertical beam over ground will be less than the forward gain of a horizontal Yagi at the same height. However, the gain of each beam over a similarly oriented dipole will be just about the same (a bit over 4 dB).

Design and Construction of the 3-Element Broad-Band Short-Boom Beam

The Boom

The 3 element short boom wideband Yagi consists of two elements that serve as a phased pair of drivers. Forward of the driver pair is a single director element. All versions of the beam have a total length of 34.75 inches from the center of the rear element to the center of the director. Therefore, you need a boom that is perhaps 38 to 40 inches long, depending upon your construction methods. An aluminum tube and a schedule-40 PVC 1 inch nominal tube are equally effective, since we shall insulate and isolate our elements from the boom with mounting plates. The prototype employed a PVC-pipe boom with a T connector for the boom-to-mast connection. The stub slips inside my main test mast, which uses 1¼ inch nominal PVC.

Element Dimensions

Table 1 lists five separate sets of dimensions for the beam, since amateurs generally have access to different material stocks. The first two sets use ⅝ inch diameter inner sections with ½ inch outer or tip sections. The middle set uses uniform-diameter ½ inch tubes throughout. The final two dimension sets use ½ inch inner sections with ⅜ inch diameter tips. The prototype in the photos uses the first set of dimensions. However, the only change in performance among the dimensions is that the fattest elements provide a very slight improvement in the SWR curve at the band edges.

Table 1 illustrates two important facts for newer beam builders. First, small design changes, such as a change in the phase line structure or a change in element diameter, can alter beam performance enough to

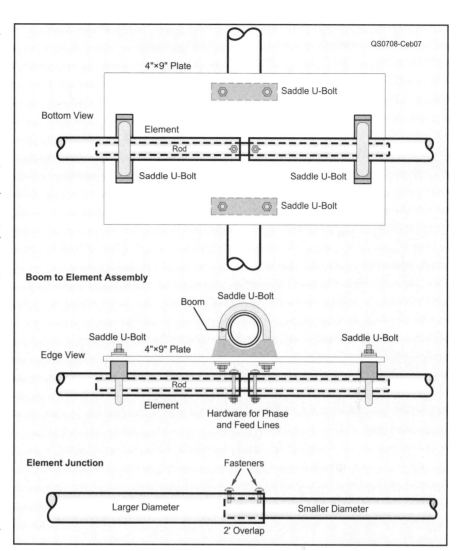

Figure 7 — Some construction details for the prototype array, including the junction of element sections and the element to boom plate assembly. The sketches apply to driver elements; omit the gap for the director.

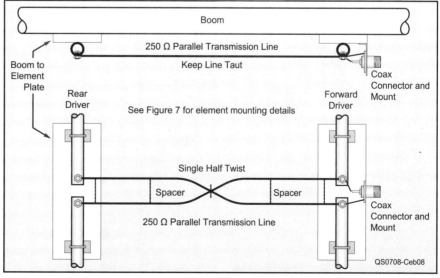

Figure 8 — The basic structure of the array feed-point and the phase lines. Except for the spacers, the same structure applies to the use of RG-63 cables for the phase lines.

require a complete redesign of the element lengths. (Element spacing is usually less critical.) Second, tapered element diameters require added length to be electrically equivalent to uniform diameter elements, even if the average diameter of the tapered element is larger than the diameter of the uniform element. Changing just the lengths of inner and tip sections can require an adjustment to the total element length for equivalent electrical performance.

If you use one of the tapered-diameter schedules, add about 2 inches to the tip lengths shown in Table 1 for insertion into the inner element section. See the bottom of Figure 7 for a typical junction. Sheet metal screws or aircraft rated rivets are among the most useful fasteners to ensure long term contact between element sections. I prefer high-quality 6063-T832 drawn aluminum tubing, available from Texas Towers and similar sources, since it is available in outer diameter increments of ⅛ inch in the US. The 0.058 inch wall thickness (just under 1⁄16 inch) allows a smooth fit but a tight joint.

Element-to-Boom Mounting

For the element-to-boom junctions, I prefer to use ¼ inch thick polycarbonate plates. For 6 meters, 9 by 4 inch plates are more than large enough. As shown in Figure 7, the chief fasteners are U-bolts with saddles, available from DX Engineering, as one source. I use saddles to prevent the U-bolt from crushing the element and to provide a space between the element and the plate. For the driver elements, you need additional hardware to handle the phase lines. The element U-bolts have a spacing of ¾ inches, while the boom U-bolts are around 1 inch to 1¼ inch tubes. Like all of the hardware (including lock washers) in the beam, the U-bolts are stainless steel.

The sketch shows a gap between element halves for each driver. The feed line and the phase line connect to each side of the gap. The exact size of the gap is not critical, although very close spacing will help keep the phase lines properly spaced. The gap is part of the overall element length and not in addition to it. To keep the element halves aligned with only two U-bolts at the plate ends, I used a length of ½ inch diameter fiberglass rod, the length of the plate, inserted into the ⅝ inch inner element sections. Almost any ½ inch diameter non-conductive rod or stiff tubing will do, although wood is susceptible to moisture.

For the director, you may use either of two mounting methods. If you do not over tighten the U-bolts, you may use a single 48 inch length of tubing for the inner element section. If you wish to guard against crushing, you can use two 24 inch lengths with an insert of

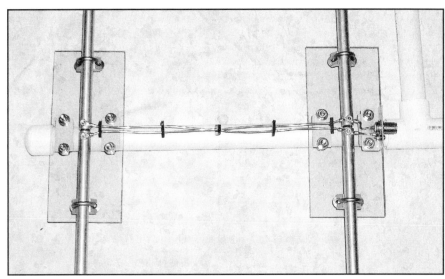

Figure 9 — A close-up photo of the phase line and driver assembly. Note the half twist in the line and the periodic spacers.

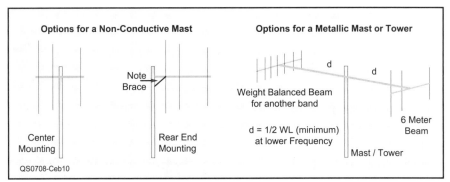

Figure 10 — Some mounting options for the 3 element wideband short-boom Yagi for 6 meters.

Table 2
250 Ω Open Wire Transmission Line Dimensions

AWG Wire Size	Wire Diameter	Center-to-Center Spacing
#14	0.0641"	0.262"
#12	0.0808"	0.330"
#10	0.1019"	0.416"
#8	0.1285"	0.525"

the next smaller aluminum tubing size that is as long as the plate. Sheet metal screws work well to ensure continuity in the element.

The Phase Lines

Since you need only 13.75 inches of phase-line (plus a bit extra for connections to the elements), you likely should make your own. Table 2 lists the center-to-center spacing for 250 Ω lines using common bare copper wire, arranged by AWG size. You will need spacers about every 3 inches to maintain the wire spacing accurately. The best way to make spacers is to drill the wire holes in a long strip of polycarbonate, Plexiglas or similar plastic. Cut the spacers to size after you complete the drilling. Do not make the holes too large; you want a tight fit. A drop of superglue at each hole will lock the spac-

ers in place. The velocity factor of this phase line will be very close to 1.0.

I do not recommend using 300 Ω TV twinlead as the phase line. Even high quality 300 Ω line has a velocity factor of about 0.8 to go with its characteristic impedance that is already 20% higher than optimal. Using a taut line will make the TV phase line about 25% longer electrically than the value needed to create the right conditions for the drivers to operate well. Two elements with a phase line use a fairly critical combination of element dimensions and spacing — along with equally critical values of phase-line characteristic impedance and electrical length — to get the job done. This involves dividing the current at the feed point so that each driver element receives the correct current magnitude and phase angle for maximum gain from the pair (in the presence of the director element) — while yielding a 50 Ω feed-point impedance.

There is an alternative way to construct the phase-line. RG-63 coax (available from such sources as The Wireman, **thewireman. com**) has a characteristic impedance of 125 Ω. Cut two 13.75 inch sections. At each end, solder the braids together and tape them to prevent contact with the elements. You then use only the center conductors to make the phase-line connections (with the single half-twist, of course). The line now forms a series-connected dual coax cable with an impedance of 250 Ω. Since RG-63 has a velocity factor of 0.84, you must adjust the lengths of the two driver elements to compensate. In Table 1, you will find alternative dimensions for both the ⅝ -½ inch and the ½-⅜ inch versions of the array. These variations on the design produce performance that is indistinguishable from the versions that use bare wire phase lines.

Figure 8 shows the connection scheme for the phase lines and the feed point. I used #8 bolts and nuts through each driver at the gap, along with ring solder lugs to fasten the phase line between doubled nuts on the bolts. Very short leads go from the forward driver connections to a coax connector mounted on a small plate that I fastened to the element mounting plate. Once I completed all final adjustments, I coated all exposed connections with one of the liquid plastics that substitutes for electrical tape. The close-up photo in Figure 9 of the phase line structure was taken before I weather-sealed the connections.

The Boom-to-Mast Connection

Although the prototype uses a PVC boom and mast, standard 1 inch or 1¼ inch aluminum tube is also suitable as a boom material. However, to minimize the metallic mass in the immediate vicinity of the forward driver, I recommend a polycarbonate plate with stainless steel U-bolts to fasten the boom to the mast. Figure 10 shows some alternative methods of mounting the beam. The two sketches at the left apply to nonconductive masts that extend at least a small distance below the tip of the lower element halves. Rear end mounting is feasible, since the beam is relatively light. However, a 45° brace is necessary to reduce boom sag.

The sketch at the right of Figure 10 shows an alternative that allows the use of a metal cross boom that is at right angles to the elements. If you have a beam for another band that is weight-balanced with the 6 meter beam, you can set up the dual mounting scheme by allowing enough room between the beams. I recommend a total starting distance of 1 λ at the lower frequency. You can then shorten the distance in small increments while maintaining proper weight distribution until you begin to notice interactions. Some pattern distortions may occur before you encounter disturbances to the feed-point impedance.

Adjustment and Performance

The beam design emerged from *NEC* software with the Leeson corrections enabled to accurately account for the tapered diameter elements on most versions of the array.[1] I tried to be as careful in the shop as at the computer. Consequently, the test version of the antenna required no post-construction adjustments. Indeed, the measured SWR curve is so close to the modeled version that I checked it several times to ensure that I was not wishfully seeing numbers that did not exist. The predicted SWR minimum occurs at about 52.75 MHz, while the prototype showed the lowest value at 52.8 MHz (give or take the tolerances of my test meters). If your minimum SWR point is lower in frequency, extend the tips of both drivers in ⅛ inch increments. If the minimum frequency is too high, shorten the driver tips in the same manner. The director, if properly constructed, should not need adjustment. Also be certain that you do not have too much metal in the boom to mast plate and that it is not too close to the forward driver. The prototype's all PVC boom and mast stub, coupled with the PVC upper section of the test mast, eliminated this concern.

The beam appears to perform just as expected, with significant forward gain (about 4 dB) over a vertical dipole (at the same height) and good rearward quieting. A gain of 4 dB can make the difference between signals that fall below or rise above the FM threshold of reception. The present design is perhaps the smallest Yagi of which I am aware that provides this level of performance.

In fact, the design is adaptable to other frequency bands that need good performance over a wide operating bandwidth. The first MHz of 10 meters and the entire 40 meter band are two such examples. Although a 40 meter version falls outside the limits of my shop and test facilities, I'll bet that I can build a horizontal version for 10 meter use in time for the new sunspot cycle.

[1] *EZNEC* models for all five versions of the array in Table 1 are available at the ARRL Web site at **www.arrl.org/qst-in-depth**. Scroll down to the "2007" section and look for the file Cebik0807.

*Licensed since 1954, L. B. Cebik, W4RNL, is a prolific writer on the subject of antennas. Since retiring from teaching at the University of Tennessee, LB has hosted a Web site (**www. cebik.com**) discussing antennas — both theoretical and practical. He has written more than 15 books, including the ARRL course on antenna modeling. Serving both as a technical and an educational ARRL advisor, he's also been inducted into both the QRP and QCWA Halls of Fame. LB can be reached at 1434 High Mesa Dr, Knoxville, TN 37938 or at cebik@cebik.com.* QST_

A Rugged VHF Beam Antenna That Resists Ice Buildup

This unique design will help you keep that Yagi up when you most need it.

Ray Abraczinskas, W8HVG

The Independent Repeater Association operates a 2 meter linked repeater system in Michigan (see **www.w8hvg.org**). Our 222 and 440 MHz band auxiliary link antennas have had many problems allowing successful operation during our cold Michigan winters. We operate twelve 2 meter repeaters continuously linked together 24/7 via these links. The system uses 51 antennas, 14 of which are 222 MHz Yagi beams. Due to the shortage of commercially available 222 MHz beam antennas available commercially, we've had to build our own for many of our linking applications.

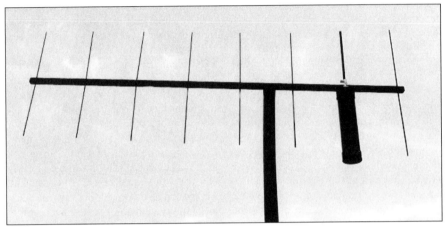

Figure 1 — A rugged 8 element 222 MHz beam antenna resists the effects of ice shorting out the gamma match and damaging the elements. The design criteria used are applicable to any beam antenna.

The Problem

During harsh Michigan winters, we discovered a major problem with the design of those VHF beam antennas in that they have an exposed gamma or T matching arrangement. During severe storms, we found that the exposed match will get coated with ice and effectively short out the antenna feed point, rendering the antenna useless until the ice thaws. It's especially problematic on high towers where the wind-chill temperature is very low.

One such commercially available antenna that caused us difficulty had a beautifully machined aluminum box attached to the boom with the T match bars protruding through plastic electrical feed-through insulators out to the driven element. Ice would simply coat over and around the feedthrough insulators and effectively short out the match. Sometimes it would take weeks or months for the ice to melt and restore operation. This, of course, was unacceptable for a wide-area linked repeater system, hopefully with 24/7 availability. There just had to be a better way.

Beam antennas can also be damaged by falling ice from higher up on a tower installation. This can often cause catastrophic failure of the antenna elements due to the heavy ice. Large ice sheets often break loose during high wind or as part of the melting process.

Every year, after a hard winter, we would

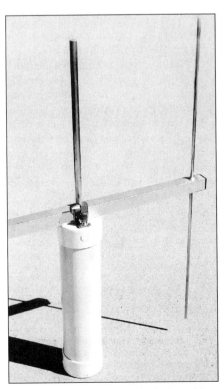

Figure 2 — A Schedule 30 PVC pipe with end caps form a shroud over the driven element and gamma match. All elements are welded or otherwise secured to the square boom. A chassis mount Type N connector and elbow are used to connect to the coax.

find that many of the thin elements on several of our beam antennas would be broken from falling ice, usually requiring replacing the entire antenna. In many cases they would still seem to work, albeit with reduced performance. However, it was evident that more rugged solid elements were required.

Some Background

There are no known commercially available 222 MHz amateur beam antennas that are specifically designed to perform while coated with ice. There are also no known commercially available beam antennas for that band that are specifically designed to reduce or resist ice buildup, especially around the feed point where it really matters.

Searching the Internet revealed that some antenna designers talk about the problem and how under certain conditions, ice buildup can alter the beam gain. In some cases, the direction of the signal can be reversed due to the ice buildup changing the director elements into reflectors.

Some designers used the phrase that an antenna must be *hydrophobic* — in other words fear or shed water — in order to reduce ice buildup. That makes sense but how does one build water aversion into an antenna?

Further investigation on the Internet revealed that certain coatings are made to shed water easier and therefore could possibly reduce the ice buildup. Coatings of epoxy, teflon or silicone were "tight skinned" and supposedly could easily shed water.

I found some information about enclosing the antenna in a protective radome as a potential solution. Commercial FM broadcast antennas and certain radar antennas use protective radomes. For a long boom amateur beam, a radome would be impractical due to increased wind loading. They would likely also add significant cost.

Quantum physics tells us that black materials radiate and absorb light energy more readily than lighter color materials. Most people know that black objects warm up faster than white objects in the sun (and they cool down faster in the dark). That's why people generally wear light colored clothes in the sunlight and also why solar heater panels are painted black inside. It seems reasonable then to assume that black antennas would absorb sunlight and melt ice faster than light aluminum colored antennas.

For many years, I have been using the do-it-yourself aluminum available in most hardware stores for making beam antennas. There are usually choices available in a rack of different sized aluminum tubes, rods, angles, channels, flat stock and sheet stock. I've used these materials to make equipment mounts, antennas and mounting brackets, including a rugged tri-band ground plane antenna described in *QST*.[1]

Building a Suitable Yagi

I wanted to use readily available materials to make our ice-resistant beam antennas. Therefore, do-it-yourself aluminum, stainless bolts and clamps and schedule 30 PVC pipe were the materials of choice.

I discovered a self-priming all-weather epoxy spray paint called VHT, available in automotive supply stores, that would aid in shedding the water as well as provide a black body for a solar heating effect. A black epoxy powder coating sprayed on the antenna might also provide a similar effect but would cost more so I opted for the epoxy spray paint. Two cans of spray paint will provide two coats.

Design Objectives

Here is a summary of the objectives I had in mind while designing the ice-resistant beam antenna. The criteria can be applied to just about any VHF or UHF beam type antenna.

■ Use lightweight aluminum available in most hardware stores.

[1]Notes appear on page 205.

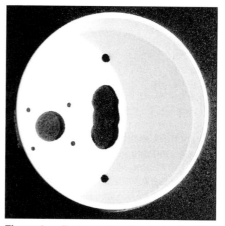

Figure 3 — End cap showing holes for the driven element weld, the Type N chassis connector and two screw holes to fasten it to the boom.

■ Use square tubing for the boom, and solid rods for the elements to make it strong.
■ Use welded construction if available (see sidebar for more information).
■ Protect the driven element match with a shroud.
■ Make it hydrophobic to shed or resist water.
■ Make it black to absorb solar energy and more easily melt ice buildup.
■ Use stainless bolts, screws and U-bolts in constructing and mounting the antenna.[2]
■ Use a Type N coax chassis fitting and elbow for low loss and water resistance.

Construction

The beam is made from 1 inch square aluminum tubing stock 72 inches long. The driven element is made from ½ inch aluminum rod and all the other elements are made from ¼ inch aluminum rod, all available at most hardware stores. The solid rod elements are more durable against falling ice than tubing. The element dimensions for 222 MHz are shown in Table 1. All these techniques should also be applicable at 146 or 440 MHz with your favorite Yagi dimensions.

The gamma matching bar is made from ⅜ inch diameter aluminum tubing. It contains a short piece of polyethylene insulated center

Table 1

Element Lengths for 222 MHz Yagi (inches)

Reflector	26⅛
Driven element	24¹⁵⁄₁₆
Director 1	23¾
Director 2	23½
Director 3	23¼
Director 4	23
Director 5	22⅝
Director 6	22⅜

conductor removed from RG-8 coax, with one end soldered to the Type N connector.

The center-to-center spacing between all the elements is 10 inches with 1 inch at each end of the boom. Square plastic caps, available at hardware stores, were used to plug each end of the boom.

The shroud covering the gamma match and driven element half is made from schedule 30 PVC pipe as shown in Figure 2. It consists of two 3 inch end caps and a short section of 3 inch pipe cut 14 inches long. Note that 3 inch PVC end caps have an actual outside diameter of 3½ inches. One end cap is drilled as shown in Figure 3 to go over the driven element weld flush against the boom. It's fastened to the boom with two #8 stainless sheet metal screws. It's also drilled to accept the chassis mount connector, which is mounted on the outside of the cap on a 1 × 1¼ inch aluminum angle 1 inch wide and drilled to accept the Type N chassis connector. The connector is fastened with four #4 stainless bolts to the 1 inch aluminum angle bracket flush against the PVC cap. The center pin of the Type N chassis connector has the RG-8 coax center conductor soldered in it and protrudes through the cap. The gamma match ⅜ inch tubing slides over the RG-8 coax center conductor and is clamped to the driven element.

The gamma match clamp can be made from two pieces of ½ inch wide ¹⁄₁₆ inch thick flat stock formed as a clamp between the ½ inch driven element and the ⅜ inch gamma tube. Two #6 stainless bolts secure the clamp after it's adjusted for the best match.

The other cap has several ¹⁄₁₆ inch moisture drain holes in it. Both caps are fastened to the PVC pipe with two #6 stainless sheet metal screws. After cutting the elements to length, chamfer the ends slightly by lightly filing.

Measure, mark and drill the boom for each element. Use a drill press to maintain alignment and straightness. Then weld each element in the boom. As an alternative method, you could fasten the elements with stainless steel panhead bolts, as described in the sidebar.

After drilling one of the PVC end caps to fit over the driven element, drill it to mount to the side of the boom with two #8 stainless sheet metal screws.

Gamma Match Construction

The gamma match tube is made from ⅜ inch diameter aluminum tubing 5 inches long. The capacitor insert is made from the center conductor of RG-8 coax and is 4 inches long. One end is soldered to the Type N chassis connector. Following assembly, the gamma tube is moved, along with the shorting clamp, for the best match — the point with the lowest SWR. Be sure and mount the beam away from metal objects

Welding Aluminum Elements

For antenna ruggedness and durability under heavy icing conditions, it's best to weld the elements to the boom. There are several ways to weld aluminum; either find someone capable, locate a friendly welding shop (in the phone book) or do it yourself using the inexpensive *Alumaloy* rods available in hardware stores or on the Internet. These allow welding with a standard propane torch. Working with them is similar to soldering copper pipe and therefore the normal propane soldering safety precautions are applicable. Make sure you wear safety glasses and heavy gloves and work in a clear safe area.

If aluminum welding is not available, an alternative construction method using stainless bolts is viable. See Figure A. After drilling the boom for the elements, prepare the elements. Put each element in a vise and lightly mark the center with a center punch, and then drill through the center of each ¼ inch

element using a number 43 drill bit. Tap each element center hole using a 4-40 tap. Check to ensure a 4-40 bolt will enter the threads. Then using a ⅛ inch bit, drill a hole in the boom centered between each element hole as shown in Figure 4. On the ½ inch diameter driven element, drill the center with a number 36 drill bit and tap for a 6-32 bolt. Check

to ensure a 6-32 bolt will enter the threads. Remove any burrs. Insert the elements into the boom and fasten each with a stainless 4-40 × ¾ inch panhead bolt and star washer. Use a 6-32 × ¾ inch stainless pan head bolt and star washer to fasten the driven element to the boom. Tighten each element bolt a quarter turn snug.

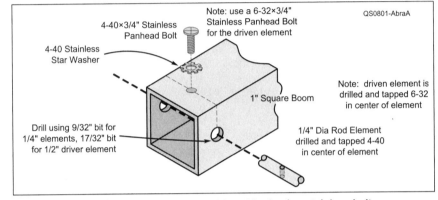

Figure A — Illustration of alternate assembly method using stainless bolts.

or hold the beam high and pointing straight up while adjusting for minimum SWR. Details of gamma construction are shown in Figure 4.

Make a 1 × 1¼ inch aluminum angle bracket 1 inch wide from 1⁄16 inch thick angle stock. This will be used to mount the Type N

chassis connector to the PVC cap and to the boom. Drill out the 1¼ × 1 inch side to the pattern of the Type N connector. The 1 × 1 inch side will mount to the boom with two #6 stainless sheet metal screws. Following final assembly, use some silicon caulk to seal

between the PVC cap, the boom and around the Type N connector.

Mast Attachment

The antenna balance point (center of gravity) is in between directors D1 and D2. This is the place where the mounting clamp should be installed.[2] The antenna is mounted vertically on a horizontal mast. The mounting clamp is thus drilled vertically through the square boom.

Finishing Touches

Following final assembly, check the SWR and set the gamma match. Do it with the shroud off. When it looks good enough, slip the shroud over and recheck the SWR. I expected some dielectric loading effects but found little difference. Then spray everything with the black epoxy spray paint (except the coax fittings). Spray the PVC end caps and pipe, both on the inside and outside, before final assembly. Fasten the end caps with two #6 stainless sheet metal screws in each cap. Spray the boom and elements with the black epoxy paint. Two coats should do it, then be careful handling the antenna to avoid scratching the black paint. Check the SWR again to confirm there is no, or very little, change.

Note that there will likely be a change in the SWR after the antenna is in its final

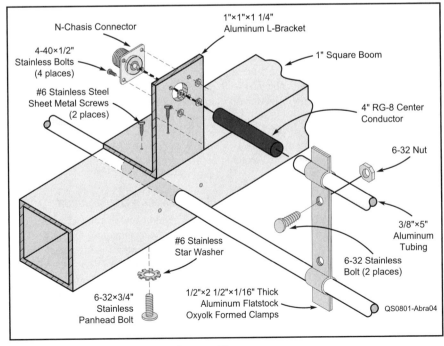

Figure 4 — Details of gamma match assembly.

position due to height and surrounding differences than when you checked it on the ground. It's the Antenna God's Law!

Finally, remember to waterproof the coax connection to the beam either by wrapping it with tape, a butyl rubber sealant, or shrink tubing. Be sure to mount the antenna with the shroud pointing down.

Performance

This antenna was installed in the fall of 2006 replacing a problematic auxiliary link beam that would continually fail to transmit during winter ice and snow storms. When we took the problem antenna down, we noticed that two of the eight elements were broken off due to falling ice.

Since installing the new shrouded beam, we've had three severe storms, one with up to an inch of ice that coated everything. The new beam antenna kept transmitting the vital link signal without failure. Although our observations are limited so far, that's all the proof we need!

Thanks to Tom Parker, KC8YOE, of YOE Antennas for helping to fabricate and weld two antennas for the link system. He welds some beautiful antennas!

Notes

[1]R. Abraczinskas, W8HVG, "A Rugged Broadband Tri-Band VHF-UHF Base Antenna," *QST*, May 2004, p 39.

[2]An excellent stainless U-bolt mast clamp is available from DX Engineering at **DXEngineering.com** or 1-800-777-0703.

Photos by the author.

Ray Abraczinskas, W8HVG, was first licensed as W3HJR in 1956, and as KA2MA in Japan in 1957 (see his listing on **www.qrz.com** *for details). He holds a BSEE and retired in 2001 as a special projects manager from Smiths Aerospace in Grand Rapids, Michigan. He enjoys ham radio, genealogy, fishing in Canada and writing. He also assists the Independent Repeater Association with building and maintaining the Michigan Link Repeater System (***www.w8hvg.org***). You can contact him at 4295 Kentridge SE, Grand Rapids, MI 49508; or* **abra@i2k.com**. QST

Constructing a Flagpole Antenna

Sometimes adversity can work to a ham's advantage.

Geoff Haines, N1GY

In the middle of the 2008 holiday season, a kind of catastrophe struck at our house. A significant amount of damage was caused by a water line that broke during the night. My wife, Audrey, and I eventually had to find a new home. This, in a strange way, turned out to be a blessing in disguise. Our new home is only about two blocks from our old one, but it is considerably newer and actually has a spare room that I immediately requisitioned for the "radio room."

Getting Back on the Air

As soon as the domestic necessities of moving and setting up housekeeping in our new home were taken care of, work began on the location of my station. Most of the furniture from the old radio room was used, if in a slightly different layout, the radios were hooked up and power was run. Some very good friends of mine from our local club, The Manatee Amateur Radio Club, volunteered to help me get the VHF and UHF antennas mounted on my roof. Coax was run to the radio room and I was soon back on the air. The only difficulty was found to be the HF side of things.

At our previous residence, I had used a commercial multi-band HF antenna for several years. It served me well and rarely needed any attention. My mounting system was an old telescopic TV type mast with

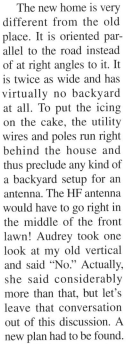

a universal joint at the base to permit the antenna and mast to be tilted to the ground when a hurricane was imminent. The mast was secured to the roof at two places and never gave us a problem.

A Horse of a Different Hue

The new home is very different from the old place. It is oriented parallel to the road instead of at right angles to it. It is twice as wide and has virtually no backyard at all. To put the icing on the cake, the utility wires and poles run right behind the house and thus preclude any kind of a backyard setup for an antenna. The HF antenna would have to go right in the middle of the front lawn! Audrey took one look at my old vertical and said "No." Actually, she said considerably more than that, but let's leave that conversation out of this discussion. A new plan had to be found.

I did notice that many of my neighbors had flagpoles in their front yards and so the thought occurred to me that maybe that was a solution to my dilemma. You will note that I have not mentioned anything about restrictive covenants. That is because there aren't any where I live. When we first moved to the development a number of years ago, I specifically asked the park owner about Amateur Radio antennas. His answer was simple: "As long as it doesn't look like the

Johnson Space Center, you'll be okay." To that end, I have steered clear of large dish antennas and HF Yagis and everyone seems happy.

Run it up the Flagpole

No, the problem here was one of simple esthetics, and the judge of what would be acceptable sleeps right beside me every night. An antenna combined with a flagpole seemed to be the right way to go. At the Orlando Hamcation in February, I purchased a remote HF automatic antenna tuner. After diligent research into what would best suit my situation I chose an ICOM AH-4 based on several factors — size, compatibility with my ICOM IC-706 MkIIG and ease of connection to the flagpole. For your station, another tuner may be more appropriate — as long as it will automatically match a wide range of loads and handle your transmitter's power.

Now I had a site (the middle of the front lawn), I had a tuner (the AH-4), and I had a plan for the radial runs under the sod. What was I forgetting? Oh yeah, the antenna/flagpole! There are several manufacturers of flagpole type antennas, and other antennas that can be disguised as a flagpole. I even visited with a fellow ham who built a flagpole around a commercial trap vertical that was featured in an issue of *QST* a few years ago.[1] I was all set to follow one of those paths when a member of our ham club mentioned that I could have an old sailboat mast from his back yard. What a find! For free, the price was right. The overall length was 22 feet. It even broke down into two sections, so it would be easy to get home. It was made of aluminum tubing, was light weight and even had some of the hardware attached so turning it into a flagpole would be simple.

Making it Happen

Initially, I thought that this would be dirt simple. Then I realized that I had to mount it so that it would stay vertical. I also had to design some way to take it down should one of our frequent hurricanes head my way. Here is where the sticky bit began. The mast has a diameter of 2½ inches at the bottom. This diameter transitions to 2 inches at the junction of the two mast sections. I checked with several vendors of tilt over mounts and all were very helpful, but none had a mount that could handle anything over 2 inches of mast diameter.

And I did want a tilt over mount. I don't know about anyone else, but I did not want to try balancing a 22 foot mast while trying to lower it gently to the ground. I wanted to be able to remove one or two bolts and smoothly walk the mast down to a horizontal position. At that point I can remove the other bolts and disassemble the mast in relative comfort.

[1] J. Ebner, N8JE, "Flagpole Vertical," *QST*, Apr 2007, p 21.

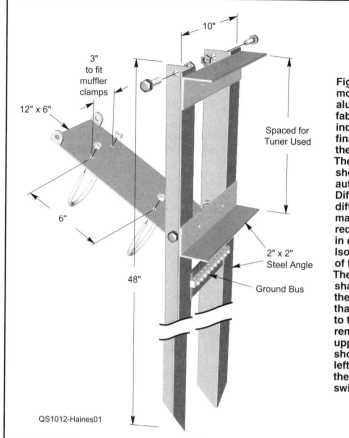

10"

3"
to fit
muffler
clamps

12" x 6"

6"

48"

Spaced for
Tuner Used

2" x 2"
Steel Angle

Ground Bus

QS1012-Haines01

Figure 1 — The mount for the aluminum mast as fabricated. Also indicated is the final location for the AH-4 tuner. The dimensions shown apply to the author's antenna. Different tuners or different antenna masts might require a change in dimensions. Isometric view of the mount. The sideways U shapes indicate the muffler clamps that hold the mast to the mount. By removing the upper two bolts (as shown) holding the left plate in place, the antenna can be swiveled down.

Figure 2 — View of the finial on top of the mast shows how a toilet tank float and a little wire can be used to extend the antenna to a full 23 feet.

Figure 3— Base of the antenna with the enclosure in place and the surrounding flowers in full bloom.

Out came the graph paper and pencils (and the erasers too, if you must know). I tried to avoid reinventing the wheel and looked closely at the various tilt mounts available commercially. From one I took the idea of a solid base plate with the antenna/flagpole attached via U bolts. I insulated the mast from the mount with a section of PVC pipe — the darker type used for electrical conduit, since the white stuff is not tolerant of too much UV light. The white PVC works fine for situations in which not too much stress is placed on it, such as a radome for a VHF antenna or the like, but with even a light weight 22 foot mast, the extra support of the slightly thicker gray PVC is appreciated.

From another manufacturer I pinched the idea of a kind of *pickle fork* mount, driven deep into the ground. If necessary, this, like most others, can be surrounded with a concrete footing to add weight and permanence to the mount. In evaluating the other flagpoles in our neighborhood, I found that most of them were simply supported by driving a PVC sleeve into the ground and placing the pole into the sleeve. Some, however, had been mounted in a concrete filled hole dug into the soil.

I figured that I would wait until the time came to actually place the mount before making that decision. More on that later.

Figure 1 shows my basic design. I deliberately oversized the bolts and used steel rather than aluminum. Not being a structural engineer, I figured the safe approach was to look at what the commercially available units were made of and go up at least two notches in size. I took my design to a local welding shop and after a few modifications suggested by the owner, he proceeded to whip up the whole thing in just about one hour. The cost was no more than some of the commercial tilt mounts on the market.

After the mount was constructed, it was time for paint. I chose to paint the mast and the mount with white metal primer first, and then finish with a good grade of exterior white enamel. The finial on the very top of the mast, to be mentioned a little later, was painted with a spray can of metallic gold color paint so that the entire assembly would look as traditional as possible.

When I began to attempt driving my steel mount into our front lawn, I quickly realized that the ground under our lawn was much harder than that of my neighbors. I immediately borrowed a post hole digger from one of the neighbors and proceeded to dig a two and a half foot deep hole with it. The hole wound up sort of oval in shape because I had to allow for the fact that the mount had two legs. After the mount was placed in the hole, with a little gravel for drainage at the bottom, I poured in a bag of quick setting concrete obtained from the local home improvement store. One gallon of water was added as per the instructions on the bag. By this time the mount had been braced and held level and perpendicular with an assortment of scrap wood braces, to be removed once the concrete had set. With all of that done, I could now begin the process of erecting the flagpole.

I let the concrete cure for more than 24 hours before I removed the wood braces. Since I had already attached the tilting portion of the mount to the bottom section of the flagpole, it was relatively easy to attach the tilting plate to the steel uprights of the mount using the two large bolts that fit into the nuts welded on the back side of the plate. With Audrey's help, I then walked the flagpole up to the vertical plane. While she steadied it, I inserted the other two bolts at the top of the plate to hold it firmly perpendicular to the lawn. Before raising the mast to its final position, I added a 12 inch extension to the top, bringing the overall length to 23 feet. ICOM specifies that length as the minimum for 10 to 80 meter coverage using the AH-4. Only about 8 inches of the whip is visible above the copper toilet tank ball that I attached to the top of the mast to make the transition to flagpole complete (see Figure 2). A short piece of wire with ring terminals soldered at both ends makes the electrical connection from mast to the finial extension. With the extension painted a nice gold color, the humble origin of the finial is completely disguised.

The End Result

The flagpole antenna looks very nice in the middle of the front lawn, surrounded as it is by flowering plants installed by Audrey and me. The planting bed is protected from the lawn service's weed whacker by a ring of concrete edging blocks (see Figure 3). The plantings also hide what few wires are above ground, completely disguising the fact that it really is an antenna with a flag on it. I purchased a very nice 3 × 5 foot flag from a local flag dealer and 40 feet of ³⁄₁₆ inch rope, along with a cleat to secure the rope about 4½ feet above the ground completing the flagpole disguise. Now to get to the bits that turn this flagpole into an HF antenna.

The AH-4 tuner is mounted to the "back" of the mount, while the tilting part of the mount is on the front. At the point where the mount disappears underground there is a flat steel strap welded across the legs of the structure. This has an electrical ground buss attached to it to accept the wire radials. The ground connection on the AH-4 is also wired to this buss bar. An 8 foot ground rod driven near the legs of the mount is also tied to this point. This ground rod is connected by a large size wire to the ground rod just outside the radio room.

The coax, ground wire and control cable are buried from the mount to the house about 6 to 8 inches deep. A direct bury rated coax was purchased for this application. The control cable is four conductor cable obtained from a local electronics supply house. I have used this type of cable before to remotely control other auto tuners on ARRL Field Days. A lightning arrestor was inserted in the coax run and connected to the ground rod near the base of the mount rather than at a point just outside the house. The ground rod at the base of the antenna was connected via a #6 AWG copper wire to both the station ground rod and the house safety ground.

The Radials Finish the Story

The radial arrangement I use cannot be called optimum. The lawn area I can use is probably no more than 40 × 30 feet, with the mast just about in the center. The screened porch of our house encroaches on this area somewhat, so the radials were laid and buried where I could. A total of 4 were placed, roughly at 90° intervals around the base, varying from 10 to 25 feet in length. I used about 100 feet of #18 AWG vinyl insulated wire from a local auto parts store. I know that is not nearly broadcast station quality, but with such a constricted site, it was the best I could do. The sod was cut using an electric edger and the wire was placed in the resulting slit trench about 1 to 2 inches below the bottom of the grass. I had originally planned to install about 300 feet of radials, but the work involved turned out to be more than I could tolerate. More may be added later if I suddenly become 25 again. The radials are all connected to the base of the antenna flagpole (see Figure 6) along with the 8 foot ground rod driven at the base of the mount.

The entire base mount is hidden by the simple expedient of taking a surplus kitchen waste basket and inverting it over the base mount, tuner and the assorted cables. At the top of the waste basket (now the bottom of the enclosure) about 4 inches was cut off to allow the top of the enclosure to sit right on the top of the base mount. A 3 inch diameter hole was cut off center in the bottom of the waste basket (now the top of the enclosure) and several cuts made outward from the hole to allow it to be maneuvered around the base without having to remove the mast first. These cuts were then secured by screwing small aluminum plates over them. If I need to work on the tuner or the connections, the enclosure can be lifted up and rotated so that it sits on the top of the mount while I make any needed adjustments to the system.

Once all this is done, I simply rotate the enclosure back to its normal position and it slides down the mast until it meets the planting bed that surrounds the base. The white plastic of the enclosure matches the white paint of the mast well and, since the flowers around the base have grown a bit, all anyone can really see is the top couple of inches of the enclosure. The enclosure is not waterproof and it was not intended to be. Really, it is just there to cover the tuner and all the wires and cables that attach to it, purely for esthetic value. If your antenna is in the middle of your front lawn, it pays to think about the esthetics of the situation.

While I do not spend a lot of time on HF and certainly am not what one could call a contester, I wanted to have an antenna that would let me use the capabilities of my radio to the degree I needed. That statement brings us to the obvious question: "So, how does it work?" Once the labor of installing radials and coax and control lines was done, the testing began.

So, How's It Play?

I am quite sure that those hams who are lucky enough to have towers and multiband Yagis on big rotators running the legal limit will be quite underwhelmed by the results. But for those of us who, for one reason or another cannot put up big towers or who have to go to stealth mode due to covenant restrictions, even a half decent antenna is better than none at all.

Given the experience I had with my commercial vertical for the past eight or nine years, I would say the results are satisfactory. With my previous setup and 100 W, I was pretty much able to work most of the stations I could hear and I find much the same to be true with the flagpole antenna. The addition of coverage on 75 meters is welcome as the previous antenna was only designed to go down to 40 meters. Because I live only a couple of miles from the Gulf of Mexico, the water table is quite high so the performance is somewhat enhanced compared to another location on higher or rockier terrain.

The point of all this is simple. If your site is less than optimum, or if antenna restrictions limit what you can set up, you do not have to forgo your HF privileges. You just have to get a little creative and hide the antenna in plain sight. Just make sure that you pay attention to the details. As someone once said: "Take care of the little details and the big picture will take care of itself."

Photos by the author.

*ARRL member Geoff Haines, N1GY, was first licensed in 1992 as N1LGI. Geoff upgraded to Amateur Extra in 2005 and received his current call sign. He retired following a career in respiratory care. Geoff currently holds several ARRL appointments in the West Central Florida Section, including Assistant Section Manager, Technical Coordinator and Net Manager among others. He is a past president of the Manatee Amateur Radio Club, and a member of several ham radio clubs both in Florida and Connecticut. In his spare time, Geoff is the editor of the quarterly e-magazine "The Experimenter" for the West Central Florida Section. Geoff is active in designing small projects such as antennas and accessories suitable for the new ham. He also finds time to update his Web site, **www.n1gy.com**, on a regular basis. Recently, his wife Audrey became licensed as KJ4YMX. Geoff can be reached at 904 52nd Avenue Blvd W, Bradenton, FL 34207 or at **n1gy@arrl.net**.*

By Allen Baker, KG4JJH

A 6 Meter Moxon Antenna

Discover 6 meters for the first time or enhance your existing operation with a rugged but portable version of this novel 2 element antenna.

I was amazed by the response to my Black Widow antenna in the May 2003 *QST*.[1] I subsequently helped quite a few builders locate the hard-to-find fishing pole spreaders and I also addressed several details about its construction. Many had never heard of this antenna configuration and enjoyed building it. While the wire version of the Moxon rectangle is a proven performer, a tubular version provides broader bandwidth and slightly more gain. The two antennas presented here are based on an article by L.B. Cebik, W4RNL.[2] The first is horizontally polarized for CW and SSB use at the low end of the 6 meter band (50-51 MHz) and the second is vertically polarized for FM use at the upper portion (52-54 MHz). For ease of reference, I refer to the first as H-POL and the second as V-POL. All materials have been chosen to withstand the elements and are available locally or via the Internet for under $100.

The Moxon Rectangle

I used the program *MoxGen*[3] to generate models at 50.5 and 53.0 MHz, using $5/8$ inch OD aluminum tubing. I then fine-tuned them with *EZNEC*[4] to allow for the different tubing sizes. The 6 meter Moxon is built from $5/8$ inch OD and $1/2$ inch OD aluminum tubing with $3/8$ inch OD solid aluminum for the corners. The detailed construction drawings, sheets and *EZNEC* models for both versions are available at **www.arrl. org/files/qst-in-depth.** Scroll down to the 2004 section and look for the file 6 meter moxon.zip. A basic outline drawing of the antenna is shown in Figure 1, while the full material list is available on the Web site. I built the antenna to the dimensions in the *EZNEC* model listed on Sheet 1.

Construction

Drawing Sheet 1 presents an overview of the antenna assembly. Each component of the antenna is identified by a letter designation (A_0, A_1, A_2, etc). After choosing which version you want to build, follow the Material Cutting Schedule to get the correct quantity, material and length. All materials are easily cut with a tubing cutter, hacksaw or band saw.

Figure 2—A bottom view of the completed antenna clearly shows the fiberglass insulators separating the driven element from the reflector.

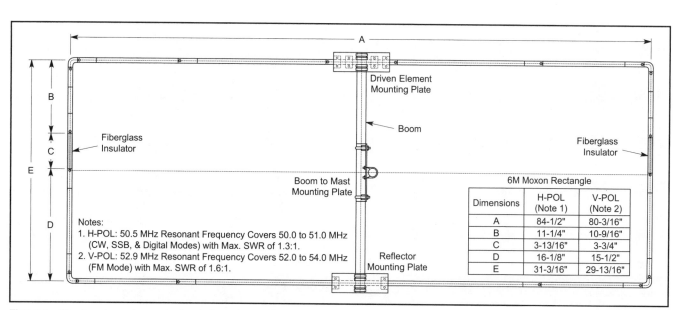

Dimensions	H-POL (Note 1)	V-POL (Note 2)
A	84-1/2"	80-3/16"
B	11-1/4"	10-9/16"
C	3-13/16"	3-3/4"
D	16-1/8"	15-1/2"
E	31-3/16"	29-13/16"

6M Moxon Rectangle

Notes:
1. H-POL: 50.5 MHz Resonant Frequency Covers 50.0 to 51.0 MHz (CW, SSB, & Digital Modes) with Max. SWR of 1.3:1.
2. V-POL: 52.9 MHz Resonant Frequency Covers 52.0 to 54.0 MHz (FM Mode) with Max. SWR of 1.6:1.

Figure 1—The 6 meter antenna design is based on a Moxon rectangle. Its basic dimensions are shown. Definitive construction details can be found on the ARRL Web site (**www.arrl.org/files/qst-binaries/6 meter moxon.zip**).

Figure 3—A top view of the antenna mounting plates.

Figure 4—A bottom view of the mounting plates. Note the insulated element support blocks that are discussed in the text.

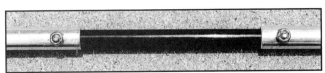

Figure 5—One of the insulators that separates the reflector from the driven element.

Figure 6—The driven element SO-239 wiring details. The driven element can also be wired directly, as outlined in the text.

After cutting, use a $^3/_4$ inch countersink bit and a file to deburr the inside and outside edges of the tubing. Add the common components (such as channel and stainless steel hardware) and you will be ready to begin assembly. All of the necessary materials are listed on Sheet 7 along with sources for each. Figure 2 gives a view of the completed antenna, without the mast.

Mounting Plates

The driven element, reflector and boom to mast plates are fashioned from structural aluminum channel. This material is overkill for this application, but this method of mounting is sturdy enough to be used on tubular Moxons up to 20 meters or more (by scaling the mounts and tubing upward). There is absolutely no flexing or bending of the mounts and the finished antenna is very solid.

The channel is easily cut with a band saw and a metal cutting blade. Cut three pieces 8 inches long and lay out all holes according to the dimensions shown on Sheets 4 through 6. It's a good idea to smooth all sharp edges on the channel with a file. I use a center punch and a drill press with a $^1/_{16}$ inch bit to get accuracy, then go back and enlarge each hole to its final dimension. Be sure to size the mast saddle clamps to match your mast and use the chart on the drawing for a drill guide. Tap the holes as specified and assemble using the stainless steel saddle clamps and radio support blocks listed. This was my first encounter with the support blocks and they provided a great way to support the elements rigidly while providing isolation from the metal brackets and boom. These blocks, actually industrial insulated tubing clamps, may also be found at hydraulic and piping distributors. Figures 3 and 4 show top and bottom views, respectively, of the completed mounting plates.

Insulators

A pair of insulators that maintain a fixed distance between the tubing ends supports the ends of the antenna elements (within dimension C on Drawing Sheet 1). The insulators are made from $^3/_8$ inch OD × 10 inch solid fiberglass and slide inside the $^1/_2$ inch OD aluminum tubing. Similarly, a $^1/_2$ inch OD × 10 inch solid fiberglass rod is used to join the $^5/_8$ inch OD tubing at the feed point. (Because tubing and fiberglass materials are usually sold in 6 foot lengths, the

shipping costs can be more than the material itself. I recommend ordering enough material for a group of builders to keep the costs down.) An installed insulator can be seen in Figure 5.

Feed Point

The installation of an SO-239 coax connector on the 6 meter Moxon adds a bit of reactance to the feed and it is best to attach the coax directly to the driven element.[5] Unfortunately, this was not practical for me, as I use this antenna for portable use and prefer to separate the coax from the antenna. I tried several methods and ended up using the channel as a mount for the SO-239 connector. In the interest of isolating the feed from the antenna, I made an insulator from the end of a $1^1/_2$ inch PVC cap and fastened this and the connector to the channel using nylon screws. Short pieces of 14 gauge insulated wire connect the SO-239 to the driven element. Apply a weatherproof sealant to the solder joints. Figure 6 shows the driven element connection.

An alternate method is to fabricate a bracket that mounts the SO-239 directly on the driven element (see Drawing Sheet 7 for details). The brackets are made from $1^1/_2$ inch × $1^1/_2$ inch × $^1/_8$ inch aluminum angle. The connector is mounted on one bracket, which is attached to one side of the driven element. Cut the head off of a 6-32 × 1 inch copper screw, file one end down to fit inside the SO-239 center pin and solder. Use 6-32 nuts on either side to clamp the second bracket, which is attached to the other side of the driven element. Apply a weatherproof sealant to the solder joint and copper materials.

Corners

Cut the $^3/_8$ inch OD aluminum rod into four 8 inch lengths and chuck each into your drill or drill press. While rotating the rod, use a file to smooth the edges to ensure a smooth fit inside $^1/_2$ inch OD aluminum tubing. The $^3/_8$ inch OD solid aluminum rod is fairly soft and easy to bend. My method is to mark the center and place a scrap piece of $^1/_2$ inch OD × 12 inch aluminum tubing over each end (to give some leverage) and slide it near the mark. I then place the $^3/_8$ inch rod over a vise-mounted $^1/_4$ inch drill bit and smoothly push the tubing down until I have a 90° bend. See Sheet 7 for a corner detail. A completed corner can be seen in Figure 7.

Fasteners

The 6-32 stainless steel fasteners were chosen to provide reasonable strength and corrosion resistance without having to drill very large holes in the tubing. The stop nuts provide a vibration-proof fastener without using lock washers.

Assembly

I prefer to assemble the antenna parts loosely and then go back and install the fasteners. Mark the center of the $^1/_2$ inch OD fiberglass rod (A_0) and $^1/_8$ inch on either side. Slide the fiberglass inside both pieces of $^5/_8$ inch OD tubing (A_1) up to the $^1/_8$ inch marks and place inside the radio support blocks on the driven element mounting bracket. Center the assembly in the bracket and drill holes and install the feed line screws. Mark the center of the $^5/_8$ inch OD aluminum tube (A_3) and mount it in the Reflector Mounting Bracket. Place a line 3 inches from the end on the four $^1/_2$ inch OD tubing lengths (A_2) and slide each into the previously mounted $^5/_8$ inch OD tubing (A_1 and A_3) up to the mark. Place a mark 1 inch from the centerline on each of the four $^3/_8$ inch OD bent corners (A_4) and insert each inside the $^1/_2$ inch OD tubing (A_2) up to that mark. Mark the centerline and a point 3 inches from each end on the $^3/_8$ inch OD fiberglass (C_1) and insert each into the $^1/_2$ inch OD aluminum (B_1 and D_1).

At this point you should have a complete antenna layout. Referring to the Moxon dimensional chart, check each ABCDE measurement and adjust the assembly until you are satisfied. Keep in mind that there should be at least a 3 inch overlap on all tubing-to-tubing and rod-to-tubing transitions. When you are satisfied, clamp the tube positions (I used tape) and drill straight through, installing the stainless steel hardware as you go. Disassemble and clean all metal-to-metal joints. Then, apply an aluminum antioxidant compound to the joints to maintain good electrical contact by preventing oxidation. Reassemble and use an ohmmeter to ensure feed-point isolation from the boom and mounting brackets.

Antenna Models

H-POL—The resonant frequency is 50.5 MHz at a height of 15 feet. This antenna is intended to cover the lower end of the 6 meter band with less than a 1.3:1 SWR, and tests conducted with an MFJ-259B antenna analyzer verified this. The *EZNEC* model predicts the antenna to have a gain of 11 dBi and front-to-back ratio of 25 dB at resonance. The H-POL antenna completed and mounted is shown in Figure 8.

V-POL—The resonant frequency is 53 MHz at a height of 15 feet. This antenna is intended to cover the upper end of the 6 meter band with less than a 1.6:1 SWR. The *EZNEC* model predicts the antenna to have a gain of 6.7 dBi and front-to-back ratio of 36 dB at resonance. The completed V-POL antenna is shown in Figure 9.

SWR Measurement

Upon completion of the H-POL version, I wanted to compare the SWR curve predicted by *EZNEC* with my MFJ-259B analyzer. At first, I was completely baffled by the results. The analyzer showed a much broader curve than I thought possible. W4RNL provided the following explanation:

"If you made the measurements at the end of a length of coax, they will be flatter than at the antenna itself, due to losses in the coax.

Figure 7—A corner of one of the elements.

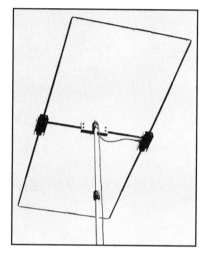

Figure 8—The completed 6 meter Moxon in the horizontal position.

These losses increase with thinner coaxes and are less with 1.2 inch diameter low loss coax cables. Hence, RG-58/U will show a flatter SWR than some of the latest coax types. This is normal behavior. As well, the longer the coax run, the greater the losses and, hence, the flatter the curve. If you are measuring the low SWR at the antenna terminals, then it becomes more likely that the flat curve is a function of equipment limitations."

Armed with this knowledge, I replaced the 50 feet of RG-8X coax that I had been using with a 3 foot run and got much better results with the analyzer. Figure 10 shows the antenna mounted and ready for testing.

Mounting

The finished antenna weighs $8^1/_2$ pounds and is light enough for my trusty painter's pole at a height of 15 feet. The antenna will mount horizontally or vertically by loosening the boom to mast plate saddle clamps and rotating the antenna (see Sheets 2 and 3). If you're industrious, you could mount the H-POL and V-POL on the same boom with different feeds.[6]

6 Meter Activity

Listen for beacons at the lower end of the band. If you hear one, chances are the band is open. Here is a short list of where I have found the most activity:

CW	50.000 to 50.100 MHz
SSB	50.100 to 50.200 MHz
PSK	50.290 MHz
FM	52.000 to 54.000 MHz (simplex and repeaters)

Testing

I decided the best way to test the antenna was to go camping during the July 4 holiday. As luck would have it, tropical storm Bill was passing through our area, so it was raining heavily. We set up camp in a light drizzle and then mounted the Moxon on the painter's pole. A quick check with NG4T (about 50 miles away) told me that the antenna was working. I was S7 on his dipole while running 30

Antenna Patterns and SWR Plots

Here are the both azimuth and elevation antenna patterns for the 6 meter Moxon antenna, including the SWR plots. These are presented for both the vertically and horizontally polarized antennas and were made at a modeled test height of 15 feet. All of the plots were made using *EZNEC* software.

EZNEC predicts a gain of 11.06 dBi for the horizontally polarized Moxon and the constructed antenna appears to verify that model. The SWR has, likewise, been confirmed.

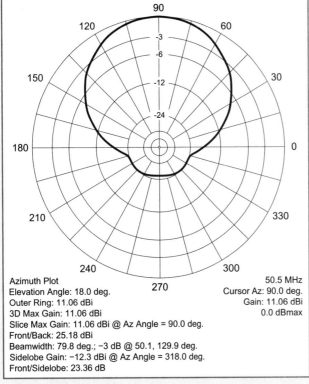

Azimuth Plot
Elevation Angle: 18.0 deg.
Outer Ring: 11.06 dBi
3D Max Gain: 11.06 dBi
Slice Max Gain: 11.06 dBi @ Az Angle = 90.0 deg.
Front/Back: 25.18 dBi
Beamwidth: 79.8 deg.; −3 dB @ 50.1, 129.9 deg.
Sidelobe Gain: −12.3 dBi @ Az Angle = 318.0 deg.
Front/Sidelobe: 23.36 dB

50.5 MHz
Cursor Az: 90.0 deg.
Gain: 11.06 dBi
0.0 dBmax

Figure A—The 6 meter horizontally polarized Moxon azimuth plot at 15 feet.

Elevation Plot
Azimuth Angle: 90.0 deg.
Outer Ring: 11.06 dBi
3D Max Gain: 11.06 dBi
Slice Max Gain: 11.06 dBi @ Elev Angle = 18.0 deg.
Beamwidth: 19.4 deg.; −3 dB @ 8.7, 28.1 deg.
Sidelobe Gain: 7.16 dBi @ Elev Angle = 64.0 deg.
Front/Sidelobe: 3.9 dB

50.5 MHz
Cursor Elev: 18.0 deg.
Gain: 11.06 dBi
0.0 dBmax

Figure B—The elevation plot for the horizontally polarized Moxon at 15 feet.

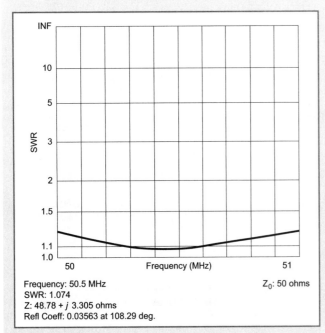

Frequency: 50.5 MHz
SWR: 1.074
Z: 48.78 + *j* 3.305 ohms
Refl Coeff: 0.03563 at 108.29 deg.

Z_0: 50 ohms

Figure C—The SWR of the horizontally polarized Moxon at 15 feet at 50.5 MHz.

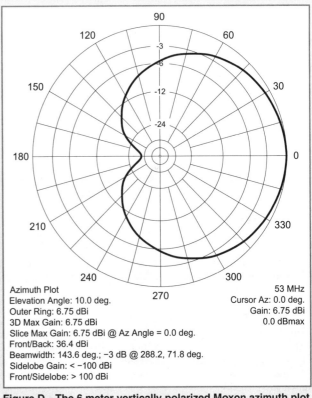

Azimuth Plot
Elevation Angle: 10.0 deg.
Outer Ring: 6.75 dBi
3D Max Gain: 6.75 dBi
Slice Max Gain: 6.75 dBi @ Az Angle = 0.0 deg.
Front/Back: 36.4 dBi
Beamwidth: 143.6 deg.; −3 dB @ 288.2, 71.8 deg.
Sidelobe Gain: < −100 dBi
Front/Sidelobe: > 100 dBi

53 MHz
Cursor Az: 0.0 deg.
Gain: 6.75 dBi
0.0 dBmax

Figure D—The 6 meter vertically polarized Moxon azimuth plot at 15 feet.

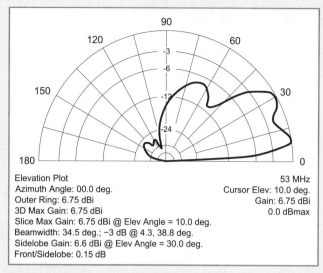

Figure E—The elevation plot for the vertically polarized Moxon at 15 feet.

Elevation Plot
Azimuth Angle: 00.0 deg.
Outer Ring: 6.75 dBi
3D Max Gain: 6.75 dBi
Slice Max Gain: 6.75 dBi @ Elev Angle = 10.0 deg.
Beamwidth: 34.5 deg.; −3 dB @ 4.3, 38.8 deg.
Sidelobe Gain: 6.6 dBi @ Elev Angle = 30.0 deg.
Front/Sidelobe: 0.15 dB

53 MHz
Cursor Elev: 10.0 deg.
Gain: 6.75 dBi
0.0 dBmax

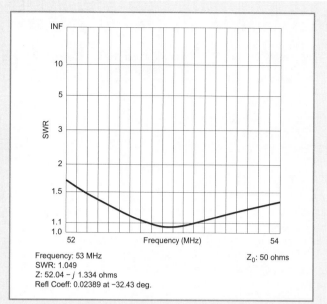

Frequency: 53 MHz
SWR: 1.049
Z: 52.04 − j 1.334 ohms
Refl Coeff: 0.02389 at −32.43 deg.

Z_0: 50 ohms

Figure F—The SWR of the vertically polarized Moxon at 15 feet at 53 MHz.

W SSB. Our contact was quickly joined by WB4GBI, who gave me a 20 dB over S9 report. It continued to rain throughout the night and the next day brought some welcome sunshine and NG4T (my brother) to the campsite. Thanks to an unusual 6 meter opening that weekend, we logged numerous contacts to California, Colorado and Texas on SSB and PSK. On FM, 6 meter repeaters were easily worked with full quieting. I am still on the lookout, however, for that first 6 meter DX contact!

Results

The antenna easily withstood the wet weather and the performance was flawless, with excellent gain, directivity and F/B ratio. The fact that the assembled antenna is small enough to fit in a pickup truck makes it a great portable for camping, Field Day, or an afternoon in the park. So start building—and discover why 6 meters is called the "Magic Band."

Acknowledgments

I would like to thank L.B. Cebik for his advice and expertise, my wife Ann for her continued encouragement and support, and the late Oddis Baker, my father, for his quest for knowledge that he passed on to me.

Notes
[1] A. Baker, KG4JJH, "The Black Widow—A Portable 15 Meter Beam," *QST*, May, 2003, pp 35-39.
[2] **www.cebik.com/6m.html**.
[3] **www.qsl.net/ac6la/moxgen.html**.
[4] **www.eznec.com**.
[5,6] See Note 2.

All photos by the author.

*Allen Baker, KG4JJH, received his license in September 2000, after a lifelong dream of becoming a ham. He holds a BS in Industrial Engineering from Tennessee Technological University and works as an Instrument and Controls Engineer for the Department of Energy in Oak Ridge, Tennessee. Allen is active on the digital modes (6 through 40 meters) and loves to experiment with antenna designs. He can be reached at **kg4jjh@arrl.net**.*

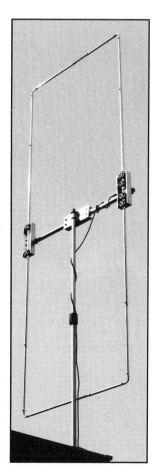

Figure 9—The Moxon mounted for vertical polarization.

Figure 10—A temporary lash-up for testing and adjustment purposes at the author's location.

An Improved Center Insulator for Wire Antennas Fed with Window Line

Richard J. Peacock, W2GFF (SK)

An antenna fed with window or open wire transmission line works better, both electrically and mechanically, if the transmission line is perpendicular to the antenna wire. This arrangement will result in minimum distortion of the antenna pattern due to coupling. In addition, the transmission line conductors will be evenly stressed and localized flexing of the leads will be minimized. The desired configuration is shown in Figure 1.

The Problem Appears

It is often impossible to meet this condition. If the transmission line leaves the antenna at an angle other than 90°, as in Figure 2, one lead will be supporting the weight of the transmission line and the other will have a slack loop. The line is free to twist around the tight lead as the wind moves the transmission line. Both wires will flex or twist locally near the attachment points. This constant flexing and twisting will eventually result in a mechanical failure of the wire connections.

Easy Solution

A solution to this problem is to use a center insulator that has the transmission line attachment points oriented 90° to the antenna wire axis. This basic principle for any open wire balanced line is illustrated in Figure 3.

This configuration automatically equalizes the strain on the two wires of the transmission line because the antenna wire will twist and the whole insulator will rotate around the axis of the antenna wire regardless of the angle at which the line leaves the antenna. With both conductors of the transmission line sharing the load equally there is negligible flexing of these leads. The jumpers between the transmission line and the antenna wire can be made with direct connections that will not see any flexing. This type of center insulator can be used with wide spaced open lines or with window line by choosing appropriate dimensions to match the line spacing.

Insulators for 450 Ω Window Line

I elected to make my insulators from polycarbonate, a very tough plastic with good resistance to UV exposure.[1] Polycarbonate can be machined easily and the cut surfaces can be readily sanded and polished with hand

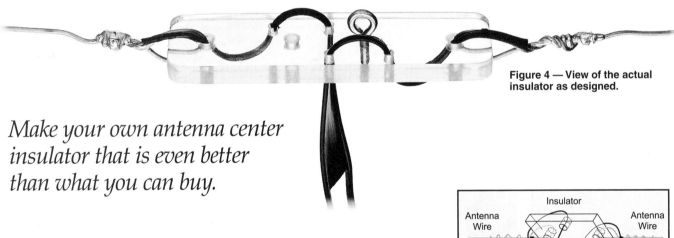

Figure 4 — View of the actual insulator as designed.

Make your own antenna center insulator that is even better than what you can buy.

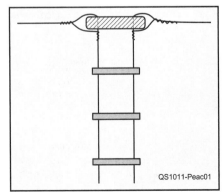

Figure 1 — The usual desired configuration of open wire or window line on the typical insulator. Note that in this position both line conductors are equally stressed.

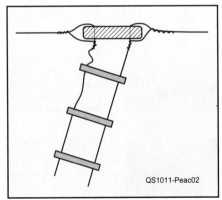

Figure 2 — What really happens as the antenna and line move in the wind. The conductors are subject to unbalanced stress and flexing.

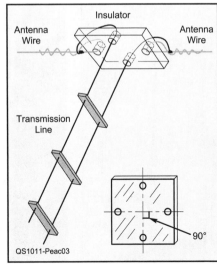

Figure 3 — Making the line attachment perpendicular to the wire access tends to equalize the stress.

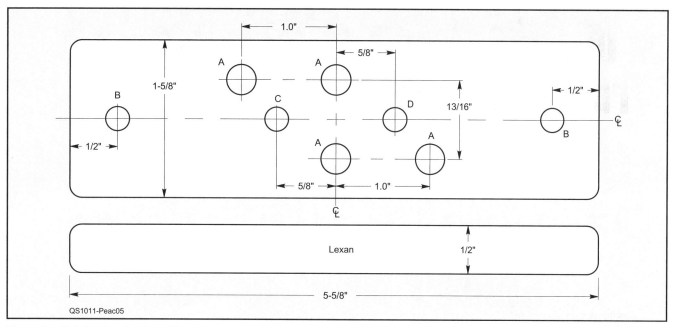

Figure 5 — Fabrication drawing of insulator shown in Figure 4. Your hole diameters may be different, depending on the diameter of the antenna and transmission line wire. My dimensions were: A, ⁵⁄₃₂ inch; B, ¼ inch; C and D, as required for eye bolt or rope line.

QS1011-Peac05

tools. It also does not shatter when dropped on a hard surface.

I have had excellent results by making insulators out of ½ inch thick polycarbonate and drilling the holes for the window line wires as snug fits. By pulling the window line cross piece tight against the insulator and looping the wires back through a second hole, there is negligible motion or flexing of the window line. The leads continue to the antenna loops where they can be soldered. Window line attachments of this type have survived several years of exposure to the weather without any indication of mechanical wear. See Figure 4 for an example of the complete assembly with this type of insulator.

Preparing the Line

Carefully plan the termination of the window line conductors. Determine how many of the window line cross pieces will need to be removed to provide sufficient separated lead lengths to solder to the antenna after looping through the holes in the insulator. Try to maintain the same insulation dimension the entire lead length. I found that this was quite readily accomplished using a band saw. Evenly trimmed insulation will be easier to install in the insulator holes. Snug fit in the holes will ensure that the transmission line will not pull away from the insulator during normal use.

Fabricating the Insulator

Detailed dimensions of my insulators are shown in Figure 5. You may wish to make some changes in hole sizes for different gauge or insulation of your antenna wire and transmission line. A drilling template is suggested for drilling small pilot holes, such as ⁵⁄₆₄ inch, in the Lexan blanks. You may later

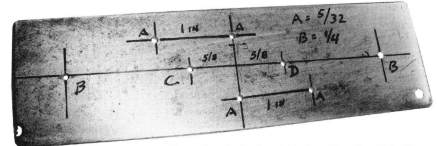

Figure 6 — A sheet metal hole drilling jig will facilitate getting all the pilot holes in the right place.

enlarge these pilot holes to suit your own preferences. A suggested template is shown in Figure 6. The total length of the insulator and the spacing of the antenna wire holes is not critical, but the overall center line between the antenna holes should be used to center the other holes. Centering the antenna wire holes about ⅝ inches from the end appears to provide sufficient material strength for tension loads. The antenna wire holes are chamfered slightly with a countersink to eliminate any sharp edges being presented to the antenna wire loops. The only critical dimension is the spacing of the two A holes that must match the spacing of the transmission line. For my 450 Ω window line this spacing is ¹³⁄₁₆ inch, and ⁵⁄₃₂ diameter was a good snug fit to the insulated conductors.

If sagging of the antenna requires attachment of a support rope, use a stainless steel eye bolt. The hole for the eye bolt can be easily tapped for the required thread. With a full thread the eye bolt will be secure and no locking nut will be required. The eye bolt should be centered with respect to the transmission line. With the eye bolt about ⅝ inch from the

transmission line attachment points there is no indication of any RF problem with about 1200 W to my antenna. If you do not want to use an eye bolt you can simply drill a hole in the same area to pass a rope line, and then tie a secure knot in the rope under the insulator.

[1]J. Wonoski, N1KHB, "An Ideal Plastic for Amateur Radio Projects," *QST*, Oct 2009, pp 42-44.

Amateur Extra class licensee Richard J. Peacock, W2GFF, became a silent key on February 6, 2010 at the age of 90. A longtime resident of Setauket, New York, he was living in Fairhope, Alabama at the time of his death. Richard retired in 1989 from AIL on Long Island, New York after 30 years of service. He was a lifelong Amateur Radio operator, an active member of the South Baldwin Amateur Radio Club, a member of the ARRL and on the DXCC Honor Roll. QST

An Experimental Look at Ground Systems for HF Verticals

In this groundbreaking work we obtain definitive results on ground system effectiveness.

Rudy Severns, N6LF

It's been over 100 years since Marconi used vertical antennas. With such a long history it would seem unlikely that anything new could be said about them. The way Amateur Radio operators use and implement vertical antennas often differs from commercial or military practice leaving amateurs with unanswered questions.

These questions can be addressed analytically or through the use of modeling and simulation, but for most of us neither is quite convincing. Actual measurements on real antennas are a lot more satisfying, at least to verify the modeling.

Some years ago, Jerry Sevick, W2FMI, (SK) published exactly this kind of information in *QST*.[1-5] Reading his articles inspired me to take another experimental look at HF ground systems. The result was an 18 month effort, partly replicating Jerry's work, but also addressing other questions such as the comparison between ground surface and elevated

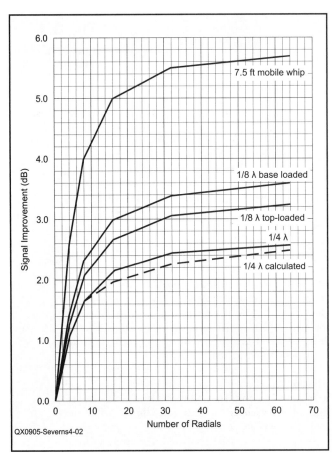

Figure 1 — Typical improvement in signal as ¼ wave radials are added to the basic ground system of a single ground stake.

radial systems. These experiments have been covered in detail in a series of seven *QEX* articles. Since not everyone wants all the gory details, this article is a summary of the more interesting results.[6]

Near and Far

It is important to keep in mind the role of the ground system associated with the radiation from a vertically polarized antenna. The radiation pattern for a vertical is strongly influenced by the characteristics of the soil in the neighborhood of the antenna. This is particularly true at lower angles for which the pattern is determined by soil characteristics out to a great distance (many wavelengths), often referred to as the *far-field* region.[7] As a practical matter we can't usually do much about conditions beyond perhaps ½ wavelength from the base of the vertical, other than select our location — we simply have to accept what's out there. We can, however, do a lot to reduce the losses in the immediate vicinity

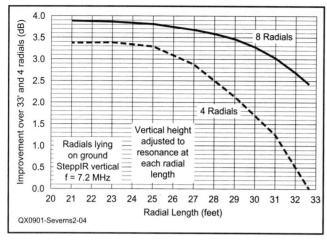

Figure 2 — Effect on signal strength of shortening radial lengths. The 0 dB reference is four 33 foot radials.

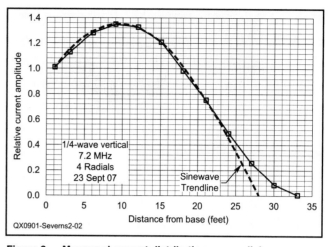

Figure 3 — Measured current distribution on a radial.

of the antenna (the *near-field* region), where the losses can be very high.[8] The purpose of the ground system is to reduce these near-field losses, increasing efficiency and allowing us to radiate as much of the antenna input power as possible, which ultimately improves our signal.

Overview of the Experiments

This work started with a 160 meter vertical with which I varied the number of ¼ wave radials and measured the change in signal strength for a fixed input power. This was interesting and educational but I realized that repeatedly laying down and picking up some 8000 feet of #12 AWG wire was not practical for more extensive investigations. I thus changed the test frequency to 7.2 MHz initially, and later added experiments for multiband ground systems (40 through 10 meters). This initial experiment also stimulated me to use the much more accurate measurement procedure that is outlined in the sidebar on the QST In Depth Web site.[9]

I went through several rounds of experiments, each one answering some questions but, of course, always generating more. In the following three sections we'll consider radials for vertical monopoles — on and above the ground and finally, radial systems for multiband verticals.

Round One — Radials on the Ground

This set of experiments used four different antennas: a ¼ wave vertical, an ⅛ wave vertical with base loading, an ⅛ wave vertical with sufficient top loading to be resonant at 7.2 MHz and a 40 meter mobile whip. I started with a single 4 foot ground stake (zero radials) and then progressively added ¼ wave radials, measuring the changes in signal strength with each increase in radial num-

ber. The results are shown in Figure 1. Note that the graph is in terms of the *improvement* in signal for a given input power for *each* antenna over the single ground stake with no radials. The graph does *not* compare the relative merit of each antenna. Obviously a short, lossy mobile whip will yield less signal, typically 10 dB less, than a full size ¼ wave vertical. The signal improvement metric gives us a direct idea of how much is gained for a given improvement in the ground system.

How Many Radials?

This graph shows several things. First it makes clear just how important a radial system is. It can make a difference of many dB in our signal strength. Keep in mind that the soil over which the experiments were done would be classified as good to very good. Over average or poor soils the signal improvements could be many dB greater than shown here. The second thing the graph shows is the point of diminishing returns. Laying down a system with at least 16 radials will give you most of the obtainable improvement. As we go to 32 and then 64 radials the improvement gets progressively smaller. It's arguable that the improvement from going from 32 to 64 radials is worth the cost and clearly the standard 120 radial BC ground system would be overkill.

A final point the graph makes is that *the shorter and more heavily loaded your vertical, the more you have to gain from improving the ground system.* The shorter the vertical, the higher will be the field intensity (for a given input power) in the near field of the antenna and the lower will be the radiation resistance. This leads to much higher ground losses, which translates to more improvement when you reduce these losses by improving the ground system.

How Long Should They Be?

Radials ¼ wave in length are known to be effective in ground systems, but I wondered what the penalty would be from using shorter radials. I was expecting to see a fairly uniform decrease in signal strength (due to an increase in ground loss) as the radials were shortened. That is *not* what I found. Figure 2 shows the results of an experiment in which I measured the signal strength while progressively shortening the radials in four and eight radial systems.

Surprisingly, shortening the radial lengths *increased* the signal strength — not by just a little bit, but by more than 3 dB. This is certainly counterintuitive, but I was seeing clues that helped explain what was happening. I noticed that with only the ground stake the resonant frequency of the vertical was much lower than expected and, as I added more radials, the resonant frequency increased slowly. Most of the change occurred between 4 and 16 radials and had pretty much leveled out by the time I had 64 radials. This suggested to me that the radials might be self-resonant below 7.2 MHz. To check this out I measured the current distribution on a radial and found it to be sinusoidal. The results are shown in Figure 3.

The maximum current point has been moved from the base of the antenna out onto the radials and this substantially increases the ground loss. The radials are resonant below the band and this affects the antenna. A wire, close to ground, can be heavily loaded by the ground, decreasing its resonant frequency. The extent of the loading will depend on the characteristics of the soil. Figure 3 shows that the maximum current point is 10 to 11 feet away from the base. Looking at Figure 2 we see that the maximum signal occurs when we have shortened the radial by this amount.

Figure 3 also illustrates a difference

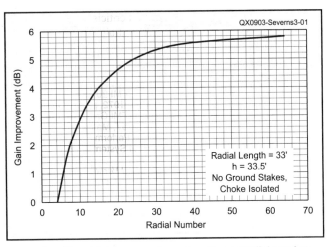

Figure 4 — Signal improvement as a function of radial number. All radials lying on the ground surface, F = 7.2 MHz.

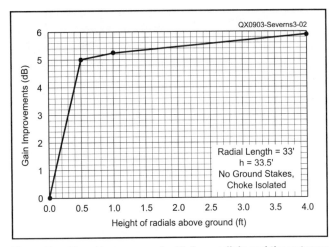

Figure 5 — Signal improvement with four radials and the antenna base at different heights. F = 7.2 MHz.

Table 1

Relative Signal Strengths for 4, 8, 16 and 32 Radials, Comparing Lengths of 33' and 21'

Number of Radials	Normalized to Four 33' Radials (dB) 33' Radials	Normalized To Four 33' Radials (dB) 21' Radials	Gain Change (dB)
4	0	3.08	+3.08
8	2.26	3.68	+1.42
16	3.76	3.95	+0.19
32	4.16	4.04	−0.12

between buried bare wire radials and radials lying on or very near the surface of the soil. The current distribution on a buried bare radial will usually decrease exponentially from the base regardless of its length.[10] You will not see the standing wave shown in Figure 3 except in very poor soils. The insulated radial lying on the ground surface behaves much more like a radial in an elevated radial system in that it has a sine wave-like current distribution. A buried insulated wire will be somewhere in between these two cases depending on the burial depth and soil characteristics.

You can also see in Figure 2 that the signal increases as the radial numbers increase. To check this out I extended the experiment to 32 radials, comparing 33 to 21 foot radials. The results are given in Table 1.

The results in Table 1 indicate that the excess loss due to radial resonance has pretty much disappeared by the time you reach 16 radials. This leads to some advice — rather than trying to determine the optimum radial length, which will vary with every installation due to soil differences, just use at least 16 radials. If you are limited by the total amount of wire available, you're better off to use a larger number of shorter radials rather than a few long ones.

I didn't have time to run an extensive set

of experiments comparing different radial length and radial number combinations (each with the same total length of wire), but I did model that situation with *EZNEC*.[11] The modeling predicted, particularly with short verticals, that it was often advantageous to reduce the length of the radials and increase their number. The modeling showed that there is a correlation between vertical height and optimum radial lengths. More details can be found in the modeling report and in the work of others.[12-15]

Round Two — Elevated Radials

Over the past few years there has been a lot of discussion about the relative merits of ground systems using a large number of surface or buried radials versus only a few elevated radials. This stems from *NEC* modeling that indicated that four radials elevated 8 feet or so above ground could be just as effective as 120 buried radials. Many of us, including me, simply could not believe that.

I decided the best way to address this question would be to directly compare two antennas, one with a large number of ground radials and the other with only a few elevated radials. The same antenna was used in both cases, a simple ¼ wave vertical. For the surface tests I used ¼ wave radials and varied the number from 4 to 64. For the

elevated tests I used four ¼ wave radials. The elevated radials were placed at 0, 6, 12 and 48 inches above ground. The results are shown in Figures 4 and 5. The 0 dB point in the graphs is normalized to the signal strength for the case of four ¼ wave radials lying on the surface (0 dB). What you see in the graphs is the improvement as you either add more surface radials or elevate the antenna and the four radials above ground.

The most striking thing shown by the graphs is that four elevated radials at a height of 48 inches are within 0.2 dB of 64 radials lying on the ground. This would seem to support the predictions from *NEC* modeling. A detailed view of the results with different elevated configurations is provided on the QST In Depth Web site.

Round Three — Multiband Ground Systems

While single band verticals are frequently used, multiband verticals are even more popular but I'd not seen any experimental work related to multiband ground systems. So I did some. The experiments were performed in two phases. The first was for radials lying on the ground and the second was for elevated radials. These represent two typical scenarios for amateurs, helping to answer a related question: "Do I put the antenna in the backyard or up on the roof?" For this series of tests I used a SteppIR III vertical.[16] The motor driven SteppIR can be adjusted to be resonant anywhere between 40 and 6 meters.

For these experiments I made up four sets of thirty-two ¼ wave radials, one set for each band (40, 20, 15 and 10 meters). I then tried several different configurations starting with sets of 32 single band radials, *one set at a time*. In this way I had a ¼ wave vertical over a ground system of thirty-two ¼ wave radials on each band. These antennas were then measured individually on each band. I then tried groups of four and eight (32 total) ¼ radials for each band, connected all at the same time. Next I tried 32 radials each 32 feet long, followed by 16, 8 and 4 at 32 feet each.

Obviously with a multiband antenna you would not run out to the antenna and change the radials whenever you changed bands! But this data can give us a feeling for any compromises resulting from the shift from monoband to multiband ground systems.

Four radials per band (16 radials in a four band system) probably represents the most common multiband ground system in general use both for elevated and ground surface radial systems, and we will use this as one measurement standard. I could have chosen many other possible combinations but those I did choose are at least reasonable. In particular I wanted to show that a few long radials don't work very well whether on the ground or elevated.

Radials Lying on the Ground

A comparison of the relative signal strength of each configuration with radials lying on the ground was made in comparison to the four radials per band case. The detailed results of this and following cases are shown on the QST In Depth Web page. In summary, however, there was little to choose among the cases (1 dB or less) until we came to the four 33 foot case that was down 2 to 4 dB from the standard four radials per band. The best performer is found with the 32 radials of 33 feet each, which is 0.4 to 1 dB better than our standard depending on the band. This case does require almost four times as much wire, however.

In the final analysis it appears that the standard ground system works just fine, but you can add more wire and get some improvement.

Vertical and Radials Elevated 48 inches

Once again the standard multiband radial system of four elevated radials appears to work well, nearly as well as the 32 radials of 33 feet each, although it has an edge of about 1.1 dB on 10 meters. As we move to fewer

long radials, however, we found a problem on 20 meters in which the gain starts to fall quickly. This is related to the fact that the 33 foot, ¼ wave, radials on 40 meters are close to ½ wave radials on 20 meters, presenting a high impedance. At eight 33 foot radials the 20 meter response is down 4 dB, and at four 33 foot radials the performance was so poor I wouldn't consider it a multiband ground system. The four long radials didn't even work well on 15 meters, on which they were close to ¾ wave long.

Elevated Versus Ground Surface Radials

How do elevated multiband and ground surface radial systems compare to each other and to a large number of radials on the ground on each band? While the details are tabulated in the In Depth Web page, some conclusions can be summarized.

The differences between a 32 radial monoband system on the ground and a four radial elevated monoband system on each band are small, as we would expect from our earlier results.

If we compare a 16 radial multiband system on the ground with the same configuration elevated, the elevated system has about a 1 dB advantage on all bands. Doubling the number of radials on the ground will reduce the differences by 0.2 to 0.3 dB. The standard multiband system works just fine if elevated, but when the radials are lying on the ground it's not quite as good. If a radial system lies on the ground, the rule is you should use more radials to achieve comparable performance.

Acknowledgments

I want to acknowledge the helping hands that Mark Perrin, N7MQ, and Paul Thompson, W8EIB, provided in the field during these experiments. My thanks also to Mike Mertel, K7IR, for the loan of a SteppIR vertical for these experiments.

In addition to creating the design for the VNA used in these experiments, Paul Kiciak, N2PK, originally suggested to me the use of a VNA for these experiments when I was moaning and groaning about more conventional techniques. Paul also

provide important criticism at several points to keep me on the straight and narrow

Notes
[1]J. Sevick, W2FMI, "The Ground-Image Vertical Antenna," *QST*, Jul 1971, pp 16-19.
[2]J. Sevick, "The W2FMI 20 Meter Vertical Beam," *QST*, Jun 1972, pp 14-18.
[3]J. Sevick, "The W2FMI Ground-Mounted Short Vertical," *QST*, Mar 1973, pp 13-19.
[4]J. Sevick, "A High Performance 20, 40 and 80 Meter Vertical System," *QST*, Dec 1973, pp 30-33.
[5]J. Sevick, *The Short Vertical Antenna and Ground Radial*, CQ Communications Inc, 2003, ISBN 0-943016-22-3. This is a compendium of Sevick's earlier work.
[6]R. Severns, N6LF, "Experimental Determination of Ground System Performance — Part 1," *QEX*, Jan/Feb 2009, pp 21-25; Part 2, Jan/Feb 2009, pp 48-52; Part 3, Mar/Apr 2009, pp 29-32; Part 4, May/June 2009, pp 38-42; Part 5, Jul/Aug 2009, pp 15-17; Part 6, Nov/Dec 2009, pp 19-24, and Part 7, Jan/Feb 2010, pp 18-19.
[7]R. D. Straw, Editor, *The ARRL Antenna Book*, 21st Edition, pp 3-11 to 3-32. Available from your ARRL dealer or the ARRL Bookstore, ARRL order no. 9876. Telephone 860-594-0355, or toll-free in the US 888-277-5289; **www.arrl.org/shop**; **pubsales@arrl.org**.
[8]R. Severns, N6LF, "Verticals, Ground Systems and Some History," *QST*, Jul 2000, pp 38-44.
[9]**www.arrl.org/qst/qstindepth**.
[10]A. Doty, K8CFU, "Improving Vertical Antenna Efficiency," *CQ*, Apr 1984, pp 24-31.
[11]Several versions of *EZNEC* antenna modeling software are available from developer Roy Lewallen, W7EL, at **www.eznec.com**.
[12]Rudy Severns, N6LF, "Vertical Height Versus Radial Length," 2008. Available at **www.antennasbyn6lf.com**.
[13]J. Stanley, K4ERO, "Optimum Ground Systems for Vertical Antennas," *QST*, Dec 1976, pp 13-15.
[14]R. Sommer, N4UU, "Optimum Radial Ground Systems," *QST*, Aug 2003, pp 39-43.
[15]A. Christman, K3LC, "Maximum Gain Radial Ground Systems for Vertical Antennas," *NCJ*, Mar/Apr 2004, pp 5-10.
[16]**www.steppir.com**.

Rudy Severns, N6LF, was first licensed as WN7WAG in 1954 and has held an Amateur Extra class license since 1959. He is a consultant in the design of power electronics, magnetic components and power conversion equipment. Rudy holds a BSE degree from the University of California at Los Angeles. He is the author of three books, over 90 technical papers and a former editor of QEX. Rudy is an ARRL Life Member and an IEEE Fellow. You can reach Rudy at PO Box 589, Cottage Grove, OR 97424 or at n6lf@arrl.net. **QST**

Nominal Characteristics of Commonly Used Transmission Lines

RG or Type	Part Number	Nom. Z_0 Ω	VF %	Cap. pF/ft	Cent. Cond. AWG	Diel. Type	Shield Type	Jacket Matl	OD inches	Max V (RMS)	Matched Loss (dB/100') 1 MHz	10	100	1000
RG-6	Belden 1694A	75	82	16.2	#18 Solid BC	FPE	FC	P1	0.275	300	0.3	.7	1.8	5.9
RG-6	Belden 8215	75	66	20.5	#21 Solid CCS	PE	D	PE	0.332	2700	0.4	0.8	2.7	9.8
RG-8	Belden 7810A	50	86	23.0	#10 Solid BC	FPE	FC	PE	0.405	300	0.1	0.4	1.2	4.0
RG-8	TMS LMR400	50	85	23.9	#10 Solid CCA	FPE	FC	PE	0.405	600	0.1	0.4	1.3	4.1
RG-8	Belden 9913	50	84	24.6	#10 Solid BC	ASPE	FC	P1	0.405	300	0.1	0.4	1.3	4.5
RG-8	CXP1318FX	50	84	24.0	#10 Flex BC	FPE	FC	P2N	0.405	600	0.1	0.4	1.3	4.5
RG-8	Belden 9913F	50	83	24.6	#11 Flex BC	FPE	FC	P1	0.405	300	0.2	0.6	1.5	4.8
RG-8	Belden 9914	50	82	24.8	#10 Solid BC	FPE	FC	P1	0.405	300	0.2	0.5	1.5	4.8
RG-8	TMS LMR400UF	50	85	23.9	#10 Flex BC	FPE	FC	PE	0.405	600	0.1	0.4	1.4	4.9
RG-8	DRF-BF	50	84	24.5	#9.5 Flex BC	FPE	FC	PE	0.405	600	0.1	0.5	1.6	5.2
RG-8	WM CQ106	50	84	24.5	#9.5 Flex BC	FPE	FC	P2N	0.405	600	0.2	0.6	1.8	5.3
RG-8	CXP008	50	78	26.0	#13 Flex BC	FPE	S	P1	0.405	600	0.1	0.5	1.8	7.1
RG-8	Belden 8237	52	66	29.5	#13 Flex BC	PE	S	P1	0.405	3700	0.2	0.6	1.9	7.4
RG-8X	Belden 7808A	50	86	23.5	#15 Solid BC	FPE	FC	PE	0.240	300	0.2	0.7	2.3	7.4
RG-8X	TMS LMR240	50	84	24.2	#15 Solid BC	FPE	FC	PE	0.242	300	0.2	0.8	2.5	8.0
RG-8X	WM CQ118	50	82	25.0	#16 Flex BC	FPE	FC	P2N	0.242	300	0.3	0.9	2.8	8.4
RG-8X	TMS LMR240UF	50	84	24.2	#15 Solid BC	FPE	FC	PE	0.242	300	0.2	0.8	2.8	9.6
RG-8X	Belden 9258	50	82	24.8	#16 Flex BC	FPE	S	P1	0.242	300	0.3	0.9	3.2	11.2
RG-8X	CXP08XB	50	80	25.3	#16 Flex BC	FPE	S	P1	0.242	300	0.3	1.0	3.1	14.0
RG-9	Belden 8242	51	66	30.0	#13 Flex SPC	PE	SCBC	P2N	0.420	5000	0.2	0.6	2.1	8.2
RG-11	Belden 8213	75	84	16.1	#14 Solid BC	FPE	S	PE	0.405	300	0.1	0.4	1.3	5.2
RG-11	Belden 8238	75	66	20.5	#18 Flex TC	PE	S	P1	0.405	300	0.2	0.7	2.0	7.1
RG-58	Belden 7807A	50	85	23.7	#18 Solid BC	FPE	FC	PE	0.195	300	0.3	1.0	3.0	9.7
RG-58	TMS LMR200	50	83	24.5	#17 Solid BC	FPE	FC	PE	0.195	300	0.3	1.0	3.2	10.5
RG-58	WM CQ124	52	66	28.5	#20 Solid BC	PE	S	PE	0.195	1400	0.4	1.3	4.3	14.3
RG-58	Belden 8240	52	66	29.9	#20 Solid BC	PE	S	P1	0.193	1400	0.3	1.1	3.8	14.5
RG-58A	Belden 8219	53	73	26.5	#20 Flex TC	FPE	S	P1	0.195	300	0.4	1.3	4.5	18.1
RG-58C	Belden 8262	50	66	30.8	#20 Flex TC	PE	S	P2N	0.195	1400	0.4	1.4	4.9	21.5
RG-58A	Belden 8259	50	66	30.8	#20 Flex TC	PE	S	P1	0.192	1400	0.5	1.5	5.4	22.8
RG-59	Belden 1426A	75	83	16.3	#20 Solid BC	FPE	S	P1	0.242	300	0.3	0.9	2.6	8.5
RG-59	CXP 0815	75	82	16.2	#20 Solid BC	FPE	S	P1	0.232	300	0.5	0.9	2.2	9.1
RG-59	Belden 8212	75	78	17.3	#20 Solid CCS	FPE	S	P1	0.242	300	0.2	1.0	3.0	10.9
RG-59	Belden 8241	75	66	20.4	#23 Solid CCS	PE	S	P1	0.242	1700	0.6	1.1	3.4	12.0
RG-62A	Belden 9269	93	84	13.5	#22 Solid CCS	ASPE	S	P1	0.240	750	0.3	0.9	2.7	8.7
RG-62B	Belden 8255	93	84	13.5	#24 Flex CCS	ASPE	S	P2N	0.242	750	0.3	0.9	2.9	11.0
RG-63B	Belden 9857	125	84	9.7	#22 Solid CCS	ASPE	S	P2N	0.405	750	0.2	0.5	1.5	5.8
RG-142	CXP 183242	50	69.5	29.4	#19 Solid SCCS	TFE	D	FEP	0.195	1900	0.3	1.1	3.8	12.8
RG-142B	Belden 83242	50	69.5	29.0	#19 Solid SCCS	TFE	D	TFE	0.195	1400	0.3	1.1	3.9	13.5
RG-174	Belden 7805R	50	73.5	26.2	#25 Solid BC	FPE	FC	P1	0.110	300	0.6	2.0	6.5	21.3
RG-174	Belden 8216	50	66	30.8	#26 Flex CCS	PE	S	P1	0.110	1100	0.8	2.5	8.6	33.7
RG-213	Belden 8267	50	66	30.8	#13 Flex BC	PE	S	P2N	0.405	3700	0.2	0.6	2.1	8.0
RG-213	CXP213	50	66	30.8	#13 Flex BC	PE	S	P2N	0.405	600	0.2	0.6	2.0	8.2
RG-214	Belden 8268	50	66	30.8	#13 Flex SPC	PE	D	P2N	0.425	3700	0.2	0.7	2.2	8.0
RG-216	Belden 9850	75	66	20.5	#18 Flex TC	PE	D	P2N	0.425	3700	0.2	0.7	2.0	7.1
RG-217	WM CQ217F	50	66	30.8	#10 Flex BC	PE	D	PE	0.545	7000	0.1	0.4	1.4	5.2
RG-217	M17/78-RG217	50	66	30.8	#10 Solid BC	PE	D	P2N	0.545	7000	0.1	0.4	1.4	5.2
RG-218	M17/79-RG218	50	66	29.5	#4.5 Solid BC	PE	S	P2N	0.870	11000	0.1	0.2	0.8	3.4
RG-223	Belden 9273	50	66	30.8	#19 Solid SPC	PE	D	P2N	0.212	1400	0.4	1.2	4.1	14.5
RG-303	Belden 84303	50	69.5	29.0	#18 Solid SCCS	TFE	S	TFE	0.170	1400	0.3	1.1	3.9	13.5
RG-316	CXP TJ1316	50	69.5	29.4	#26 Flex BC	TFE	S	FEP	0.098	1200	1.2	2.7	8.0	26.1
RG-316	Belden 84316	50	69.5	29.0	#26 Flex SCCS	TFE	S	FEP	0.096	900	0.8	2.5	8.3	26.0
RG-393	M17/127-RG393	50	69.5	29.4	#12 Flex SPC	TFE	D	FEP	0.390	5000	0.2	0.5	1.7	6.1
RG-400	M17/128-RG400	50	69.5	29.4	#20 Flex SPC	TFE	D	FEP	0.195	1400	0.4	1.3	4.3	15.0
LMR500	TMS LMR500UF	50	85	23.9	#7 Flex BC	FPE	FC	PE	0.500	2500	0.1	0.4	1.2	4.0
LMR500	TMS LMR500	50	85	23.9	#7 Flex CCA	FPE	FC	PE	0.500	2500	0.1	0.3	0.9	3.3
LMR600	TMS LMR600	50	86	23.4	#5.5 Solid CCA	FPE	FC	PE	0.590	4000	0.1	0.2	0.8	2.7
LMR600	TMS LMR600UF	50	86	23.4	#5.5 Flex BC	FPE	FC	PE	0.590	4000	0.1	0.2	0.8	2.7
LMR1200	TMS LMR1200	50	88	23.1	#0 Copper Tube	FPE	FC	PE	1.200	4500	0.04	0.1	0.4	1.3

Hardline

	Part Number	Nom. Z_0 Ω	VF %	Cap. pF/ft	Cent. Cond. AWG	Diel. Type	Shield Type	Jacket Matl	OD inches	Max V (RMS)	1 MHz	10	100	1000
1/2"	CATV Hardline	50	81	25.0	#5.5 BC	FPE	SM	none	0.500	2500	0.05	0.2	0.8	3.2
1/2"	CATV Hardline	75	81	16.7	#11.5 BC	FPE	SM	none	0.500	2500	0.1	0.2	0.8	3.2
7/8"	CATV Hardline	50	81	25.0	#1 BC	FPE	SM	none	0.875	4000	0.03	0.1	0.6	2.9
7/8"	CATV Hardline	75	81	16.7	#5.5 BC	FPE	SM	none	0.875	4000	0.03	0.1	0.6	2.9
LDF4-50A	Heliax – ½"	50	88	25.9	#5 Solid BC	FPE	CC	PE	0.630	1400	0.02	0.2	0.6	2.4
LDF5-50A	Heliax – ⅞"	50	88	25.9	0.355" BC	FPE	CC	PE	1.090	2100	0.03	0.10	0.4	1.3
LDF6-50A	Heliax – 1¼"	50	88	25.9	0.516" BC	FPE	CC	PE	1.550	3200	0.02	0.08	0.3	1.1

Parallel Lines

	Part Number	Nom. Z_0 Ω	VF %	Cap. pF/ft	Cent. Cond. AWG	Diel. Type	Shield Type	Jacket Matl	OD inches	Max V (RMS)	1 MHz	10	100	1000
	TV Twinlead (Belden 9085)	300	80	4.5	#22 Flex CCS	PE	none	P1	0.400	**	0.1	0.3	1.4	5.9
	Twinlead (Belden 8225)	300	80	4.4	#20 Flex BC	PE	none	P1	0.400	8000	0.1	0.2	1.1	4.8
	Generic Window Line	450	91	2.5	#18 Solid CCS	PE	none	P1	1.000	10000	0.02	0.08	0.3	1.1
	WM CQ 554	440	91	2.7	#14 Flex CCS	PE	none	P1	1.000	10000	0.04	0.01	0.6	3.0
	WM CQ 552	440	91	2.5	#16 Flex CCS	PE	none	P1	1.000	10000	0.05	0.2	0.6	2.6
	WM CQ 553	450	91	2.5	#18 Flex CCS	PE	none	P1	1.000	10000	0.06	0.2	0.7	2.9
	WM CQ 551	450	91	2.5	#18 Solid CCS	PE	none	P1	1.000	10000	0.05	0.02	0.6	2.8
	Open-Wire Line	600	0.95-99***	1.7	#12 BC	none	none	none	**	12000	0.02	0.06	0.2	—

Approximate Power Handling Capability (1:1 SWR, 40°C Ambient):

	1.8 MHz	7	14	30	50	150	220	450	1 GHz
RG-58 Style	1350	700	500	350	250	150	120	100	50
RG-59 Style	2300	1100	800	550	400	250	200	130	90
RG-8X Style	1830	840	560	360	270	145	115	80	50
RG-8/213 Style	5900	3000	2000	1500	1000	600	500	350	250
RG-217 Style	20000	9200	6100	3900	2900	1500	1200	800	500
LDF4-50A	38000	18000	13000	8200	6200	3400	2800	1900	1200
LDF5-50A	67000	32000	22000	14000	11000	5900	4800	3200	2100
LMR500	18000	9200	6500	4400	3400	1900	1600	1100	700
LMR1200	52000	26000	19000	13000	10000	5500	4500	3000	2000

Legend:

**	Not Available or varies	N	Non-Contaminating
***	Varies with spacer material and spacing	P1	PVC, Class 1
ASPE	Air Spaced Polyethylene	P2	PVC, Class 2
BC	Bare Copper	PE	Polyethylene
CC	Corrugated Copper	S	Single Braided Shield
CCA	Copper Cover Aluminum	SC	Silver Coated Braid
CCS	Copper Covered Steel	SCCS	Silver Plated Copper Coated Steel
CXP	Cable X-Perts, Inc.	SM	Smooth Aluminum
D	Double Copper Braids	SPC	Silver Plated Copper
DRF	Davis RF	TC	Tinned Copper
FC	Foil + Tinned Copper Braid	TFE	Teflon® Type IX
FEP	Teflon® Type IX	TFE	Teflon®
Flex	Flexible Stranded Wire	TMS	Times Microwave Systems
FPE	Foamed Polyethylene	UF	Ultra Flex
Heliax	Andrew Corp Heliax	WM	Wireman

BNC CONNECTORS

Standard Clamp

1. Cut cable even. Strip jacket. Fray braid and strip dielectric. ***Don't nick braid or center conductor.*** Tin center conductor.

2. Taper braid. Slide nut, washer, gasket and clamp over braid. Clamp inner shoulder should fit squarely against end of jacket.

3. With clamp in place, comb out braid, fold back smooth as shown. Trim center conductor.

4. Solder contact on conductor through solder hole. Contact should butt against dielectric. Remove excess solder from outside of contact. Avoid excess heat to prevent swollen dielectric which would interfere with connector body.

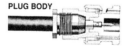

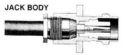

5. Push assembly into body. Screw nut into body with wrench until tight. ***Don't rotate body on cable to tighten.***

Improved Clamp

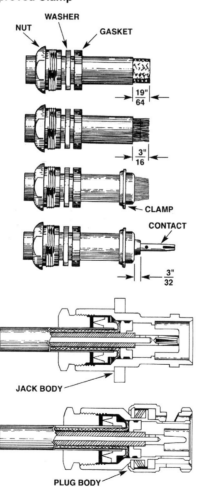

Follow 1, 2, 3 and 4 in BNC connectors (standard clamp) except as noted. Strip cable as shown. Slide gasket on cable *with groove facing clamp*. Slide clamp *with sharp edge facing gasket*. Clamp *should* cut gasket to seal properly.

C. C. Clamp

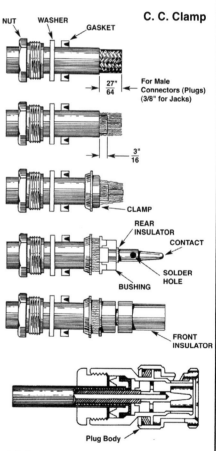

For Male Connectors (Plugs) (3/8" for Jacks)

1. Follow steps 1, 2, and 3 as outlined for the standard-clamp BNC connector.

2. Slide on bushing, rear insulator and contact. The parts must butt securely against each other, as shown.

3. Solder the center conductor to the contact. Remove flux and excess solder.

4. Slide the front insulator over the contact, making sure it butts against the contact shoulder.

5. Insert the prepared cable end into the connector body and tighten the nut. Make sure the sharp edge of the clamp seats properly in the gasket.

Coaxial Cable Connectors

UHF Connectors

Military No.	Style	Cable RG- or Description
PL-259	Str (m)	8, 9, 11, 13, 63, 87, 149, 213, 214, 216, 225
UG-111	Str (m)	59, 62, 71, 140, 210
SO-239	Pnl (f)	Std, mica/phenolic insulation
UG-266	Blkhd (f)	Rear mount, pressurized, copolymer of styrene ins.

Adapters

PL-258	Str (f/f)	Polystyrene ins.
UG-224,363	Blkhd (f/f)	Polystyrene ins.
UG-646	Ang (f/m)	Polystyrene ins.
M-359A	Ang (m/f)	Polystyrene ins.
M-358	T (f/m/f)	Polystyrene ins.

Reducers

UG-175	55, 58, 141, 142 (except 55A)
UG-176	59, 62, 71, 140, 210

Family Characteristics:

All are nonweatherproof and have a nonconstant impedance. Frequency range: 0-500 MHz. Maximum voltage rating: 500 V (peak).

N Connectors

Military No.	Style	Cable RG-	Notes
UG-21	Str (m)	8, 9, 213, 214	50 Ω
UG-94A	Str (m)	11, 13, 149, 216	70 Ω
UG-536	Str (m)	58, 141, 142	50 Ω
UG-603	Str (m)	59, 62, 71, 140, 210	50 Ω
UG-23, B-E	Str (f)	8, 9, 87, 213, 214, 225	50 Ω
UG-602	Str (f)	59, 62, 71, 140, 210	—
UG-228B, D, E	Pnl (f)	8, 9, 87, 213, 214, 225	—
UG-1052	Pnl (f)	58, 141, 142	50 Ω
UG-593	Pnl (f)	59, 62, 71, 140, 210	50 Ω
UG-160A, B, D	Blkhd (f)	8, 9, 87, 213, 214, 225	50 Ω
UG-556	Blkhd (f)	58, 141, 142	50 Ω
UG-58, A	Pnl (f)		50 Ω
UG-997A	Ang (f)		50 Ω

Panel mount (f) with clearance above panel

M39012/04-	Blkhd (f)	Front mount hermetically sealed
UG-680	Blkhd (f)	Front mount pressurized

N Adapters

Military No.	Style	Notes
UG-29,A,B	Str (f/f)	50 Ω, TFE ins.
UG-57A.B	Str (m/m)	50 Ω, TFE ins.
UG-27A,B	Ang (f/m)	Mitre body
UG-212A	Ang (f/m)	Mitre body
UG-107A	T (f/m/f)	—
UG-28A	T (f/f/f)	—
UG-107B	T (f/m/f)	—

Family Characteristics:

N connectors with gaskets are weatherproof. RF leakage: –90 dB min @ 3 GHz. Temperature limits: TFE: –67° to 390°F (–55° to 199°C). Insertion loss 0.15 dB max @ 10 GHz. Copolymer of styrene: –67° to 185°F (–55° to 85°C). Frequency range: 0-11 GHz. Maximum voltage rating: 1500 V P-P. Dielectric withstanding voltage 2500 V RMS. SWR (MIL-C-39012 cable connectors) 1.3 max 0-11 GHz.

BNC Connectors

Military No.	Style	Cable RG-	Notes
UG-88C	Str (m)	55, 58, 141, 142, 223, 400	

Military No.	Style	Cable RG-	Notes
UG-959	Str (m)	8, 9	
UG-260,A	Str (m)	59, 62, 71, 140, 210	Rexolite ins.
UG-262	Pnl (f)	59, 62, 71, 140, 210	Rexolite ins.
UG-262A	Pnl (f)	59, 62, 71, 140, 210	nwx, Rexolite ins.
UG-291	Pnl (f)	55, 58, 141, 142, 223, 400	
UG-291A	Pnl (f)	55, 58, 141, 142, 223, 400	nwx
UG-624	Blkhd (f)	59, 62, 71, 140, 210	Front mount Rexolite ins.
UG-1094A	Blkhd		Standard
UG-625B	Receptacle		
UG-625			

BNC Adapters

Military No.	Style	Notes
UG-491,A	Str (m/m)	
UG-491B	Str (m/m)	Berylium, outer contact
UG-914	Str (f/f)	
UG-306	Ang (f/m)	
UG-306A,B	Ang (f/m)	Berylium outer contact
UG-414,A	Pnl (f/f)	# 3-56 tapped flange holes
UG-306	Ang (f/m)	
UG-306A,B	Ang (f/m)	Berylium outer contact
UG-274	T (f/m/f)	
UG-274A,B	T (f/m/f)	Berylium outer contact

Family Characteristics:

Z = 50 Ω. Frequency range: 0-4 GHz w/low reflection; usable to 11 GHz. Voltage rating: 500 V P-P. Dielectric withstanding voltage 500 V RMS. SWR: 1.3 max 0-4 GHz. RF leakage –55 dB min @ 3 GHz. Insertion loss: 0.2 dB max @ 3 GHz. Temperature limits: TFE: –67° to 390°F (–55° to 199°C); Rexolite insulators: –67° to 185°F (–55° to 85°C). "Nwx" = not weatherproof.

HN Connectors

Military No.	Style	Cable RG-	Notes
UG-59A	Str (m)	8, 9, 213, 214	
UG-1214	Str (f)	8, 9, 87, 213, 214, 225	Captivated contact
UG-60A	Str (f)	8, 9, 213, 214	Copolymer of styrene ins.
UG-1215	Pnl (f)	8, 9, 87, 213, 214, 225	Captivated contact
UG-560	Pnl (f)		
UG-496	Pnl (f)		
UG-212C	Ang (f/m)		Berylium outer contact

Family Characteristics:

Connector Styles: Str = straight; Pnl = panel; Ang = Angle; Blkhd = bulkhead. Z = 50 Ω. Frequency range = 0-4 GHz. Maximum voltage rating = 1500 V P-P. Dielectric withstanding voltage = 5000 V RMS SWR = 1.3. All HN series are weatherproof. Temperature limits: TFE: –67° to 390°F (–55° to 199°C); copolymer of styrene: –67° to 185°F (–55° to 85°C).

Cross-Family Adapters

Families	Description	Military No.
HN to BNC	HN-m/BNC-f	UG-309
N to BNC	N-m/BNC-f	UG-201,A
	N-f/BNC-m	UG-349,A
	N-m/BNC-m	UG-1034
N to UHF	N-m/UHF-f	UG-146
	N-f/UHF-m	UG-83,B
	N-m/UHF-m	UG-318
UHF to BNC	UHF-m/BNC-f	UG-273
	UHF-f/BNC-m	UG-255

US Customary Units and Conversion Factors

Linear Units

12 inches (in) = 1 foot (ft)
36 inches = 3 feet = 1 yard (yd)
1 rod = $5\frac{1}{2}$ yards = $16\frac{1}{2}$ feet
1 statute mile = 1760 yards = 5280 feet
1 nautical mile = 6076.11549 feet

Area

1 ft^2 = 144 in^2
1 yd^2 = 9 ft^2 = 1296 in^2
1 rod^2 = $30\frac{1}{4}$ yd^2
1 acre = 4840 yd^2 = 43,560 ft^2
1 acre = 160 rod^2
1 $mile^2$ = 640 acres

Volume

1 ft^3 = 1728 in^3
1 yd^3 = 27 ft^3

Liquid Volume Measure

1 fluid ounce (fl oz) = 8 fluid drams = 1.804 in
1 pint (pt) = 16 fl oz
1 quart (qt) = 2 pt = 32 fl oz = $57\frac{3}{4}$ in^3
1 gallon (gal) = 4 qt = 231 in^3
1 barrel = $31\frac{1}{2}$ gal

Dry Volume Measure

1 quart (qt) = 2 pints (pt) = 67.2 in^3
1 peck = 8 qt
1 bushel = 4 pecks = 2150.42 in^3

Avoirdupois Weight

1 dram (dr) = 27.343 grains (gr) or (gr a)
1 ounce (oz) = 437.5 gr
1 pound (lb) = 16 oz = 7000 gr
1 short ton = 2000 lb, 1 long ton = 2240 lb

Troy Weight

1 grain troy (gr t) = 1 grain avoirdupois
1 pennyweight (dwt) or (pwt) = 24 gr t
1 ounce troy (oz t) = 480 grains
1 lb t = 12 oz t = 5760 grains

Apothecaries' Weight

1 grain apothecaries' (gr ap)
   = 1 gr t = 1 gr
1 dram ap (dr ap) = 60 gr
1 oz ap = 1 oz t = 8 dr ap = 480 gr
1 lb ap = 1 lb t = 12 oz ap = 5760 gr

Conversion

Metric Unit = Metric Unit × US Unit

(Length)

mm	25.4	inch
cm	2.54	inch
cm	30.48	foot
m	0.3048	foot
m	0.9144	yard
km	1.609	mile
km	1.852	nautical mile

(Area)

mm^2	645.16	$inch^2$
cm^2	6.4516	in^2
cm^2	929.03	ft^2
m^2	0.0929	ft^2
cm^2	8361.3	yd^2
m^2	0.83613	yd^2
m^2	4047	acre
km^2	2.59	mi^2

(Mass)   (Avoirdupois Weight)

grams	0.0648	grains
g	28.349	oz
g	453.59	lb
kg	0.45359	lb
tonne	0.907	short ton
tonne	1.016	long ton

(Volume)

mm^3	16387.064	in^3
cm^3	16.387	in^3
m^3	0.028316	ft^3
m^3	0.764555	yd^3
ml	16.387	in^3
ml	29.57	fl oz
ml	473	pint
ml	946.333	quart
l	28.32	ft^3
l	0.9463	quart
l	3.785	gallon
l	1.101	dry quart
l	8.809	peck
l	35.238	bushel

(Mass)   (Troy Weight)

g	31.103	oz t
g	373.248	lb t

(Mass)   (Apothecaries' Weight)

g	3.387	dr ap
g	31.103	oz ap
g	373.248	lb ap

Multiply $\longrightarrow$

Metric Unit = Conversion Factor × US Customary Unit

$\longleftarrow$ **Divide**

Metric Unit ÷ Conversion Factor = US Customary Unit

Reflection Coefficient, Attenuation, SWR and Return Loss

Reflection Coefficient (%)	Attenuation (dB)	Max SWR	Return Loss, dB
1.000	0.000434	1.020	40.00
1.517	0.001000	1.031	36.38
2.000	0.001738	1.041	33.98
3.000	0.003910	1.062	30.46
4.000	0.006954	1.083	27.96
4.796	0.01000	1.101	26.38
5.000	0.01087	1.105	26.02
6.000	0.01566	1.128	24.44
7.000	0.02133	1.151	23.10
7.576	0.02500	1.164	22.41
8.000	0.02788	1.174	21.94
9.000	0.03532	1.198	20.92
10.000	0.04365	1.222	20.00
10.699	0.05000	1.240	19.41
11.000	0.05287	1.247	19.17
12.000	0.06299	1.273	18.42
13.085	0.07500	1.301	17.66
14.000	0.08597	1.326	17.08
15.000	0.09883	1.353	16.48
15.087	0.10000	1.355	16.43
16.000	0.1126	1.381	15.92
17.783	0.1396	1.433	15.00
18.000	0.1430	1.439	14.89
19.000	0.1597	1.469	14.42
20.000	0.1773	1.500	13.98
22.000	0.2155	1.564	13.15
23.652	0.2500	1.620	12.52
24.000	0.2577	1.632	12.40
25.000	0.2803	1.667	12.04
26.000	0.3040	1.703	11.70
27.000	0.3287	1.740	11.37
28.000	0.3546	1.778	11.06
30.000	0.4096	1.857	10.46
31.623	0.4576	1.925	10.00
32.977	0.5000	1.984	9.64
33.333	0.5115	2.000	9.54
34.000	0.5335	2.030	9.37
35.000	0.5675	2.077	9.12
36.000	0.6028	2.125	8.87
37.000	0.6394	2.175	8.64
38.000	0.6773	2.226	8.40
39.825	0.75000	2.324	8.00
40.000	0.7572	2.333	7.96
42.000	0.8428	2.448	7.54
42.857	0.8814	2.500	7.36
44.000	0.9345	2.571	7.13

Reflection Coefficient (%)	Attenuation (dB)	Max SWR	Return Loss, dB
45.351	1.0000	2.660	6.87
48.000	1.1374	2.846	6.38
50.000	1.2494	3.000	6.02
52.000	1.3692	3.167	5.68
54.042	1.5000	3.352	5.35
56.234	1.6509	3.570	5.00
58.000	1.7809	3.762	4.73
60.000	1.9382	4.000	4.44
60.749	2.0000	4.095	4.33
63.000	2.1961	4.405	4.01
66.156	2.5000	4.909	3.59
66.667	2.5528	5.000	3.52
70.627	3.0000	5.809	3.02
70.711	3.0103	5.829	3.01

$$\rho = \frac{SWR - 1}{SWR + 1}$$

where $\rho = 0.01 \times$ (reflection coefficient in %)

$$\rho = 10^{-RL/20}$$

where RL = return loss (dB)

$$\rho = \sqrt{1 - (0.1^X)}$$

where $X = A/10$ and A = attenuation (dB)

$$SWR = \frac{1 + \rho}{1 - \rho}$$

Return loss (dB) = $-8.68589 \ln(\rho)$
where ln is the natural log (log to the base e)

Attenuation (dB) = $-4.34295 \ln(1 - \rho^2)$
where ln is the natural log (log to the base e)

Index

Notes

Notes

Notes

FEEDBACK

Please use this form to give us your comments on this book and what you'd like to see in future editions, or e-mail us at **pubsfdbk@arrl.org** (publications feedback). If you use e-mail, please include your name, call, e-mail address and the book title, edition and printing in the body of your message. Also indicate whether or not you are an ARRL member.

Where did you purchase this book?　☐ From ARRL directly　　☐ From an ARRL dealer

Is there a dealer who carries ARRL publications within:

　☐ 5 miles　　☐ 15 miles　　☐ 30 miles　of your location?　　☐ Not sure.

License class:

☐ Novice　　☐ Technician　　☐ Technician with code　☐ General　　☐ Advanced　　☐ Amateur Extra

Name _____　ARRL member?　☐ Yes　☐ No

_____　Call Sign _____

Address _____

City, State/Province, ZIP/Postal Code _____

Daytime Phone　(　　)　_____　Age _____

If licensed, how long? _____

Other hobbies _____　E-mail _____

_____

Occupation _____

For ARRL use only		SASS
Edition	2 3 4 5 6 7 8 9 10 11 12	
Printing	1 2 3 4 5 6 7 8 9 10 11 12	